Donald J. Trump An American Dilemma

When the Daily Stormers Sang

Robert Osenenko, Ed.D.

Donald J. Trump An American Dilemma

Grateful acknowledgment is made to Daniel de la Cruz Díaz-Valdés and Universidad Complutense, Madrid, for use material.

Library of Congress Certificate of Registration February 25, 2019

1. Biography 2. Political theory. 3. Discourse 4. Religion and Politics 5. Post-Soviet History 6. Identity (Culture)

Notice: Any similarity of opinion between this narrative and the United States government, Department of Defense, or any of its contractors is purely coincidental.

Table of Contents

Prologue 5

Emotions and Character 19

QANON and Its Antecedent 35

A Path Backwards 55

Vladamir Lenin and Yuri V. Andropov 81

Father Dearest A Hero's Quest 109

The Captive Queen 117

The Daily Stormers Song 131

Only as He Understood Love 139

National Socialism's Policy Integration with Republican Platform 151

Conclusion 163

The Commercial Insurgency 166

Appendix A: Between Democracy 175

Appendix B: Words of War 177

Appendix C: Language of The Reich 181

Bibliography 183

Index 223

When the Daily Stormers Sang, 11 August to 12, 2017, this would forever change the American landscape. No such social movement to change a nation existed without its songs. Obscure people of all kinds started to compete by replacing historical figures of the Stormer's past. In an objective presentation focused on the American history of fascism, this unique biography will include Stormer's history and its antecedents. It will conclude by revealing the outcome of this competition. Thereby foretelling the future of this movement.

Visuals surrounding the Unite the Right was dangerous. This marked a first in American history in that it was also a commercial event. Having little to do with the original industrial-inspired Nazi's signified the merger of a mafia presence in commercial industries. It could even be said that the places where President Vladamir Putin invested trillions of dollars in American business and Wall Street interests would be invisible in the coverage of distracting rallies. Together the Nazis and mafias who met in the 1980s at a series of White House conferences converged on Charlottesville, Virginia.

One purpose of this book, the second in the series, is to establish a framework on the intent and identity of who is Adolph Hitler. While creating a narrative of the different and diverse perspectives of the era. Using biographical information, these aspects of this book stand on the shoulders of the perception of the extreme right in America.

The idea of regenerating a part of the Nazi psychological and behavioral infrastructure did not originate in the United States. We know it was initially conceived by the philosophical advisers surrounding Vladamir Putin as an idea of creating disunity in the West. Both among the NATO membership and the people who inhabit former Nazi enclaves throughout Eastern Europe and Midwest America. This revealed itself when President Putin's Spetsnaz (Special Forces) were dispatched to Slovakian forests to recruit neo-Nazi biker gangs.

The state-sponsored training resulted in their use during the Russian seizure of Crimea as patrols under Spetsnaz management. Not only was Russia interested in sowing discord in the European Union, but its covert use of the thieves-in-law organized criminal merged with their international interests. Their continued involvement in drug cartels formerly used as Soviet-funded militia in South and Central America is part of their expansive investment portfolio. The second purpose of this book is to unforget the role of Republican Conservatives and their ambitious attempts to control commercial interests worldwide.

Primarily these efforts are immediately identified as psychological operations requiring little or no state funding. This is mainly due to their ability to advise neo-Nazis, and the cartels on how to rely on sovereign organized criminal methods in the host country. This had the advantages of being dangerous in their location. To this point, Russian dissenters point out that Mr. Putin's illegal industry in Russia surrounding the energy sector has led to investment holdings in various United States corporations. Urging the American government to take some action to divest itself from Mr. Putin.

Dissenters acknowledged how relaxed the United States had become in financial regulations, making it more attractive than Switzerland. Once considering when the U.S. State Department exposed the Nazi treasure. Likely the money Mr. Putin placed in banking institutions also served a dual purpose. Russia could hide its wealth in the United States. They could also use it to direct beneficial actions.

The countries which were the coziest with Russia wanted to repeat Third Reich ambitions by allowing their presence in its Heartland and Rimland borders. A family would be installed in each country Russia held investments to conduct President Vladamir Putin's daily operation, as was his predecessor's case. History teaches us about the expectations and rewards of these arrangements going back to Vladamir Lenin, Leon Trotsky, and others who invested in American industry, particularly the energy sector. Parents in Russia's circle of friends participated in profits and ill-gotten gains. Their children would receive assets such as attendance in the best schools and a seat at the table-of-advisors about Russia's future opportunities and its communist partners. Overall, the family's future was filled with hopes and imageries of Russian dominance. Where upcoming events did not match expectations, such as family leaders and associates hanged or shot in the town square or when they recalled Moscow or its suburbs where they languished as retired spies.

This is a story about Trump's one diminutive family who risked it all for Russia and its future dreams. Their entire life story would be pinned on the hope of When the Stormers Sang first, and when they repeated those verses in Washington D.C. Behind the scenes of the families, Russia influenced. Race theorists are pushing the Republican National Committee into Russia's *Fourth Political Theory*. It encompasses three sectors. The current presidency, National Socialist (Nazi) affiliations, and Russia. Not in official legitimization but coordination of agreement.

Golden Dawn, stated heirs of Nazism, have endorsed this plan.[1] Yet, for some reason, American scholars only compare Nazism to Adolph Hitler and not the new "Good Hitler" being presented to conservative youth by Russia's *Fourth Political Theory*. The latter form is recently responsible for mass numbers of killings in the United States.

---

[1] Balezdrova, Anastasia. "Golden Dawn and Russian neo-Nazism." *GR Reporter*. 15 Apr. 2014.

Suggesting there may be some connection between Trump's speech, his campaign to revive Nazi lore, and the numerous efforts to impose himself on the cover of *My New Order* by the ISHI Press in New York.

One of the worst kept secrets in the Kremlin is it hosts neo-Nazi groups and extremist education and training. The person these groups herald the most is President Donald J. Trump and his Republican Conservatives. Witness accounts of his bedside reading of *Mein Kampf* have also placed him in the camp of a rumor of being an aspirational neo-Nazi American Führer.

Even Adolph Hitler had to pass through the passions and fire of three organizational stages. This sequence included the pronouncement and propaganda, transformation of religious institutions, merging military interests with strong well-seasoned militias followed by the seizure of power and dictatorship. Republican Conservatives have instead adopted the Trump family to do their bidding in exchange for financial support. The same messaging President Vladamir Putin made public.

Post-World War II, there have been attempts at understanding the personality type like Adolph Hitler in hopes of gaining insight. Their success has overlooked important unintentional conclusions. The most serious of the missed information has been the assumption that the Third Reich idea was on the decline as neo-liberalism increased. This view largely ignored neoliberalism that plants the seed to allow National Socialism to rise again via its class privileges, Conservative policies ignoring public need, economic immunity to high-income criminals, and tearing down moral restraints.

At Nuremberg, the West point of view that racial theory and corporatist imperialism began the war is forgotten.[2] In its aftermath, this

---

[2] Heller, Kevin and Gerry Simpson. *The Hidden Histories of War Crimes Trials.* Oxford University Press; 1 edition. Oxford University Press. 30 Dec. 2013. Also

carries a taboo that to openly discuss what the National Socialist Movement is today leads to too much curiosity. The reasons for this include what Judy Scales-Trent identifies as the United States' "racial purity laws."[3] The United States has not passed legislation to eradicate many of its shared prejudices adopted by Nazi Germany. It still hopes to continue the image of a racialized nation.

In the mid-1990s, Nazi gold that investigators realized was used for the Fourth Reich was stirred by President Bill Clinton. Russian soldiers used intelligence operatives of aspiring Nazis to conduct military operations. In the United States, 20,000 voters chose to elect a Nazi through the Republican National Committee process. The Democratic party has had its problems in this regard with extremist groups on the left. [4]

Nevertheless, National Socialism grew along parallel routes with the 45th Republican President that encourages it. The exponential growth is concerning. I wish to point out that National Socialism is a structural organization that serves governments, individuals, religious groups, industrial capitalists, and oligarchs. In its early years, it depended on crime to survive. The pre-violent stage of National Socialism is most susceptible to becoming influenced, reshaped, and made unrecognizable to untrained eyes. This book may change that by remembering what the United States has forgotten.

One should be alarmed because the culture has invoked the loss of citizenship as a primary weapon of racial purity. The 45th President also

---

read Oxford University Online "Capitalism's Victor's Justice? The Hidden Stories Behind the Prosecution of Industrialists Post-WWII." by Grietje Baars..

[3] Scales-Trent, Judy. "Racial Purity Laws in the United States and Nazi Germany: The Targeting Process.", 23Hum. Rts. Q.259 (2001). Available at: https://digital-commons.law.buffalo.edu/articles/826. University at Buffalo School of Law Digital Commons @ University at Buffalo School of Law. Human Rights Quarterly. 23 (2001) 259-307 © 2001 by The Johns Hopkins University Press.

[4] Israel, Josh. "20,000 Republicans just voted for an actual Nazi." *ThinkProgress.* 21 Mar. 2018.

cites his personal sovereignty philosophy as an exact passphrase to his white supremacist supporters. Among the limitation of law to prosecute subversion at Nuremberg and the resting shield it created over industrialists and lower criminals, we must not forget that the Nazi movement itself was founded on support from both below socioeconomic levels and above type of mutual consent.

Lately, there has been some movement away from justice after the war; nonetheless, the United States' responsibility is to finally make the matter right through structured settlement agreements.[5] The world's industrial leaders, if they are penitent, should not be allowed to quickly give their money away but structure settlements to make specific restitution. They should not follow the central injustice with another. [6] During the war, industrialists who helped the Nazis also supported the 45th President after his announcement on *My New Order's* cover. Namely the energy sector that also supplies Mr. Putin with his profits.

Among recent anti-American conspiratorialists were President Vladamir Putin and *New Russian Empire* Ideologue Aleksandr Dugin, Andranik Migranyan, Ph.D., and Steve Bannon.[7] Ideologue Aleksandr Dugin wrote a concept of rising fascism using models from what is envisioned as the Fourth Theory similar to the Reich, a parallel with mild fascism without anti-Semitism violence and racial discrimination without racism. It involves speech as a weapon in the first lap of the Russian assault on its enemies. Those who know history immediately identify this ideology as Bolshevist by Vladamir Ilyich (Ulyanov) Lenin to gain otherwise resistant groups.

---

[5] Isidore, Chris. "Krispy Kreme owners admit to family history of Nazi ties." *CNN*. 25 Mar. 2019.

[6] Baars, Grietje "Capitalism's Victor's Justice? The Hidden Stories Behind the Prosecution of Industrialists Post-WWII.".

[7] Allen-Ebrahimian, Bethany. Et.al. "Nazi Sympathizers Pushing to Take Over Europe's Spy Agencies. " *The Daily Beast.* June 26, 2018.

It works in India, which has one of the most virulent shifts of Nazism. It has revised all history texts. Shrenik Rao explained this Hindu development in "Hitler's Hindus: The Rise and Rise of India's Nazi Loving Nationalists."[8] In Europe, its name is "the Good Hitler" theory and spreads in South America, Alexander Ross Reid. "Opinion: Hitler in Brasilia: The U.S. Evangelicals and Nazi Political Theory Behind Brazil's President-in-waiting."[9] Aleksandr Dugin predicts the destruction of the United States by converging it with Eastern European politics. What we see used is the military maneuver using the two-pronged approach.[10] The first most significant impact is on youth who haven't been learning about history.[11] Next are those with financial self-interest.

The Dugin narrative even includes the Russian Conservative terror-gothic image of the end of civilization. However, Dugin predicts this will not be extraterrestrial warfare but will be instigated in a far bloodier battle by mankind, millenarianism.[12] Russians believe that National Socialism (Nazi) can be materialized into a new rebranded Nazism as The Fourth Political Theory and spurn one, two, three sequences of coups like their victorious Bolsheviks.

---

[8] Rao, Shrenik. "Hitler's Hindus: The Rise and Rise of India's Nazi Loving Nationalists." *Haartz*. 14 Dec. 2017.

[9] Ross Reid, Alexander. "Opinion Hitler in Brasilia: The U.S. Evangelicals and Nazi Political Theory Behind Brazil's President-in-waiting." *Haaretz*. 28 Oct. 2018.

[10] "U.S. and Coalition Forces." *Counterinsurgency in Afghanistan: RAND Counterinsurgency Study--Volume 4*, by Seth G. Jones, RAND Corporation, Santa Monica, CA; Arlington, VA; Pittsburgh, PA, 2008, pp. 87–110. *JSTOR*, Open Access..

[11] Heinze, Kristin and Carsten Heinze. "The Educational Conceptualization of the Ethnic Community Volksgemeinschaft in National Socialist Primers by the Example of Presentations of Adolf Hitler – Methodical Prospects." In History of Education & Children's Literature IX, 2 (2014), pp. 185-200. ISSN 1971-1093 (print) / ISSN 1971-1131.

[12] Dugin, Alexander. And Alain Sorel. *The Fourth Political Theory*. Arktos Media Ltd. 16 July 2012.

Their strong populist debut happened in Crimea, Charlottesville, Virginia and Pittsburgh, Pennsylvania, and other locations that demonstrated neo-Nazi interference can be mobilized to significantly disrupt the West. This reconstructed view of Nazism is prevalent among students from Australia to Berlin. President Trump and Russian ideologues want people to see Russia as anti-Hitler as a coverup to their intelligence maneuver to those who do not make the logic behind this Russian approach.

One of Adolph Hitler personality's unique aspects is that he critiqued the landscape of ideas and tampered with a population's sense of place. Often incorporating a widespread population thought into his. They might be surprised by their similarity to "Good Hitler." So, let's recall the Public Speech given by Adolf Hitler in Munich, November 1941.

> "I have learned a great deal from Marxism as I do not hesitate to admit … The difference between [Marxists] and myself is that I have really put into practice what these peddlers and pen-pushers have timidly begun. The whole of National Socialism is based on it. Look at the workers' sports clubs, the industrial cells, the mass demonstrations, the propaganda leaflets were written especially for the comprehension of the masses: all these new political struggle methods are essentially Marxist in origin. All I had to do is take over these methods and adapt them to our purpose."[13] Adolph Hitler's statement about the United States was equally indicting.

> "I know that people do not like to hear all this, but anything more thoughtless, more hare-brained than our present-day citizenship laws scarcely exists. There is today one state in which

---

[13] Hitler, Adolf. *Public Speech*. Munich, November 1941. Cited in *The Bulletin of International News*, Royal Institute of International Affairs, XVIII, No 5, 1941, p 269.

at least weak beginnings toward a better conception are noticeable. Of course, it is not our model German Republic, but the American Union, in which an effort is made to consult reason at least partially. By refusing immigration on principle to elements in poor health, by simply excluding certain races from naturalization, it professes in slow beginnings a view which is peculiar to the folkish state concept."[14]

History records from 1919 to 1938, the majority of the United States was vehemently against most forms of fascism, and these recollections and transitions are told through the voice of documents. In the modern post-war era, Americans began to reconstruct a narrative about legislative sub-agencies and political foundations. Consequently, through world events, the rise of communism and Soviet-Russia psychiatry, in particular, waged an information war that significantly impacted the culture. The first time it surfaced was when Nazi Germany was defeated.[15] In the following years, a series of events were considered psychologically uncanny, the way the 2016 campaign looks a lot like the 1920-1930s in Germany in schizoid theme messaging and isolationism.[16]

Throughout history, the United States has always included its subversives and deviants in society, and they still were used by our enemies. This never surprised the United States as it occurred during several ideological transitions. Everything can be gained by examining deviance from explaining what similarities and differences there are to the past. The 45th President brings to bear the social and historical

---

[14] Hitler, Adolph. *Mein Kampf.* Volume Two: The National Socialist Movement. Chapter 3. Subjects and Citizens. Munich: Verlag. Frz. Eher.
[15] Pick, Daniel. ""In pursuit of the Nazi mind?" The deployment of psychoanalysis in the Allied struggle against Germany" *Psychoanalysis and history* vol. 11,2 (2009): 137-57.
[16] Gray, R. "Freud and the Literary Imagination." Lecture Notes: Freud, "The Uncanny" (1919).

forces from this forgotten era of the American portrayal of Adolph Hitler, Rudolf Hess' agent Fritz Kuhn, well-known fascist George Sylvester Viereck, and the first opposition to American National Socialism during the President Ronald Wilson Reagan administration from conservative Peter Viereck. Though scorned, ridiculed, and disavowed after their deaths, their lives unquestionably impact the lives of all Americans today.

1920 America had resolved several issues that established its identity. It decided to unify the States, enact genocide on Native Americans, conduct revolutions in South and Central America using corporations like AT&T, maintain the master-slave relationship through a brutal plantation system, an unstable economy, and justifying it with eugenics. The Negroes were thought of like 50% human. In 1920 the American economy was prosperous and dubbed "The Roaring 20s." However, in the Midwest, severe drought and poor farming practices led to one of the most massive migrations in the nation to the Coasts, the Dust Bowl. Today fascist groups have moved back into the Midwest, hoping to reignite heirs to the 1920s National Socialist (Nazi). The eugenics movement returned.[17]

According to Adolph Hitler, this was destiny to aggravate American strife. A goal that coincided with his perception that Americans were similar to alienated Germans. In 1920 the first arrival of Adolph Hitler's Nazis came to the United States by way of the German Embassy in New York City. Their first assault was against Congress to prevent them from entering World War II, which Adolph Hitler predicted to Anton Drexler at this early stage of his political career. To a large extent, the happenings in Europe and the social discontent was

---

[17] Camera, Lauren. "Lawmaker Calls on DeVos to Resign." *US News*. 01 Apr. 2019.

objectified by Americans. News reports were unable to tell the "feeling" story. Republican Conservatives, due to the money, sided to support Nazism.

Adolph Hitler was viewed at best as an entertainer, a person competing with Charlie Chaplin for popularity. Many people in the street considered him ludicrous, funny, and girlish in his Bavarian shorts, feminine legs, and small stature. He wanted to be portrayed as a successful artist that would someday become an architect and rebuild Germany. This goal was replaced by despair as he failed to attain recognition and resigned himself as a criminal that would join the German Workers Party and Anton Drexler, a moderate fascist. This is the history that began the American perspective in the evolution of National Socialism (Nazi). A relatively peaceful Adolph Hitler and Anton Drexler using manipulation and clandestine politics smattered with paranoia. On a larger scale, Hitler's insiders stole banks, killed millions, and thoroughly corrupted himself so that he became bewildered, unstable, and virtually useless to his followers and corporate investors.

This view of Adolph Hitler changed as the United States Army took somber notice. The Beer Hall Putsch 8-9 November 1923 marked the failed takeover of Bavaria, Germany, and technically the United States began to suspect revolutionary motives were at play. Instantaneously the Army sent a dispatch to the White House, and the German Embassy went under surveillance. The FBI started a counterintelligence operation surveilling all activities that could be construed as Nazism.

When World War II survivors say that the White House's operations look like these early days of Adolph Hitler, this is what is meant. It is a definitive statement, a judgment that carries the weight of human experience. Survivors have not received the response that their warning deserves. Even news coverage one could expect is over objectified. This book gives another view that includes a compilation of experience and viewpoint, comparing the history of 1919-1938 to 2016. This history takes place using a refined look, "this happened, and then that happened; that happened because this happened first." World War II survivors are not talking about their reality alone.

We find Friedrich Trump arriving in New York, where both Lev Bronstein (Leon Trotsky) and Adolph Hitler, a first-time politician, are discussed. Vladamir Ilyich Ulyanov Lenin has just paid college for Armand Hammer (M.D.). Elizabeth Christ Trump, a Bavarian, with her son Frederick Jr. in New York, New York. Elizabeth Christ Trump, a matriarch, began "Elizabeth Trump & Son" with her son Frederick Christ Trump. He is just starting to mature in the real estate business and listens to the scurry of a passing Ku Klux Klan Memorial Day 1927 rally.

While the radio back at work and The New York Times reports on the Nazi movement in New York where the Silver Shirts are beginning a rampage of violence, and the Jewish community is fighting back. Frederick Christ Trump saw and heard about the Nazi movement as it geared up to February 1939 when it held the Madison Square Garden Hitler Rally. It would become an inseparable part of their family legacy that ultimately led to Donald J. Trump, her grandson, on the cover of the revised New World Order by Adolph Hitler. Eventually leading to exploration in what is the appeal of the Führer and its interloper sexuality. There has to be a return to what the U.S. Army World War Two profiles stated, "about the man and his vision," that strangely has become relevant. This history appealed to Donald J. Trump, only motivating him later to act on his resentment toward all people. No evidence exists Donald J. Trump had any close normative relationship. This is the first part of the story that led *The Stormers to Sing* of the Trump Presidency.

The Adolph Hitler the Trump's portended to be was fictional and digitized. In some respects, Hitler's story was taken captive and placed into submission to fulfill and serve the plan of announcing the beginning of the 45th Presidency's election campaign. The announcement first appeared by Donald J. Trump on the cover of *My New Order* by ISHI Press in a calculated chess move. This political attempt to connect and reconstruct is also an aggressive offense on the universality of how the world recalled the bloody era of the Third Reich. From the broad palette of political ideas, only Adolph Hitler was considered suitable for Republican Conservatives to take ultimate advantage of a decline in Second World War witnesses.

The concept itself to change a nation's national Memory is not new for the United States. Suggesting that there were people among the Republican Conservatives and government that had deeper ties to the Third Reich than suspected. Opening the political debut on the cover of a new *My New Order* spoke volumes about where their platform was heading. Donald J. Trump, a member of the Screen Actors Guild, could portray Hitler in a fictionalized way. No one knew whether he had the emotional depth and understanding to follow up on the required cruelty as President.

The aftereffect of Adolph Hitler's pattern to incorporate alien and foreign thoughts into German policy was twofold. There would never be any possibility of creating a purely native German ideology based on the Daily Stormers Sang made from the "blood and soil" below. In itself, this contradiction would lead the truth to be told and negate, disannul, and manufacture doubt for the National Socialist Government, causing its downfall. Following is an accurate nonfiction account of Adolph Hitler before becoming dictator. It serves as a baseline for what we know from his early experience to clarify his misinformation and relatively short life.

In Adolph Hitler's case, he endured over 1,000 beatings by his father, Aloi. He was a small stature boy in Vienna in May 1913, avoiding the draft being too small and weak. August Kubizek, his best friend, recounted 1904. Adolph Hitler remembered when 16 speaking with another voice in a trance. Adolph Hitler broke into a historical analysis of Germany and its people who needed a complete rebellion. After he became *Führer,* he reminded August Kubizek, "Yes, I've never forgotten it; because that's where it all began . . ."[18] While he spoke to August Kubizek, Adolph held his hand. On 03 August 1914, after petitioning the government, Adolph Hitler was inducted. Adolph Hitler's sexuality was the subject of clinical assessment.[19] Salvatore Dali imagined Adolph Hitler as a woman who ravished him and was enveloped by his own sado-masochism as he created World War II just to cover himself in the rubble.[20]

Adolph Hitler's attraction in the early years before the 1920s found the Nazi party was small compared to Germany's opposition parties. Some people supported the Nazis, mostly among a cadre of women active in its political affairs. After the extensive publication of Adolph Hitler's so-called Hitlerputsch, he became almost a household name in Europe and overseas. Crime only increased his popularity. Through Providence, Adolph Hitler met Joseph Goebbels. It was not until

---

[18] Kubizek, August. *The Young Hitler I Knew: The Definitive Inside Look at the Artist Who Became a Monster.* Arcade; Reprint edition 13 July 2011.
[19] Murray, Henry. "Subject: Adolph Hitler" CIA File. *Central Intelligence Agency.* Declassified. 18 May 2000.
[20] Maylon, John. Art Cyclopedia Oct. 2000.

Rudolph Hess was assigned that Nazism came into United States Conservatism based on racial theory.

Women were attracted to the Nazi party during these initial stages. After revisions of the Nazi platform, they were still expected to continue their open admiration of Adolph Hitler. The Nazi party was successful in moderating the campaign generating even greater positivity after writing them out. Those voting rights promised had dropped and no longer extended to women through the party. Recognized without monetary support from women, the party could not exist. Still, amid this risky and daring move, the party pursued the publication and popularization of the "little German housewife," especially among the men. The female support that party leaders believed would dwindle did not. German women accepted their subservience to male sovereignty.

Attempting to be loyal to his geographic and racial ties, Adolph Hitler endeared himself to his ethnic sense of community by appealing to the Völkisch ethnics. He was aware that the fellowship of his ethnic community and peasant upbringing had few limits. Adolph Hitler summoned intelligent German thinkers far advanced in academics compared to himself. Knowing he had the small membership of Nazi supporters to expand German lands, he needed to nationalize his appeal by broadcasting more speeches. Ernst Hanfstaengl, nicknamed "Putzi," a Harvard graduate who worked for Franklin Deleanor Roosevelt, made this analysis to the Office of Strategic Services and Adolph Hitler. Ernst Hanfstaengl attempted to explain to Allied officials that the Nazi state existed not just in an economic structure. He helped Hitler develop a marching cadence for the Harvard football team within a personality structure, Mein Kampf's funder. He later fled Germany to become a speechwriter for President Roosevelt.

> "There is only so much room in a brain, so much wall space,
> as it were, and if you furnish it with your slogans, the

opposition has no place to put up any pictures later on because the apartment of the brain is already crowded with your furniture." Hanfstaengl added, "Hitler admired the use the Catholic Church made of slogans and tried to imitate it."[21]

Wilhelm Reich explains it in his theoretical analysis of how deep, broad appeals can lead to loss of individual identity. He writes this theory, "Even more essential, however, is the *identification* of the individuals in the masses with the "führer." The more helpless the "mass-individual" has become, owing to his upbringing, the more evident is his identification with the führer, and the more the simple need for protection is disguised in the form of a feeling at one with the führer."[22]

The state's absolute power over the church replaced Holiness's image in denominational institutions. In its theology, Emil Lengyel describes, the Third Reich aspired not to be perpetrators and victims, but utopians as what he promises before the Reichstag fire's crime in his nationalist speeches. This did not prevent Adolph Hitler's participation in supporting the violent murders by the Freikorps, ex-veterans that killed suspected communists, and numerous others they suspected as communistic. Adolph Hitler began to moderate and conform to the social and political situation as the people were not seeking a dictator.[23] In its Third Reich stage, Germany will become transformed into the Holy Roman Empire's image, and Adolph Hitler refers to Mein Kampf as the Bible of National Socialists.

A Rhenish group of Christians in 1937 passed this resolution, "Hitler's word is God's law, the decrees, and laws, which represent it

---

[21] Langer, Walter C. Psychological Analysis of Adolph Hitler. CIA File. *Central Intelligence Agency*. Declassified August 1999.

[22] Reich, Wilhelm. William Steig, Ralph Manheim. *Listen, Little Man*. Published 1946. Noonday/Farrar, Straus & Giroux (NYC).

[23] Lengyel, Emil. "The Battlecries of Hitlerism Modified as Election Nears." *The New York Times*. 10 July 1932.

possess divine authority."[24] Adolph Hitler used youth rallies to prepare them as The Reich next generation. In The Atlantic, reporting by Timothy Ryback said, "Hitler's Forgotten Library: You can tell a lot about a person from what he reads. The surviving—and largely ignored—remnants of Adolf Hitler's personal library reveal a deep but erratic interest in religion and theology."[25] Adolph Hitler studied how the religious mind worked and bowed to authority.

Adolph Hitler mentally and emotionally worked every day for over ten years overseeing the past Bundesrat governance's slow deterioration. Its imperialist structure transitioned to the Weimar Republic, a developing democracy. These structural social pillars were also reasonable indications of how the German people developed their daily behaviors and how they related to the state. In its democratic phase, in 1924-1929, the German people had success in forming a government. Its economic structure and participation were acceptable between the "towns and country." Joseph Goebbels made it quite clear in the Nazi Nuremberg Rally that the people should dismiss this idea of majority government involvement as an impediment.

In the community town square streets, some intellectuals began to see what was taking shape and were migrating to other countries, but most Jews had no place to go. Adolph Hitler and his propagandists made clear that intellectuals were not needed in Germany as they were primarily in the way. Privileged Gitta Sereny, fourteen years old, remembered this and took individual steps to maintain her independent

---

[24] Langer, Walter C. Psychological Analysis of Adolph Hitler. CIA File. *Central Intelligence Agency*. Declassified August 1999.

[25] Ryback, Timothy W. "Hitler's Forgotten Library: You can tell a lot about a person from what he reads. The surviving—and largely ignored—remnants of Adolf Hitler's personal library reveal a deep but erratic interest in religion and theology." *The Atlantic*. May 2003.

sovereignty. Her defense was free and unrestricted speech placing herself in great danger of being gassed.[26]

In this time, several commissioned reports in the Allied Intelligence Services, such as the Office of Strategic Services (OSS), sustained the mind of Adolph Hitler's malignant narcissism and decompensation of his personality. Among his closest staff, aside from those that wanted to murder him, others tried to love him and would die for him. The madness of the people as Germany became economically smaller and had much less influence over its future. He and Alfred Rosenberg plotted to rob gold and treasure throughout Europe. They pondered the wealth from Soviet-Russian imperialists. Fiscally it took more money to run The Reich inefficiently as it had previously and was, in fact, a provisional military, financial system without an earning structure for ordinary people.

The devastating dissolution of the working Weimar Republic into an authoritarian ideological structure incapacitated the German government. Not able to sustain the logistical support it required. Seeking resources to maintain Germany, plans were initiated, based on its imperialistic past using military officers with that background, with as much success, which is to say their battles were not sustainable. The same corruptible practices emerged, and the elite survived well above the common soldier. Like before, murders were still routine. Princes Philip and Christoph von Hessen-Kassel, who heavily collaborated with Adolph Hitler lastly were killed by him.

Adolph Hitler and the German regime were striking back at the press for not writing complimentary stories. It was apparent to the observer that Adolph Hitler had very few ideas about governing but had taken the parts and pieces of scattered and sometimes conflicting

---

[26] Sereny, Gitta. "My Journey to Speer." *The Independent*. 30 Sept. 1995.

thoughts picked up along the roadside. Katherine Blunt of Elon Journal measured Hitler's rise in this way. This research showed the actor in Adolph Hitler and his exploitation of a "spiritual and physical terror," used in particular a combination to exploit and confuse listeners. Of utmost importance was the usage of the Volksempfänger, the people's radio broadcast all the time the voice of Adolph Hitler and his propaganda was run 24 hours per day while he shut down the news presses.

Emil Lengyel of *The Times* saw Hitlerism as described by supporters as "the political expression of the spiritual yearnings of a great epoch." Germany will become Adolph Hitler. He explained, as the natives in the wild, utterly independent without the need for anything, "autarky." Hitlerism will create a new economy, "The Third Reich will, therefore, endeavor to cut adrift. Imports will be restricted to a bare minimum. Nazi Germany will laugh at the resultant anger in other producing countries."[27]

Adolph Hitler envisioned a German government that burnt to the ground to save it. Interjecting vague concepts to the German people, such as alternative national identity. A Darwinist view was alleging that non-white "races" were geschichtslos, a people without history and origin. In time, the German system itself was geschichtslos, and Adolph Hitler began to doubt whether all Germans were as pure a race as he once thought, which started a campaign to compare their brains.

Gita Sereny wrote of her childhood experience after confronting her neighbors humiliating her Jewish doctor in Vienna, "It was extraordinary: within two minutes, the jeering crowd had dispersed, the brown guard had gone, the "street cleaners" had melted away. "Never do that again, "Dr. Berggrun said to us sternly, his small, round wife next to

---

[27] Lengyel, Emil. "The Battlecries of Hitlerism Modified as Election Nears." *The New York Times*. 10 July 1932.

him, nodding fervently, her face sagging with shock and exhaustion. "It is very dangerous." They gassed them in Sobibor in 1943."[28]

Jews who previously went to the American Embassy in Austria recalled being ordered to comply with Adolph Hitler's orders to prevent Jewish escape. The United States stood as reactionary as ever. To prevent Judaism from destroying the United States, diplomats attached quotas and began to work with the Nazi government by denying the majority of visas.[29] It was these political positions that Adolph Hitler stated to his inner circle that they would not take the example of their German racial policies, but those of the United States.

During the war, the soul of the German nation was wounded. By reverting to previous plans and in the most ravaged areas as possible and imaginable, a distant dream of greatness. Reminiscing, the German community and its social fabric became unrecognizable by Adolph Hitler, who had become a stick figure walking the streets of Vienna, Austria, with security. Gitty Sereny saw some of the meaningful times, recalling her childhood friend saying, "What happened to the promised freedom? The proud nobility and nationalism?" [30]

After the war, a lack of writers and authors had apparent effects on reading. Civics and national education had the most challenging time, and how people related to authority figures accelerated paranoia. Christian organizations cooperating under the Reich manipulated their way into the government, attempting to sideline Antifa, the anti-fascists. It was a conglomeration of attempts to rebuild the "New Germany." A problematic era recalled by Dr. Walter C. Langer as the era of a

---

[28] Sereny, Gitty. "My journey to Speer." *The Independent*. 30 Sept. 1995.
[29] Taylor, Melissa Jane. "Bureaucratic Response to Human Tragedy: American Consuls and the Jewish Plight in Vienna, 1938–1941." Holocaust and Genocide Studies. *Oxford University Press*. Volume 21, Number 2, Fall 2007, pp. 243-267. United States Holocaust Museum..
[30] Ibid.

Madness of the Nation filed as a study mentioned in mass psychology under "irrational societal behavior." In conjunction with its racial and economic conspiracy, it was judged by the Allies as a criminal conspiracy, war crimes, and terror.

Adolph Hitler also served in World War I with distinction, and during this combat tour, he came into contact with the little man inside him he identified as his Providence. For the rest of his life, he had never taken action unless "the voice" urged him to go ahead. His time in prison for treason against Germany began on 26 February 1924. Due to the Hitlerputsch that served as the auditorium for his speeches. The Nazi party chose the judges for the trial that drew attention to his sentence, which he conceived as "martyrdom" for the German people's benefit. Judges allowed Adolph Hitler to cross-examine witnesses against him. He often argued that World War I was wrong for democratic political forces that opposed German imperialism to undermine the German people's will. His first speech was directed at the judges who felt compelled to release him early.

The trial was the first of many exhibitions that tested Adolph Hitler's lie theory that there was some kernel of truth in every grotesque lie, and this kernel once turned into a boulder, gave such weight on the mind that it overcame doubt. His emotional outbursts changed his sentence from five years with the possibility of early parole to months. The other co-conspirators received light sentences. He emerged confident that his career would follow politics and persuasion. This first judicial judgment did not reveal Adolph Hitler as an overwhelming force but a fearful and weakened judiciary. Going back in time, let's look at the development of Hitler the Man not made for peacetime.

The first twenty years or so after leaving the Army, he spent in psychological recovery. Historians called them the "calm years." Adolph

Hitler did not isolate but carried on a series of social experiments while going into and out of prison. He hardened his beliefs from the veteran experience and studied the reaction of instigating several small uprisings. Using various art forms, incorporating several graphics, flag designs, and uniforms into a military strike force's horrifying vision. Still, he favored a nationalistic theme in an appeal of building back Germany from World War One.

Inspired by Western and American capitalists, he enthralled investors who built the first designs of a military fleet, tank vehicles, and machinery. After making progress on imagining a stronger Germany, the nationalist vision began to form something more hateful, spiteful, and uncontrollable. For a short time, he and Rudolph Hess, Deputy Führer, took steps to pressure the United States out of the growing effort to push back Germany from creating war. In the following paragraphs, Adolph Hitler, the inexperienced nationalist and a political leader, took on a personality that combined previous German leaders' aspects.

Mein Kampf was the ultimate portrayal of Adolph Hitler as a historical figure. [31] At this time, Anton Drexler had begun to form the Nazi party; he was a machine automation specialist, a railway toolmaker, and a locksmith. Drexler could not expand the party resulting in Adolph Hitler taking the reins. Still, no one attributed him as Hitler but the adult small formed boy Adolph, Alois, and Klara Hitler's son. With the increased popularity in the coming years, he was considered a comic figure practicing an act at the local bars. Until he started "Hitler's Beer Hall Putsch," *The Stormer* uprising.

---

[31] Murray, Henry A. "Analysis of The Personality of Adolph Hitler." Office of Strategic Services (OSS). *Central Intelligence Agency Archive.* Copy No. 14 of 30. Harvard Psychological Clinic. October 1943.

Adolph Hitler's father Alois married a cousin, and forthwith came Adolph Hitler's family. He was a German peasant, a small man, with little actual work experience and tendencies to become incoherently hysterical. Working as an espionage agent for the emerging Reichswehr after military service and the Soviet putdown in Munich, Adolph Hitler encountered Anton Drexler. Educationally Adolph Hitler was only interested in history and geography, possessing no additional skills adequately. He could not proceed to pursue his aspirations as an architect. His description is elaborate, lonely, self-isolating, and loathsome by Henry A. Murray.[32] There were competing theories about Adolph Hitler's emotional stability as he proceeded. Some of the most serious entertained his assassination.

Professor Max von Gruber of the University of Munich, the eugenics expert known throughout Europe, made this observation note of Adolph Hitler in law court 1923, which was publicly accessible at the time. In the modern era, Joseph Goebbels' story about Adolph Hitler assessed his superiority, but nothing like he appeared in reality.

> "It was the first time I had seen Hitler close at hand. Face and head of inferior type, crossbreed, having a low receding forehead, ugly nose, broad cheekbones, little eyes, dark hair. An expression not of a man exercising authority in perfect self-command but of raving excitement. In the end, an expression of satisfied egotism."[33]--- Professor Max von Gruber

Despite his unattractiveness, *the voice* he called *Provenance* (auditory guidance while awake) drew some charisma and a government position. Those that bend to his will Adolph Hitler feels contempt. Their submission revolts him, indicating he would respect them were they to

---

[32] Ibid.

[33] Langer, Walter C. "Psychological Analysis of Adolph Hitler." CIA File. *Central Intelligence Agency*. Declassified August 1999.

behave masculine. The crowd he addresses is established in such a timely fashion to be part of the day after they have worked hardest and unlikely to resist, so he claims they are feminine in their characteristics. In rationalization of the way he becomes abusive, he uses vulgarities hurled at them. His speeches reflected partial statements that Alois, his father, made toward him during his many beatings. Adolph Hitler took on the task of murdering his close friends. His half-niece Geli Raubal either killed or drove her to commit suicide. Followers who disagreed with Adolph Hitler were no exception and were sent to the front. Adolph Hitler was behind at least two plots to kill his manager associates in aeronautic accidents.

Psychologically ordinary Adolph Hitler has some recognized abilities and is not an imbecile operating in areas he designates, such as speeches and specific basic military strategy. His capacity to give simple analysis to what others find in complex situations is observed as uncanny, attacking others at the time of their greatest vulnerability and intuitively reading oppositional emotions. This passive-aggressiveness and paranoia added to his cunning. He was smart enough to romanticize the people by playing to their feelings of weaknesses and vulnerabilities. His close fans, too, are selective, not intellectuals. He believed in mutual non-intimate love affairs among men, especially in Joseph Goebbels, and may have been polymorphous. Psychoanalysts considered him schizoid; on this basis, he carefully selected his intellectual advisors.

Adolph Hitler's policy with the wealthy was loaded with the higher echelon. Election rigging and manipulation characterized the German voting system that brought him into office.[34] Some touting of his

---

[34] Kershaw, Ian. "How Hitler Won Over the German People." *Spiegel.* And Spiegel Online. January 30, 2008.

"accomplishments," Joseph Goebbels magnified each military maneuver into an overwhelming success. Until after 1939, the real heavy lifting of the war led to massive confrontation and battles. His economic achievements turned into rubble as sickness, food shortages, and the outcome of his ruination of the German government became incapable of sustaining itself, an impression of Leon Goldensohn, psychiatrist and Nazi suspect interviewer at Nuremberg.[35] Albert Speer pointed out Adolph Hitler's tragic toxicity and the system as an openly shared account. The well-established German government, from all indications, had a well-run administration, but after Adolph Hitler, decisions slowly moved from factual and evidence-based findings to ideological choices. Adolph Hitler embossed his beliefs imposing military rule while the government needed to support it he destroyed. Were it not for his generals, the war would end early as a political failure with superb choreography and acting.

Joseph Goebbels was to Adolph Hitler, an abnormal attachment that ultimately cost his wife and children's lives plus the imaginary world they created. Adolph Hitler thinks about himself most of the time and pens his policies at the discussion table. Nicolas Fairweather noted that Adolph Hitler was considered remarkably ethnocentric, to put it mildly. He was opposed to Socialism and Communism as most conservatives of his time. Primarily he thought the German people were a "chosen people" that needed to be ruled and the Jews eradicated. Adolph Hitler believed democratic governments and political institutions had failed to pursue total extermination.[36] In his concept of life, since the Jews were a tiny minority and he was the authority, it stood,

---

[35] Goldensohn, Leon and Robert Gellately, from *The Nuremberg Interviews*. 14 Apr. 1946. Reprint edition Vintage. 25 Oct. 2005. ISBN-10: 1400030439.
[36] Fairweather, Nicolas. "Hitler and Hitlerism: Germany Under the Nazis." *The Atlantic*. April 1932.

they should be eradicated not for what they had done but for the mere reason he could exploit them economically and industrially as slaves.

One month later, Nicolas Fairweather was able to derive the policy direction he was taking as Adolph Hitler believed he was infallible. Within a month, after speaking with Nicolas Fairweather, Adolph Hitler has been reassured that he is on the right path. He has decided on the opening of the first concentration camp, Dachau, in March 1933. Adolph Hitler conceals Dachau to Nicolas Fairweather. Mr. Fairweather expressed several doubts about Adolph Hitler's sanity and wrote, "Hitler does not believe in objective thinking about national questions. He is impatient of cold, intellectual considerations."[37]

The dictatorial nature of Adolph Hitler began to emerge, and the personality cannot be hidden by his nationalism. There are insufficient comprehension and minimal ability to grasp abstract ideas, which may cause his limited ability to succeed in his personal endeavors, painting, and architecture. However, the skills he has are used forcefully and without restraint as an excellent tribal leader. The sum of this profile is Adolph Hitler closely resembles his followers. Karl Marx's portrayal describes 'the dictatorship of the proletariat and the formula for making a great communist nation.'[38]

Here's what we know about Adolph Hitler's speeches recalling that it was Joseph Goebbels that propagandized many of his presentations. Practicing his famous speeches, he spent the construction of their fundamentals during his five months in prison. There were sixteen speeches from 1919 to 1926, with an attendance of 7,000 each. Up to three hours of practice for the most formal statements to only minutes for informal gatherings averaged around fifty hours of preparation.

---

[37] Ibid.
[38] Ibid.

Still, Adolph Hitler had no one to copy. It was a purely personal inspiration.

The early development of the Nazi party's popularity went rough, and Adolph Hitler was viewed as an entertainment figure before he became violent and consolidated his power using military support. Robert Wilde from *ThoughtCo* explained membership in the Nazi party went from minimal participation to overwhelming support by 1928, just ten years. Adolph Hitler took the criticism. He looked like a character out of silent movies.[39] People were making reference to Charlie Chaplin and having a good laugh imitating him in the street. Albert Speer correctly described Adolph Hitler as the first dictatorship plot that directly confronted the structure of technical and scientific globalism, later described by A. Khoshkish as the myth of fascism.[40]

Though Adolph Hitler eventually developed consensus and spoke with supporters, it proved caustic, and he could not establish a mode of rational governance. Adolph Hitler's ability to manipulate conservative politicians at the same time routing his opponents who believed in social democracy and communism was masterful on the one hand. It also had a clear emphasis on conservative thought that was earthbound and apocalyptic in gothic governance images where one beast advanced at the expense of brutally consuming another. Albert Speer, the dictatorial supporter, and architect described how Adolph Hitler spoke about how

---

[39] Wilde, Robert. "The Early Development of the Nazi Party." *ThoughtCo.* 14 June 2018.

[40] Speer, Albert. "His final statement to the Nuremberg court." 31 Aug. 1946. Trials of The Major War Criminals. Before the International Military Tribunal. 14 November 1944- 01 October 1946. Published Nuremberg, Germany 1947. See Khoshkish, A. *The Socio-Political Complex: An Interdisciplinary Approach to Political Life* (Pergamon international library of science, technology, engineering, and social studies). Pergamon; 1st edition 22 Oct. 2013.

Germany was formed into a myth during the Nuremberg Trial proceed-
ings. Ultimately becoming choreographers of its fall.

> "Hitler's dictatorship differed in one fundamental point from
> all its predecessors in history. His was the first dictatorship in
> the present period of technical development, a dictatorship that
> made full use of all technical means for the domination of its
> own country. Through technical means like the radio and the
> loud-speaker, eighty million people were deprived of inde-
> pendent thought. It was thereby possible to subject them to the
> will of one man."[41]

Nicholas Fairweather placed this in the context that people may
have felt Adolph Hitler lived in the past. Adolph Hitler had learned to
romanticize the past to the point where he dominated it in false cultural
representations about making himself great. Adolph Hitler's conception
and policies of the global threat imposed by liberal trade policies have
already been outdated. The fault in Adolph Hitler's policies is based on
the elimination of economic rivalry. A rivalry which, if suitably pursued, could enhance mutual cooperation. Adolph Hitler dismissed this
as a corrupt liberal notion not to be taken seriously by The Reich.[42]

Before he took over police powers, Adolph Hitler did not view himself as a dictator, "Our task is to give the dictator, when he comes, a
people ready for him!" Hitler, in a speech on 4 May 1923. He learned
that through controversy, he could enthrall people. Still, it had to be a
constant infusion of violence, and this he got by making the people not
better citizens but war criminals, particularly the Christian church.
Adolph Hitler was adding Christians to the enemies list. Adolph Hitler
was convinced by others to become a dictator, and the voice in his head

---

[41]Ibid.
[42] Fairweather, Nicholas. "Hitler and Hitlerism: Germany Under the Nazis." *The Atlantic*. April 1932 Issue.

Providence. Economics experts and industrialists well-funded the Reich, including IG Farben, the chemical company that designed Zyklon B gas. The U.S. robber-barons turned criminal.

Adolph Hitler was a child of a cruel father and out of sequence so far as his place in time. His arguments were based on the past. Due to military service at the front, he was absent from what was occurring elsewhere in Germany. Adolph Hitler was apparently a candidate for war trauma treatment based on his exposure to combat. The emergence of a second Adolph Hitler that he called *Providence* was a disturbing mental health development. Adolph Hitler often would do nothing unless Providence instructed him to. These command instructions were widely accepted by others surrounding him, questioning whether he and they were utterly stable.[43] Although his speeches have received some notoriety, it is not out of the question that this thunderous clamor, which was sometimes incoherent that did not always make sense to the modern ear, was more of an expression of his early abusive and schizoid life.

---

[43] Langer, Walter C. "Psychological Analysis of Adolph Hitler." CIA File. *Central Intelligence Agency*. Declassified August 1999.

Listen carefully to the QANON, and an attendant listener will hear the antecedent evangelical positions. Leaving the Gospel fundamentalism of Reverand Billy Graham and Benjamin Smith of Philadelphia themes considered undeniable are made into fallacy. From pedophilia campaigns, abortion and infanticide, prosperity teachers, distancing from the traditional political presentation, and numerous other positions have been turned on their head into common lies. Many are also derivative of Prime Minister Benjamin Netanyahu's King Cyrus pagan posts regarding the Trump family in the Old Testament. QANON has obtained a new role in the Conservative sphere of an enforcer of distorted church doctrine that carries along with it an apocraphyl message of the archaic state of mind seen in fictional Gothicism. QANON is also a psychological program as it borrows from fictionalized apocraphyl themes and dresses these heroes as nonfiction characters who play out as pagan emissaries of Trump.

Three developments in the world are creating an image in many minds. The intense description of Three Frogs of deceit in Revelation 16 came from the dried river Euphrates. Deep inside of President Trump's psyche, he has been nurtured and influenced by political forces to accept his role as King Cyrus, a pagan king of the Old Testament.[44] President Putin has been consulting with "Babooshka" (Grandmother) Baba Vanga, who has given him spiritual messages to follow a world dominion path. Both being of similar unhealthy mental stability. John

---

[44] Burton, Tara Isabella. "The biblical story the Christian right uses to defend Trump." VOX. 05 Mar. 2018.

Lockett of *The Sun* wrote, "Lord of The World." Psychic Baba Vanga, who predicted the 9/11 terror attacks, also foretold 'unstoppable' Vladimir Putin will one day rule Earth." [45] In this view of Dominionism, the world is carved into thirds. One of the major proponents of these occult and futuristic Apocalyptic views has been Michael Pence and Franklin Graham, the supporter of Republican Conservative and neo-Protestantism.

They are not undone by Benjamin Netanyahu, who has publicly announced being influenced by a mystic interpreter, writes Carlo Strenger, who wrote "Netanyahu and the Mystics of Safed." Mr. Strenger drew an analogy between some of Benjamin Netanyahu's best delusions as Winston Churchill. Talmudic scholars suggested his leadership would most likely result in the massacre at 'Bar Kochba,' the Romans' catastrophic loss when the Jews were nearly annihilated.[46]

In a pivotal position between these leaders stands a conspiratorial Vice President, Michael Pence that routinely interacts with atheist Christian White Evangelicals that support President Trump. Mr. Pence appears conspiratorial because he is busy at work involved in a transition. First, he is helping to create a new identity for Christian White Evangelicals. Second, he is working toward integrating these Evangelicals into a political base for Republican conservatives with an adjustment. This political base is known throughout the world as the neo-Protestant movement. Their primary objective is to ruin and spoil cultural achievement.

Like the others that are influenced by mysticism, Michael Pence addresses neo-Protestants with a contrary belief. Shalom Goldman,

---

[45] Lockett, Jon. "Lord of The World. Psychic Baba Vanga who predicted 9/11 terror attacks also foretold 'unstoppable' Vladimir Putin will one day rule Earth." *The Sun*. March 19, 2018.

[46] Strenger, Carlo. "Netanyahu and the Mystics of Safed." *Haaretz*. 17 June 2011.

who follows Mr. Pence, carefully describes his religious beliefs as the "Heartland Christian." Shalom Goldman thought, "As a religion scholar, Julie Ingersoll noted in her 2015 book *Building God's Kingdom: Inside the World of Christian Reconstruction,* this branch of evangelical thought advocates "dominion theology." The biblical worldview that points to how neo-Protestants are to exercise dominion over creation, especially over people for whom they deem themselves responsible, e.g., constituents and unbelievers. Coincidentally this view removes all of the restrictions globalists now have to drill oil and unrestricted global warming legislation.

Vice President Michael Pence was influenced by Hal Lindsay, a dispensationalist.[47] One of the reasons why these views feel so bizarre and confusing is that they are all extra-Biblical. Stephen R. Sizer called Hal Lindsay The *Father of Apocalyptic Zionism.* Michael Pence's theocracy has subsumed Judaism into a nationalist structure of a Christianized Zionism. This has set up the narrative that President Trump's nationalism is juxtaposed to a nationalist Zionism. The conflict is apparent that neo-Protestant white nationalists have a reason to hate the nationalist Zionist. Either think each is vying for world domination.

Under the intellectual leadership of Rousas John Rushdoony (1916-2001), a reconstructionist, Professor Ingersoll's words define this movement, he "laid an intellectual foundation that would shape the twenty-first-century Christian subculture, developing what would become the religious right's critique of the American social order, and plotting strategies to bring about change." Rushdoony advocated the institution of Old Testament "Biblical Law" and New Testament civil

---

[47] Sizer, Stephen R. 'Lindsey's Literalistic Dispensationalist Hermeneutic', *Hal Lindsey: The Father of Apocalyptic Zionism* (updated 11 April 1999. See also Julie J. Ingersoll, *Building God's Kingdom: Inside the World of Christian Reconstruction* (New York: Oxford University Press, 2015).

law in the U.S. "You can have two kinds of law," he told an interviewer."[48] In modern terminology, the wars these worldviews create are environmental and commercial in nature, each nation surviving within its own boundary.[49]

In part, environmental warfare is already happening in the Middle East via climate change and terrorism. Dominionism will push the region off a cliff. There is also a social psychological side to the Environmental Modification Convention, ENMOD. It can be used to terrorize populations, such as when Yugoslavia forces used uranium to gain political and ethnic leverage, which was considered an environmental war. When we hear that NATO should be disbanded, the result of that takes the teeth out of the ENMOD treaty and releases new possibilities for those with specific self-destructive goals.

This decline of NATO fits the Aleksandr Dugin narrative, including the end of civilizations. Dugin predicts this will not be extraterrestrial warfare but will be instigated in a far bloodier battle by mankind, millenarianism.[50] Aleksandr Dugin, in his philosophical and ideological state, is not far removed from R.J. Rushdoony. The Fourth Theory is, in practicality, self-destructive with a modern fascist face of one person in charge.

When President Dwight Eisenhower was about to leave office, he had already instituted the Operation Wetback program, the most

---

[48] Goldman, Shalom. "Mike Pence on the "American Heartland" and the Holy Land." *Patheos*. 20 July 2016.

[49] ENMOD. The Center for Media and Democracy. "Environmental warfare." Source Watch. Note: The 1977 Treaty is the "United Nations General Assembly Resolution 31/72, TIAS 9614 Convention on the Prohibition of Military or Any Other Hostile Use of Environmental Modification Techniques." Environmental Modification Convention.

[50] Dugin, Alexander. And Alain Sorel. *The Fourth Political Theory*. Arktos Media Ltd. 16 July 2012.

extensive mass deportation. It was a signal in history that something changed in American beliefs along the Mexican border. There was a domestic war igniting between two of the active pillars in society, the United States government, and businesses who were bulking up their power. The government power was beginning to exert control over companies had not seen in environmental, tax, and trade; now, this regulation was entering the field of labor and exercising standards. Exploitation and commodifying nonunion labor are central to the profits.

Manjari Chatterjee Miller, in *The Role of Beliefs in Identifying Rising Powers,* offers historical debate. What is the role of beliefs in domestic and international relationships? Some of the world's greatest thinkers have concluded that societies split into a republic and an empire cannot sustain its consensus. As a belief, Dominionism brought different viewpoints that were already disproven. The elimination, punishment, and removal of races could not be justified, which led to cause the rest of civilization falling.[51]

President Nixon's election coincided with the common belief in American politics by electing officials intuitively. Unfortunately, one could also see that reporters who had once been issuing the news by educating the public began writing intuitively. Such important issues like the Vietnam War focused primarily on the event, but not its cause. Most combat veterans realized that War politics was an expression of two powers, a combined authoritarian interest of government and business.

Daniel K. Williams wrote in *God's Own Party* President Nixon's strategic trajectory toward Christian White Evangelicals, not unlike what is seen today. Using politics and interjecting it to the level where

---

[51] Miller, Manjari Chatterjee; "The Role of Beliefs in Identifying Rising Powers." *The Chinese Journal of International Politics.* Volume 9. Issue 2. 1 June 2016. pp. 211–238.

it cost lives and impacted millions of people to win neo-Protestants who were anti-liberals established patterns from the pulpit relegated to a political gospel not based on personal integrity and strict action.[52] President Nixon began work on justifying his Southern Strategy, which nationally polarized politics as white and black. In the sublime, it was communicated as the master-slave relationship.

The statistics never showed promise during Conservative Republican administrations. The labor statistics showed that in Lyndon B. Johnson, known for his Immigration and Nationality Act and Civil Rights in 1965, 53% of the economy led with manufacturing, by Ronald Reagan in 1988 was 39 percent, and George W. Bush in 2004 only 9%. By this time, Corporations had a well-developed dependency with the Republican Conservatives readied to cut their home base in the United States adrift and move to China. Behind this change in government policy stood the archaic United States Department of Commerce, the agency responsible for overseas economic opportunities that never reigned in a declaration that United States corporations only had a responsibility to stockholders, not employees.

There was no grassroots revolt to enforce clawback and punitive fines for abandoned plants. It took until 2011 for manufacturing changes to gather sufficient opposition when Senator Bernie Sanders took to the floor and rebuked the Senate for its free trade policies, reported by Aaron Belford, of *The Progressive*.[53] So when was the time Americans wanted to Make America Great Again? Was it when they were silent? This was the primarily white silent reactionary profile of

---

[52] Williams, Daniel. *God's Own Party: The Making of the Christian Right*. Oxford Scholarship Online. September 2010. ISBN-13: 9780195340846.
[53] Belford, Aaron. "A Look at The Record: Bernie Sanders in 2011 Denounces Free Trade Pacts." *The Progressive*. 13 Oct. 2011.

constituents that eventually developed into the Christian dominionist theonomy.

Still, the Republican Conservatives managed to blame and a large portion of the guilt over the China incident on all the people and their "liberal if not communistic labor unions." Republican Conservatives were so successful at finding the scapegoat that they promoted another fallacy. Capitalist expansion and exodus would still bring democracy wherever it went, emphasizing this belief was more potent than China and its perceived inferior people.

New social and political campaigns began to emerge starring celebrity preachers from the Southern Strategy. In the Moral Majority, Jerry Falwell, Jr., Pat Robertson, Christian Broadcasting Network, and 700 Club started what amounted to a political campaign to win elections in a televised social club atmosphere. Regina Nippert wrote in explaining the locals' feedback, "*Mixing Christianity and Politics Is Killing the Church*." Christian White Evangelicals brought the first message of being an individual "king" to agitate neo-Protestant Christians.[54]

Republican and Democratic Conservatives dealt with Southerners to whom they closely aligned. Pentecostal tent preachers like the Assembly of God A.A. Allen, Rev. Robert W. Schambach, and Benjamin Smith Sr., Pastor of Deliverance Evangelistic Church in Germantown, Pa., all after the famed Oral Roberts were disputed by the new apostatized Christian White Evangelicals. In response to white supremacy and nationalism, the social gospel was born and reframed into tent-preaching with the strong support of the Civil Rights church movement. It was not capable of emphasizing the separation of state and church. It

---

[54] Nippert, Regina, "Mixing Christianity and Politics Is Killing the Church." *The Hill*. 29 May 2015.

had not incorporated a defense for the Constitution, just a racial theory of the Republican and Democratic Conservative message. A message that missed what James Madison clarified.

James Madison explains why the church should not run with the state:

> "Because the establishment proposed by the Bill is not requisite for the support of the Christian Religion. To say that it is, is a contradiction to the Christian Religion itself, for every page of it disavows a dependence on the powers of this world. Nay, it is a contradiction in terms; for a Religion not invented by the human policy must have pre-existed and been supported before establishment by an individual policy. It is moreover to weaken in those who profess this Religion a pious confidence in its innate excellence and the patronage of its Author. And to foster in those who still reject it, a suspicion that its friends are too conscious of its fallacies to trust it to its own merits." ---James Madison. 1785 speech to the Virginia General Assembly.

The fearsome threesome Jerry Falwell, Jr. in the Moral Majority, Pat Robertson, was a perfect Christian White Evangelical match and Richard M. Nixon. It helped elect President Ronald Reagan, a populist. Ian Haney-Lopez of *Salon* news showed, steeped in the racial theories of eugenics and the Southern Strategy, race theory, and Presidential Reaganomics was publicized as "*The racism at the heart of the Reagan presidency.*"[55] Wilhelm Reich, MD wrote in 1946 about conservative race theory, "Race theorists, who are as old as imperialism itself, want to achieve racial purity in peoples whose interbreeding, as a result of

---

[55] Haney-Lopez, Ian. "The racism at the heart of the Reagan presidency." *Salon*. 11 Jan. 2014.

the expansion of world economy, is so far advanced that racial purity can have meaning only to a numbskull." [56]

One example of American politics with religious Conservatism was seen in South Africa. In 1986 the Evangelical Alliance published their writings: *Evangelical Witness in South Africa: South Africans critique their theology and practice* by 132 Concerned Evangelicals. The group talked through their frustrations that "our evangelical family has a track record of supporting and legitimizing oppressive regimes here and elsewhere and have tended to assume conservative positions which maintain the status quo." [57] Overall it was difficult to participate in an alliance that pronounced conservative Christian viewpoints while falling under exploitation by their fellow brethren.

Similar problems were reported in former Axis powers and American allies of Romania previously in exile, Hungary, Czechoslovakia, Slovakia, and Poland. [58]Like in the United States' religions, the most famous of these is the European Christian Political Movement (ECPM), founded in November 2002 in Lakitelek, Hungary, a country with a fascist tether by strong past alliances to Positive Christianity. Viktor Mihály Orbán is the prime minister and leader of the national conservative Fidesz party and friends with President Trump.[59]Viktor Mihály Orbán, once a liberal, now moves among the extreme right where national purity priorities of Slobodan Milosevic remain popular.

---

[56] Reich, Wilhelm. William Steig, Ralph Manheim. *Listen, Little Man.* First Published 1946.
[57] "Evangelicals and Apartheid." 11 Dec. 2013. *Evangelical Alliance.* 176 Copenhagen Street London N1 0ST Tel: 020 7520 3830 (Mon - Fri, 9am - 5pm) Fax: 020 7520 3850.
[58] Ibid.
[59] European Christian Political Movement (ECPM) founded in November 2002 in Lakitelek, Hungary.

Viktor Mihály Orbán is reported on by Gabor Ivanyi of *Euronews, "There's nothing Christian about Orban's democratic values*." Writing that, one minister sees the unfortunate "export of Hungarian illiberalism (newly called Christian Democracy)." He says because the "Refusal, starvation, creating bureaucratic and legal hurdles, and spreading false news about asylum seekers is particularly anti-Christian behavior."[60] Long before Viktor Mihály Orbán, the United States neo-Protestant movement set the table for his approval among dominionist Christians. This shows a purpose to cross-culturally seed the United States with Hungarian policy. Zero Tolerance in the President Trump administration is derivative of this Hungarian system.

Seeking to change the worldview that has become so nationally disregarded and unpopular, Conservatives latched onto speakers like Corrie Ten Boom (her heartwarming stories and elder charm) and Dr. Francis Schaeffer's as personal members of their reactionary family. To take the first step in recreating Christian fundamentalism, Dr. Francis Schaeffer became a household name. He continued to remain so after his death in 1984. In Christian Evangelical churches across America, the beloved Dr. Francis Schaeffer, the precursor to R.J. Rushdoony, made an inroad dead. He was the first to draw on Reformation as the incident that ended church domination by corrupting it with the church aesthetics movement. Its regard for science, nakedness, and vulgarity he perceived was expressed in its art form.

Perhaps to rescue Christian Evangelicals from displays of intimacy, Dr. Shaeffer sought to Reconstruct Christianity into a reformist view for the neo-Protestant churches. Dr. Francis Shaeffer thought the

---

[60] Ivanyi, Gabor. "There's nothing Christian about Orban's democratic values." Euronews. 09 May 2018.

explanation of the future lay in the past. He would redefine the story of history in favor of Christianity and not a surprise the "Christian White Evangelical" movement. He reframed the collective knowledge of historical events into the framework of a so-called Christian Reconstruction era; this period was supposedly a partial rebuilding of the losses Evangelicals had accrued in the illegitimacy of the relatively severe 1960s.

Dr. Schaeffer, on the other hand, defined social development regarding Christian and non-Christian truth. He asserted that worldviews such as Dr. Jung could not be valid because he was not Christian. A widely accepted view of Christian White Evangelicals derived not from Biblical validation but also prejudgment toward unbelievers. Christian White Evangelicals extended this belief to all forms of science unless the outcome results originated from a Christian who was, by extension, guided by God, who is all-knowledgeable. The idea is the empowerment of individual Christians as sovereign beings discounting man as fallible.

Dr. Francis Schaeffer's philosophy ("Presuppositional Apologetics - Wikipedia.") is presuppositional, intending to mean that in justifying and defending the faith, one believes Christianity is the only "…basis for rational thought. It claims the Bible is a revelation and attempts to expose flaws in other worldviews. Apart from presuppositions, any sense of any human experience, and there are no reasons to discuss worldviews with a non-Christian." This secularized Christianity paved the way for an even more virulent nationalist and supremacist view.

R.J. Rushdoony's solution to the racist dilemma as Dr. Schaeffer's convictions gave way to further the spread of Christian radicalism. Rev. Rousas John Rushdoony, an Armenian-born religious (1916–2001), came to the United States. He believed that heaven on Earth could be possible only if it were institutionalized. Most of those that underwent

Christian Reconstructionist theology continued the Dr. Schaeffer outline later transferred themselves into the R.J. Rushdoony camp.[61] Their position was advanced by Christian Zionists, who proceeded to support wall concepts in Israel.[62] Dr. Schaeffer and Rushdoony clarified their sociological views with Biblical perspectives, many rejected.

This worldview did not extend to Christian Classical Covenant Theology throughout the United States, a grouping that was not in favor of the Christian Reconstructionist theory of R.J. Rushdoony.[63] Christopher Ladd at *Forbes* explains in "*Pastors, Not Politicians, Turned Dixie Republican.*" [64] In the United States, Judith Goldstein of Humanity in Action *The Presence of the Past: Confronting the Nazi State and Jim Crow* raises societal comparison between Nazi Germany and the United States that follows what they used to call Positive Christianity, a political gospel.

Judith Goldstein's documents that accepted differences in the cultures did not negate the distinct similarities. She prominently describes racial theory and practice, policies, and other societal reinforcers that, in their continuity, still threaten American democracy.[65],[66] A prominent concern is the fear by white women that black or brown people were given freedoms. This generated fear among whites; they would seek retribution for generations of what whites did to them. This portrayal

---

[61] Rushdoony, R.J. *Sovereignty.* Vallecito, CA: Ross House Essays, 2007. pp. 149-153.

[62] Sizer, Stephen. *Christian Zionism: Road-map to Armageddon?* IVP Academic. ISBN-10: 0830853685. 01 Jan. 2006.

[63] Ibid.

[64] Ladd, Christopher. "Pastors, Not Politicians, Turned Dixie Republican." *Forbes.* 27 Mar. 2017.

[65] Goldstein, Judith S. *Presence of the Past: Confronting the Nazi State and Jim Crow.* In Humanity in Action: Collected Essays and Talks, pp. 32-42. New York: Humanity in Action Press, 2014. ASIN: B00MOIO318.

[66] Abramsky, Sasha. "As Trump consolidates his power, the history of 1930s Germany repeats itself." Sacramento Bee. 18 Mar. 2018..

of revenge racism haunted most romantic visions in Republican conservatives as vehement opposition to the voting rights act. It is evident in portions of Aleksandr Dugin's viewpoints that trend to theonomy.

Martyn Percy of *The Guardian* reported on "*To know Donald Trump's faith is to understand his politics*." To understand President Trump's relationship to Christian White Evangelicals, "Start with his inauguration ceremony. Pastor Paula White was one of the clergies nominated to pray for Trump on the day. A televangelist and exponent of the "health, wealth and prosperity" movement, she preaches the "prosperity gospel." An unorthodox approach to Christianity that says God wants people to be productive and makes them wealthy. So, the richer you are, the more obvious it is that God loves you, and the stronger your faith is."[67] The total of how far the Christian White Evangelical had sunk so low no longer recognizing that God's value of people is according to heart, not wealth.

Pastor Paula White is giving a traditional line of Republicanism used by robber barons who justified their wealth and the poverty of their workers, stating, "our riches are God's will." It is a derivative from the 19th Century belief of Thomas Carlyle, who asserted history is only a continuous record of great men's experiences.

In this conception, their "us and them" world, such admiration fit neatly to the Christian White Evangelical. The inseparable relationship between a robust male power and a victim relationship that is abusive and supported becomes not just a discussion of male admirability and nobility but sovereignty. Robber baron's actions followed, with strict controls over labor practices. Creation Ministry explains the belief system like this in their article by Jerry Bergman, "Darwin's critical

---

[67] Percy, Martyn. "To know Donald Trump's faith is to understand his politics." *The Guardian*. 06 Feb. 2018.

influence on the ruthless extremes of capitalism."[68] In the classic *Behemoth*, Franz Neumann describes the capitalist corporation as the National Socialism (Nazi) vehicle that rests on an economic engine.[69] Male sovereignty is at the core of neo-Protestantism.

Nancy D. Wadsworth, in "*The racial demons that help explain evangelical support for Trump.*" explains in VOX, "But these sympathetic critics fail to grapple with the idea that Trump's racism and misogyny might resonate with the evangelical base, which happens to constitute about 35 percent of the GOP coalition. Racism and intolerance are more woven into the fabric of evangelicalism than these Christian critics care to accept."[70]

Frank Schaeffer, Jr. made the case against theonomic construct as dangerous in his article *With God On Our Side-Christian Zionism Exposed.*[71] Notably, it was taken up by Steve Bannon to justify vengeance on all Muslims for the 11 September 2001 attacks on World Trade Center. Through several attempts, this justification for attacking Arab nations and individuals was by the vis-à-vis equivalent to a revenge formula that annihilated an entire ethnicity by a single act. By a contrived belief system behind it, one could make it theocratic and legally sounding, but its framework's origin was not Biblically supported.

---

[68] Bergman, Jerry. "Darwin's critical influence on the ruthless extremes of capitalism." Creation Ministries International. *Journal of Creation* 16(2):105–109—August 2002.

[69] Neumann, Franz L. *Behemoth: The Structure and Practice of National Socialism 1933-1944.* Ivan R. Dee; Book Club Edition. 16 May 2009). ISBN-10: 1566638194.

[70] Wadsworth, D. Nancy. "The racial demons that help explain evangelical support for Trump." *VOX.* 30 Apr. 2018.

[71] Schaeffer, Frank. "With God on Our Side-Christian Zionism Exposed." *HuffPost.* 25 May 2011.

Steve Bannon uses these themes in creating mental images of the gothic white avenging angel, i.e., Donald J. Trump. [72,73]

Barry Hankins, *Francis Schaeffer, And the Shaping of Evangelical America* essentially states Dr. Schaeffer as a populist minister and theologian lost a great deal of credibility not standing against President Nixon to oppose the message "win at a racial cost." Therefore, his religious views fell more in line with neo-Protestantism. Tom Heneghan reports on the ordinary citizens that participate in the 'Neo-Protestant' challenge seen in France's political upheaval.' Mr. Heneghan goes on to say, "For Regis Dubray, that approach echoes some economic positions of the U.S. Republican Party and of the evangelical "neo-Protestants" who support it."[74]

It is a shallow faith absent of spirituality and sanctification', two doctrinal requirements of the traditional Christian religion. Therefore, as a light-faith, it lends heartedly to populism among the ordinary people that want to hear about God but not experience spiritual transformation and be called out on deviations of immorality. It does, however, serve a purpose to the Republican Conservatives. Who goes after them for support by cultural considerations, namely being white, feeling individually powerless, economically abandoned, and isolated, some of the critical elements necessary for totalitarian regimes' influence? So far as the Gospel requirement of "Living in Truth," they want no parts of that.

---

[72] Schaeffer, Edith. *The Tapestry: The Life and Times of Francis and Edith Schaeffer.* pp. 258-59. W Pub Group; Special memorial ed edition. 01 May 1985. ISBN-10: 0849930162.
[73] Hankins, Barry. *Francis Schaeffer And the Shaping of Evangelical America.* Library of Religious Biography. pp. 193-196. Eerdmans. 03 Nov. 2008. ISBN-10: 0802863892.
[74] Heneghan, Tom. 'Neo-Protestant' challenge seen in France's political upheaval.' CRUX Taking the Catholic Pulse. 13 Sept. 2017. Religious News Service.

Frank Schaeffer, Jr., in "With God on Our Side-Christian Zionism Exposed," explained the religious right's psyche subject to various ethnic and state justification for a genocidal solution and kill-on-sight posture in the Middle East. The worst of this was how the Republican Conservative's political goals stuck like an adhesive to its theocratic ambitions, and they exploited these positions to the maximum limit.[75]

In his book about *American Fascists*, Chris Hedges stated these earthly political goals as a conspiracy to establish a series of philosophies that spoke of brutal forceful Christian reform resulting in select unbelievers' extermination.[76] It was a totalitarian belief system that expressed itself as the Muslim ban of Stephen Miller.

Vice President Michael Pence identifies with the R.J. Rushdoony theonomy movement, openly addressing the planet's dominion. Dominionism is defined by Frederick Clarkson in "*Dominionism Rising: A Theocratic Movement Hiding in Plain Sight*." He wrote God has called on the Christian White Evangelical and Republican Conservatives to dominate. In this psychological conception, Conservatism and especially Republican Conservatives are contacted by God to exercise dominion over unbelievers. They are endowed by state-sponsored mystification based on terrestrial foundations by a leader imbued with their approval as a type of a Christian Führer undoing worldly populations.[77]

It must be noted that President Trump asked several times in his speeches, he expected his supporters to rally for him by violence. These memories in Trump to activate power are unique to his specific identity. President Trump added the icing on the cake when he sanctioned

---

[75] Schaeffer, Frank. "With God on Our Side-Christian Zionism Exposed." *HuffPost.* 25 May 2011.
[76] Hedges, Chris. *American Fascists: The Christian Right and the War on America.* Free Press. 2006. p.13
[77] Clarkson, Frederick. "Dominionism Rising: A Theocratic Movement Hiding in Plain Sight." *Political Research Associates.* 18 Aug. 2016.

a violation of Crimes of Humanity.[78] Leaders called for their supporters to initiate violence on their behalf to attain and remain in the executive office.[79,80] Like other fascists who believed he could create the environment to cut Germany adrift from international commerce, liberals oppose. Still, in reality, it could not reverse, and Nazism was an already outdated ideology.[81]

> "Hitler objects, particularly to the complications of modern industrial life. He wants to get back to simpler and more personal conditions. His mind, like Gandhi's, turns longingly to times that are dead; both have committed themselves to an outgrown form of social organization, identifying the virtues of an older order with its exterior features."[82]

Logistically several things have been learned about neo-Protestants. They are centralized in the United States and politically indistinguishable from the Republican Conservatives. They are located in Romania, Hungary, Czechoslovakia, Slovakia, and Poland (the Visegrád states).[83] They are also entering a majority in France. These locations have in common that they are heavily involved in reactionary politics, organizing, and participating in social disturbances. Neo-Protestantism saw itself as a social force aligned with Western investors

---

[78] Associated Press. "U.N. Human Rights office to U.S.: Halt Trump policy separating kids from parents at border." *USA Today*. 05 June 2018.

[79] "Trump predicts 'riots' if Republicans deny him the nomination." *BBC News*. 16 March 2016.

[80] Keneally, Meghan. "A look back at Trump comments perceived by some as encouraging violence." *ABC News*. 19 Oct. 2018.

[81] Lengyel, Emil. "The Battlecries of Hitlerism Modified as Election Nears." The New York Times. 10 July 1932.

[82] Fairweather, Nicholas. "Hitler and Hitlerism: Germany Under the Nazis." *The Atlantic*. Archive. April 1932 Issue.

[83] Bernbaum, John A. "Four Scenarios for Post-Soviet Russia." The February 1995 revised paperback edition of *Russia 2010* is available. Random House Publishers. Maryland. 1995.

who believed white evangelicals would spread democracy and corporatism. Most of their strategy was the expansion of virulent capitalism that secondarily did spread Bibles and fascism. Also, there seems to be a communication infrastructure that emanates from Billy Graham Ministries seen in the writings of John A. Bernbaum, "Four Scenarios for Post-Soviet Russia."[84]

It is important to catch an image of this Christian transformation that has drastically altered the portrayal of Christ. Carl G. Jung, who discussed man's soul's observation, did not obtain it from the cliché of "born again" or the Thule Society, those dark thinkers associated with National Socialism's elite. Carl G. Jung draws the reader into a vision of a creature in the hidden conscience that lay until awoken. One sees him in mass murderers and sadists, masochists, and the name Carl G. Jung calls him is Wotan. Vasily Grossman wrote about his ability to awake what is dark, divide and separate, pressure stronger nations to overwhelm weaker ones, and so forth.

Fascism and the Southern Strategy's sublime image was a gothic view of the world that Clare L. Spark, Ph.D., wrote, was ingrained in their conservative mind.[85] The vision of Christ in Republican Conservatism was turning apocryphal and secular. It had distorted the views of personal salvation by turning into the salvation of the one-man leader. Any opposition to the leader meant that revenge was being planned against him and resisted at every stage.

Once depicted in tops of steeples across the world, the Gothic image is a special warning to civilization, the Gargoyle. This statue was

---

[84] Ibid.

[85] Spark, L. Clara. "Klara Hitler's Son: Reading the Langer Report on Hitler's Mind." *Social Thought and Research*, Volume 22, Number 1&2 (1999), pp. 113-137.

meant to terrify the true nature that lies in human apocalyptic visions. It stood as a warning of evil. This artistic but forbidden attraction underlines the reactionary system of what Glenn Yeadon and James Q. Whitman give evidence to the affinity to apocalyptic visions it produced as *The Nazi Hydra in America*. Carl G. Jung was careful, but, in his assessment, in the Shadow, he gave another hint. It was the unconscious other. In gothic literature, he was portrayed as the outcome of the masses, the monster. —political and religious populist nightmare.

Descriptions of the Wotan in literature are carefully interwoven into self-righteous phrases of the National Socialist (Nazi) and reactionary in a language like 'an obstructive presence,' the evil ambitions of the self-tortured soul, and other metaphor. Mankind was responsible for creating all its Adolph Hitler's. Instead, to be reminded of the terror-gothic image they represent. [86] The spiritual context of man's propensity to imagine then believe a lie is written in a letter to the ancient Thessalonians under the Roman Empire. "...God will send them strong delusion that they should believe a lie."

In Russia, the gothic concept was altered again, reconceptualized into the work in their Embassy. Marie-Danielle Smith from the *National Post* laid out the Russian Embassy's role in instigating Nazi images of the gothic sublime. Although Russia has repeatedly taken offense at what it defines as American Russophobia, Canada caught them. Raising questions on Russian involvement in Charlottesville, Virginia, using the modus operandi. In Canada, the Nazi theme was used against the Jewish citizenry to portray a false accusation of Nazi monuments. Marie-Danielle Smith writes, "Recent posts from the official Twitter account of Russia's Embassy to Canada included images of

---

[86] Chiu, Allyson. "Trump revives 'Willie Horton' tactic with ad linking illegal immigrant killer to Democrats." *The Washington Post.* 01 Nov. 2018.

Ukrainian monuments at an Oakville, Ontario cemetery and an Edmonton, Alberta community hall. "There are monuments (sic) to Nazi collaborators in Canada, and nobody is doing anything about it," one Tweet said." The Russian Embassy got nowhere because of Canada's fact-checkers. This behavior showed the practice of using Nazi fear World War II and the Holocaust as state-sponsored terrorism as recent as 2017.[87] These conglomerations of confused beliefs pressure the individual to draw away. Some chose to evade others to express their anger.

---

[87] Smith, Marie-Danielle. "Russia Tweets About 'Nazi' Monuments in Canada Amid Ongoing Concerns Over Political Interference." *National Post*. 30 Oct. 2017.

KGB foreign officer Mr. Vladamir Putin was brought into higher echelon politics of Russia starting in 1999 as Prime Minister. Then he was retained from 2000-2008 then again from 2008-2012. Vladamir Putin became President in 2012. Historically the Soviet Union became the Russian Soviet Federative Socialist Republic and is now popularly called Russia. One of Russia's hallmarks since Vladamir Putin is his re-characterization of the intelligence services, the Spetsnaz (Special Forces), and the repeated use of Leon Trotsky's *French Turn* in his foreign relations. One of Mr. Putin's notable achievements is to bring real-life to film through the art of Marxism's phantasmagoria.

An article about the evolution and return to the Soviet past of repression is outlined in a section by Lamond James, "The Origins of Russia's Broad Political Assault on the United States."[88] Russia has resorted to several interventions it has had in its arsenal from the Soviet days and deploys them through various agents' personages. In his popular opinion, President Reagan said: "Every time I start negotiations with the Soviets, the diplomat dies." Three decades later, Mr. Trump killed his nuclear deal.

Europe wonders whether President Trump will take steps against dark forces to disrupt the West or work in conjunction with President Putin. Michael Kelley's reporting amplified concerns, "Europe's Russian Nightmare Is Starting to Come True. " [89] It has become apparent

---

[88] James, Lamond. "The Origins of Russia's Broad Political Assault on the United States." *Center for American Progress.* 03 Oct. 2018..
[89] Kelley, Michael B. "Europe's Russian Nightmare Is Starting To Come True. " *Business Insider.* 12 May 2014.

that Republican Conservatives are convinced that President Putin has become a member of their political party from their poll numbers. Natalie Andrews wrote, "Senate Republicans Block $250 Million Election Security Measure."[90] Peter Beinart of *The Atlantic* reported, "Trump Shut Programs to Counter Violent Extremism." The stage has been set, and the players are in motion to create a friendly Russian state compliant and authoritarian like some Visegrad states a satellite.

President Trump has become violent in his language and insists his supporters will riot to defend Republican Conservatives in front of Christian ministers who promised to sway voters, writes Lois Beckett of *The Guardian*.[91] The mental disturbance began to erupt as President Trump repeated a more widening conspiratorial theory that people are rioting because "We want Trump!"[92] President Trump wants others to incite riots for him during France's economic distress. President Trump wishes his speech's power can cause compliance, and one wonders where this came from. President Trump is not behaving like an American nor a Russian. We see for the first time Donald J. Trump exposing his dark thoughts of destruction.

Lois Beckett of *The Guardian* suggests between the lines whether there are extremist problems, with U.S. Senate Republicans Mitch McConnell and Rand Paul. They are Russia-leaning active in the coal debate. Matthew Heimbach of the Traditionalist Worker's Party, a man on the street, gave a new explanation of how the National Socialist (Nazi) platform of moderate Nazism became doctrine in

---

[90] Andrews, Natalie. "Senate Republicans Block $250 Million Election Security Measure." *The Wall Street Journal.* 01 Aug. 2018.
[91] Beckett, Lois. "Donald Trump warns of 'violence' if Republicans lose midterms." *The Guardian.* 28 August 2018.
[92] Nakamura, David, Min Kim, Seung, McAuley, McAuley, James. "In World War, I remembrance, France's Macron denounces nationalism as a betrayal of patriotism." *The Washington Post.* 11 Nov. 2018.

Charlottesville, Virginia. The reason given is to be palatable to the new American National Socialist (Nazi).[93] This mentality has been absorbed into the Republican National Committee's identity partly by planning, acclimation, or evolution.

Matthew Heimbach, known in Europe as the *Little Führer,* is a criminal figure in the Charlottesville, Virginia case was talking from prepared Republican Conservative lines. Speaking to a waitress, he said, "Their political party had been misrepresented, Heimbach explained to the waitresses. They're not the KKK. They're focused on family and faith and local control, on fighting the international corporations who came into Appalachia and took all the profits from Kentucky's coal."[94] Mr. Heimbach was referencing the National Socialists (Nazi), but it coincided with what Republican Conservatives have long held. The short speech outlined neatly what Republican-Conservative U.S. Senate Republicans Mitch McConnell and Rand Paul had said on the campaign trail. It was also a line heard from neo-Protestants who "have God on their side." Apparently, the new National Socialist (Nazi) plan is much like its past with a friendlier and intellectual face of Republicanism coal.

Andranik Migranyan, Ph.D., was touring the United States and wound up at times, testifying to Congress about terrorism and unrest, which is curious. Andranik Migranyan, Ph.D., is an Armenian-born Russian politologist once stationed in New York at the Offices of Institute for Democracy and Cooperation, a government-organized non-

---

[93] Beckett, Lois. "Is there a neo-Nazi storm brewing in Trump country?" *The Guardian.* 04 June 2017.
[94] Ibid.

governmental organization (GONGO) based in 655 3rd Ave Suite 2010-19, New York, NY 10017.[95]

Dr. Migranyan is a graduate of Moscow State Institute of International Relations, an elite background through which he achieved some honors from President Vladamir Putin. Sr. Migranyan is considered legitimate in what he states: he tells the truth about a lie of mild Nazism.[96] There is no mild National Socialism (Nazi) or soft fascism. Dr. Andranik Migranyan asserts he can remove Adolph Hitler's Apocryphal nature and is known globally as the messenger of President Putin's "Good Hitler" Conservatism of Anton Drexler.

Russia's use of subversive groups, primarily the National Socialist (Nazi), because of their long history of operating in the United States is their wedge.[97] In "The Origins of Russia's Broad Political Assault on the United States," Lamond James covers additional avenues of offenses that show how great President Putin's strategy is and how necessary President Trump is to its implementation.

Russia also uses a crime network described by the Organized Crime and Corruption Reporting Project. They award Vladamir Putin and Viktor Mihály Orbán top place as corrupt politicians. Stating, "Vladimir Putin and his siloviki fused a Cold War mentality with modern organized crime strategies and technology to create a new level of transnational organized crime. The Russian-backed money laundering platforms have exploited the lack of transparency in the global financial and offshore company registration systems to create a new criminal financial infrastructure used by crime groups from as far away as Mexico

---

95 Krastev, Nikola. "In the Heart Of New York, Russia's 'Soft Power' Arm Gaining Momentum." *Radio Free Europe-Radio Liberty.* 15 Feb. 2009.
96 Beckett, Lois. "My six years covering neo-Nazis: 'They're all vying for the affections of Russia'." *The Guardian.* 17 Feb. 2018.
97 James, Lamond. "The Origins of Russia's Broad Political Assault on the United States." *Center for American Progress.* 03 Oct. 2018.

and Vietnam."[98] Instead of using Russia to launder its crime profits, it uses foreign corporations.

Paul Goble reported in *The Interpreter* Andranik Migranyan's ideology, and philosophy is not confronted in a Congress under Republican Conservative control. Dr. Migranyan's position was published in "*Izvestiya*" in April 2014. Before Congress, he expressed the view that Ilya Milshteyn of *Grani.ru* says coincides with the *US Supreme Court*'s decision to legalize gay marriages. Given Moscow's attitudes on homosexuality, he implies, Migranyan once in Moscow may have to defend his statement that the "US civil rights have improved."[99]

Andranik Migranyan, Ph.D.'s position on what is called the "Good Hitler" used in the United States, is not original to the United States. It was a message that originated in 1920 to the 1940s by George Sylvester Viereck. George Sylvester Viereck, author of *The House of The Vampire*, the poet of *The Songs of Armageddon*, and labeled pro-Nazi by Congress, had this to say at Madison Square Garden with Fritz Kuhn. It sounds like the modern "Good Hitler" message of Andranik Migranyan, Ph.D.

> "I am not and will never be an anti-Semite. I am an admirer of Franklin D. Roosevelt. This does not imply that I agree with every one of his policies. Similarly, my admiration for Hitler does not compel me to subscribe to every article of his creed. It is possible to sympathize with National Socialism without embracing anti-Semitism."[100]

---

[98] Radu, Paul. "Vladamir Putin Wins OCCRP's Person of Year for 2014." Organized Crime and Corruption Reporting Project.
[99] Goble, Paul. "Russian Defender of Hitler No Longer to 'Defend' Human Rights in US." *The Interpreter*. 29 June 2015.
[100] Viereck, George Sylvester. "Speech at Madison Square Garden." 17 May 1934. RG 59, Box 4729, Folder 3, *National Archives and Records Administration*.

In his book on *Kaiser*, George Sylvester Viereck said this paltering statement about his unapologetic motives of supporting Germany while saving America, which helped Adolph Hitler's attempt to keep America out of World War II. George Sylvester Viereck was Kaiser's relative who said this when Isadore Greenbaum jumped on stage to protest.

> "My principal motive in releasing this volume at this time is not to forgive the Kaiser or to whitewash Germany but to save America. The land to which my grandfather came in 1848, the land where my mother was born, the land of my children, from the peril of yielding to the insidious wiles of foreign influence and of disregarding, for the second time, the last will of Washington."[101]

Lois Beckett points out in *The Guardian* about Nazi groups, *'They are all vying for the affections of Russia.'*[102] We know that American National Socialists (Nazi) like Mr. Heimbach have traveled to Russian border states, getting pointers on a unified political approach that crosses continents. Most of President Trump's speeches are heard in Romania, Hungary, Czechoslovakia, Slovakia, and Poland. President Trump's addresses coincide with the policies in these states and President Putin. Steve Bannon has been working on a new fascist movement there on behalf of Russian interest, which to date means Russia is the world's largest country by area, whose 87 percent of wealth is held by the wealthiest 10 percent. A curious position that Steve Bannon endorses and Republican Conservatives support as the new fascism of elitism.

Romania is one of the post-Soviet states with liaison tethers with American Nazi groups often connected to Basheer al-Assad. Ann

---

[101] Ibid.

[102] Beckett, Lois. "My six years covering neo-Nazis: 'They're all vying for the affections of Russia'." *The Guardian*. 17 Feb. 2018.

Maria Touma of *Balkan Insight* wrote, "Charlottesville Nationalist Leader Inspired by Romanian Fascism."[103, 104] In the former Bloc countries, the neo-Protestant groups receive funding from American backers in ideological material, booklets and pamphlets, mobilization technique guidance, and finance. the group's title is "The National Liberals Party." It established a foundation for future intermeddling and exchange of information at the Congressional level with that ongoing interaction. Liberal in name but its agenda described by Florin Poenaru, "Now, under the neo-Protestant pressure, the party resembles more the traditional conservatism of the American Republicans before Trump."[105]

Florin Poenaru points out in his investigation, "Friends and Foes. Traditional and Alt-Right in Romania." Liviu Dragnea's social democrat leader from Romania tries to unravel the justice system there in the manner of President Donald J. Trump. He has aligned his political positions directly with Republican Conservative areas such as fundamentalism, is anti-immunization, and has hostility against George Soros and folkloric nationalism Trump-style. He says he wants to make Romania great again and often cites an occult conspiracy of spirits to undermine him. Many of his statements evoke Gothic nationalism. He was a guest at President Trump's inauguration.[106] Liviu Dragnea is now a Republican Conservative of a specific type but is not "c" conservative in his thinking; he has subsumed many of his personal beliefs. Liviu Dragnea has affections for President Trump, apparently continuing to communicate under the shadows of darkness.

---

[103] Touma, Ann Marie. "Charlottesville Nationalist Leader Inspired by Romanian Fascism." *BalkanInsight*. 15 Aug. 2017..
[104] Pfaff, William. "Is Romania's New President A Fascist?" *Chicago Tribune*. 22 June 1990.
[105] Poenaru, Florin. "Friends and Foes. Traditional and Alt-Right in Romania." *Lefteast*. 24 Oct. 2017..
[106] Ibid.

Alana Goodman found Republican Conservative presence in Romania's political process and Russia's involvement in Congress. Sen. Rand Paul named his principal foreign advisor an aide to President Putin one *Dimitri Simes,* a particular favorite of Russian interests. It apparently did not matter to Sen. Paul that the United States heavily sanctioned Alexey Pushkov, a Russian government official closely associated with Dimitri Simes over Ukraine.[107] Sen. Rand Paul expresses support to hand over Syria to President Putin.

Senator Rand Paul is leveraging the type of influence Paul Manafort wielded so expertly. It certainly did not help matters that President Trump passed secret documents to Russia in the Oval Office on videotape. *The Center For The National Interest* documented the association between Sen. Rand Paul advisor Dimitri K. Simes and Andranik Migranyan, Ph.D. in this memo.[108]

National Socialist (Nazi) rebranding is not a new endeavor. This was proven after President Putin's contacts explained, "With certain modifications, this ideology is being used by Russia's current leadership. It is not an accident."[109] There is no conflict with Republican Conservatives. Adolph Hitler Youth recruitment is being sighted in the United States.[110] This indicates the effectiveness of Russian subversion

---

[107] Goodman, Alana. "Rand Paul's Russian Connection." *The Washington Free Beacon*. 20 Aug. 2014.

[108] Memo Reading: "Seminar with Russia's Andranik Migranyan. On June 22, 2015. Andranik Migranyan, Director of Russia's government-connected Institute for Democracy and Cooperation, spoke about U.S.-Russian relations at a Center seminar moderated by President Dimitri K. Simes. Russian Ambassador Sergey Kislyak also participated in the discussion." A summary of the meeting is available. Center for The National Interest, 1025 Connecticut Avenue NW Suite 1200, Washington, DC 20036.

[109] MacFarquhar, Neil. "Russia Revisits Its History to Nail Down Its Future." *The New York Times*. 11 May 2014.

[110] Swenson, Kyle. "Suspects in five killings reportedly linked to macabre neo-Nazi group." *The Washington Post*. 29 Jan. 2018.

tactics among American youth. It also shows those families can no longer assume that sending their kids to church offers the same protection from political ideology as it once did.

In the Russian discourse about the Victory Day history, Kseniya Kirillova of *Euromaidan* interviewed a foreign agent defector who alluded to Russian intelligence services' conspiratorial nature. During the Presidency of François Maurice Adrien Marie Mitterrand and during President Reagan's administration, the French underwent an attack by the Nazi's. It was sanctioned by the Central Committee of The Communist Party.[111] That was when the United States actually called them Nazis. National Socialist (Nazi) operatives have infiltrated youth movements, churches, and different levels of society. The proof of this is in the following victim reports.

Janet Reitman, *Rolling Stone wrote,* "All-American Nazis: How a senseless double murder in Florida exposed the rise of an organized fascist youth movement in the United States."[112] Christian White Evangelical parents in the United States assessed the impact secularized religion could have on their Atomwaffen Division members' children. Kyle Swenson reported the details about Atomwaffen in "Suspects in five killings reportedly linked to the macabre neo-Nazi group." [113] A group being influenced as a possible terror faction often using the terror-gothic images of fascism.

Now Russian influence such as the influence campaign by President Vladamir Putin and *New Russian Empire* Ideologue Aleksander

---

[111] Kirillova, Kseniya. "I was told we should work with fascists: former KGB officer Zhirnov." *Euromaiden*. 03 Dec. 2018.

[112] Reitman, Janet. "All-American Nazis How a senseless double murder in Florida exposed the rise of an organized fascist youth movement in the United States." *Rolling Stone*. 02 May 2018.

[113] Swenson, Kyle. "Suspects in five killings reportedly linked to macabre neo-Nazi group." The Washington Post. 29 Jan. 2018.

Dugin, and Andranik Migranyan, Ph.D. as well as the American Presidency of Donald J. Trump and Steve Bannon are in question.[114] President Trump repeatedly says he does not accept the United States intelligence reports but those of Russia. Perhaps he knows there is a change underway among Romania, Hungary, Slovakia, Poland, and even the Czech Republic, as Bethany Allen-Ebrahimian wrote, "Nazi Sympathizers Pushing to Take Over Europe's Spy Agencies."[115] By association, President Trump's statement on Charlottesville, Virginia, was not benign. It is of little notice that President Vladamir Putin hosts National Socialists (Nazi) in Moscow, President Donald J. Trump states in the United States.

Alexei Anatolievich Navalny is a Russian opposition leader against President Vladamir Putin. His supporters shed light on the United States' posture of protecting its white-collar criminals by issuing immunity laws. Pointing to Mr. Putin, Dr. Migranyan, and Aleksandr Dugin, they have transformed themselves into actors of a greater conspiracy. One which sheds light on the non-prosecution of the Trump Organization and what it hides. Mr. Nalvany has exposed that Mr. Putin and his allies have invested one trillion dollars in the American economy, where it is safe from Russia's investigatory scrutiny. The allegation also exposes Roman Abramovich, Denis Bortnikov, Andrey Kostin, Mikhail Murashko, Dmitry Patrushev, Igor Shuvalov, Vladimir Solovyev, lastly, the Alisher Usmanov - one of the critical enablers and beneficiaries of Russian kleptocracy, with significant ties/assets in the West. In the imagination of how these men actually fit into the political theatrics of Mr. Putin's regime and his inner circle, they are reminiscent

---

[114] Allen-Ebrahimian, Bethany. Et.al. "Nazi Sympathizers Pushing to Take Over Europe's Spy Agencies." *The Daily Beast.* June 26, 2018.
[115] Ibid.

of the Wannsee Conference of elites that met to discuss the end of human races.

Psychographics and the Apocalypse's portrayal weighs heavily against *hope and change* during the years of President Obama. There is no international law against one nation's attack on another's sovereignty either in the United States or the United Nations member states through social disinformation and influence campaigns.[116] Presidential Candidate Hillary Clinton wanted more change, but it was explicitly psychological and focused on Mr. Putin's disinformation campaign against her during the Benghazi hearings. The threat is not solely based on physical warfare with bombs and armament but using existing prejudices in society and using technology to aggravate public anxiety. Combining these two factors makes decisive victories and has become effectively psychological intrusions to undermine the United States government's individual enforcement branches. Immediately, President Trump has come on board with assailing all institutions' enforcement duties to make them respond to him, not Congress.

The correct propaganda will cause the society to lose its fighting spirit and intensify calls for citizens to lay down their arms. It seemed like an absurd reality just two years ago, but this is how the weak win asymmetrical warfare has already brought severe causality to the United States. It is being encouraged by the White House by calling Russia to win the election. The correct response from Republican Conservatives was to speak out. Many Republican Conservatives were organizationally receiving money from Russian sources for their

---

[116] Waxman, Matthew. "Cyber Strategy & Policy: International Law Dimensions." Testimony Senate Armed Services Committee. *Lawfare*. 01 Mar. 2017..

campaigns, according to Ruth May, "How Putin's Oligarch's Funneled Millions into GOP Campaigns."[117]

The defense of the public consciousness lies in using and exercising the existing tools of reasoning and truth. Russell Means, Ph.D., the American Indian Movement activist and the leader, spent many resources traveling and warning the people that the American culture was dying from the inside out. His point is illustrated in *Welcome To The Reservation.*

Russell Means, Ph.D., said Americans were losing their ability to apply their critical thinking skills. Limiting their interest in reading, slowing in the ability to problem-solve, and becoming a nation unfaithful to its activist past. This resulted in an inability to address the underlying issues and conflicts of today. The ability to criticize then become criticized was once a mainstay of Americanism. Now it has reached its bottom, and criticism has turned into a childish accusation. In its essence, Dr. Means stated that Americans were losing their ability to survive the modern era, unwilling to strive.

Republican Conservative thinker Peter Viereck's (1950) warning became profoundly true after Charlottesville, Virginia, when Republican Conservatives offered no resistance to the National Socialist (Nazi) rally of Unite the Right. The world saw acquiescence, violence, and death. National Socialists (Nazi) is the only faction with administrative support to function as an umbrella organization and the only one with backing in the White House. Neither should they be underestimated by their small numbers today. Recall the message of Peter Viereck, "Political anti-Semitism is no isolated program," he wrote in letters to the editor, "It is the first step in an ever-widening revolt of mob instinct

---

[117] May, Ruth. "How Putin's Oligarch's Funneled Millions into GOP Campaigns." *The Dallas Morning News.* 08 May 2018.

against all restraints and liberties. It is the thin opening wedge for the subversion of democracy, Christianity, and tolerance in general."[118] Edward Hunter, author, and correspondent reported on the Soviet disinformation and influence efforts directed at the religious values in an enemy target state stated the following.[119]

> "I see, primarily, as part of this softening up process in America, the liquidation of our attitudes on what we used to recognize as right and wrong, what we used to accept as absolute moral standards. We now confuse moral standards with dialectical materialism's sophistication, with a Communist crackpot theology, which teaches that everything changes. What is right or wrong, good or bad, everything changes. So, nothing they say is good or bad. There is no such thing as truth or a lie, and any belief we held was received as a mere, *you are unsophisticated.* They do not say this in so many words, except to those who are already indoctrinated in communism."[120]

> "For analytic philosophy, nothing is final, absolute, sacred. It reveals the transitory character of everything and in everything; nothing can endure before it except the uninterrupted process of becoming and of passing away, of endless ascendancy from the lower to the higher."[121]

After seventy years of being exposed to situational ethics, no wonder relationships have dramatically been altered. The relationship between work and competency has been impacted by a dramatic demand

---

[118] Reiss, Tom. "The First Conservative: How Peter Viereck inspired-and lost-a movement." *The New Yorker.* 24 Oct. 2005.

[119] Hunter, Edward. *Testimony.* Committee on Un-American Activities, House of Representatives, Eighty-Fifth Congress, Second Session, 13 Mar. 1958, Printed for the use of the Committee on Un-American Activities. United States Government Printing Office, Washington 1958.

[120] Ibid.

[121] Engels, Fredrick. "The End of Classical German Philosophy." 1886.

to conform. Rather than an expectation of performance and accuracy, employers sometimes purposely exclude individual thinkers. Responsiveness to hierarchy and alertness to their needs is much more important than getting the work done. Non-conformity is perceived as insubordination and critical thinking as anti-social. The overriding need to "get in line" with administratively imposed standards alters a person's identity and self-worth.

The United States public has stood by while society is undermined vis-a-vis its weak education system and deactivated its dissent, mentioned by John Horsfield of the *Alliance Research Group* in "Social Civil Disobedience-Social Change."[122] This was illustrated by Mr. Hunter, who explained the need for dissent in the United States. Though many ordinary people do not attribute the subtle perception of societal changes. A case in point was school segregation in the 2000s when resegregation occurred at a steady pace. It was more important to conform to routines than get high marks.

> "The Communists have been in operation for a full generation, taking strategic advantage of the American principles, exploiting the best sides in our characters as vulnerabilities, and succeeding for a generation in changing the characteristics of Americans. I remember when I was a young man, every personnel department was looking for leadership qualities. What was sought was a man's capacity as an individual to achieve new things. Today that is not even considered by personnel departments in their employment policies. They ask, instead, if the man 'gets along' with everybody. They do not ask what his individuality is; they ask how he conforms. When we raise a young man to believe that he must get on with everyone at all costs. We have put him into a state of mind that almost

---

122 Horsfield, John. "Social Civil Disobedience-Social Change." 2017 *Alliance Research Group* 3212 Cutshaw Ave Ste 210, Richmond, VA 23230.

guarantees, if he falls into the hands of an enemy such as the Communists, that he will react as he had been raised, to try 'to get on,' because he must not be 'antisocial.'"[123]

President Trump's competitive popularity has been in decline inside Soviet-Russia taking President Putin down as well, according to Eric C. Nisbet of *The Conversation,* summarized his reporting as follows:

In Russia, President Trump's percentages were (10% favorable), Self-centered (77%), Dangerous (58%), and Charismatic (49%).[124] Russia is more experienced in this political arrangement. Though a deficit, both have excelled in exporting fascism. [125] Edward Hunter, in 1958 explains how intelligence assets were selected, "They picked the ones they figured would be most useful to them from among these. Cunning was all that was needed, along with a complete disregard for ethics, no special intelligence. They have based their technique primarily on the complete abandonment of morality."[126] The test to identify an asset is an easy one. Just listen to the similarity in what they say and what they do when they follow everything the leader says.

Though Mr. Trump has community knowledge about communism from his associates, his most intricate understanding comes from the immediate influence. It is a filtered and acceptable account not to

---

[123] Hunter, Edward. Committee on Un-American Activities, House of Representatives, Eighty-Fifth Congress, Second Session, 13 Mar. 1958, Printed for the use of the Committee on Un-American Activities United States Government Printing Office, Washington 1958.

[124] Nisbet, Eric C., and Olga Kamenchuk. "3 charts explain how Russians see Trump and US." *The Conversation.* 13 July 2018.

[125] Kirillova, Kseniya. "I was told we should work with fascists: former KGB officer Zhirnov." *Euromaiden.* 03 Dec. 2018..

[126] Hunter, Edward. Committee on Un-American Activities, House of Representatives, Eighty-Fifth Congress, Second Session, March 13, 1958, Printed for the use of the Committee on Un-American Activities United States Government Printing Office, Washington 1958.

offend the listener—portrayals of the ideal. Edward Hunter's testimony about trade and the economy alluded to Russia's consistent strategy toward the United States. It explains why President Putin tolerates President Trump for "better days."

> "This is a strategy. The Kremlin is merely giving the United States a choice in surrendering by the voluntary change of attitude, to avoid more destructive ways of surrender. Unfortunately, in the United States, large elements, mainly among our non-Communist population, have been softened up into believing that if we can stall in this situation, it will take care of itself. The Reds have succeeded in inducing business communities to look to Soviet trade as a means of restoring prosperity."[127] Edward Hunter was perhaps making reference to Dr. Julius Hammer of the Bronx, New York pharmacy.

In his domestic situation, the United States President Donald J. Trump is causing an abandonment of its role and go autarky (isolationist). He continues to influence the relationship between the Russian Federation and NATO states. President Trump's policies have weakened the defense programs in places that guard against insurgents.

Viktor Suvorov, aka Vladimir Bogdanovich Rezun, former Russian agent, identifies the Spetsnaz as controlled and administratively commanded by the GRU/FSB intelligence services and the Russian armed forces commands.[128] They came into operation publicly in 1949 as partisan resistor fighters against the invasion by Germany. Spetsnaz operations are both covert and overt. The identity and function have always been controversial. One can identify them by the type of activities

---

[127] Ibid.

[128] Suvorov. Viktor. *Spetsnaz: The Inside Story of the Soviet Special Forces*. W. W. Norton & Company. 01 Sept. 1988. ISBN-10: 9780393335576.

signature they leave behind. Recently they have appeared hacking the 2016 elections. They are members of the Russian Special Forces under Intelligence Commanders, while some have been activated during retirement.

Members of the Spetsnaz have been increasingly taken to defensive and offensive positions throughout the world, infiltrating daily human activities. Also, right in the United States and publicly alluded to in the Russia Investigation as "12 Russian military hackers" who disrupted the 2016 election. A fascinating twist on this, which one would have expected to come from President Putin, has come from President Trump assailing the United States Russia Investigation as a conspiracy against him by "13 angry Democrats," signaling they are equally dangerous. President Trump tried to use his speeches to divert attention away from Spetsnaz. In so doing, did he hope to dissuade United States intelligence from himself? It appears that this assault against the U.S. is a counterintelligence action by President Trump.

The origin of Spetsnaz was a designation as intercontinental infiltrators and "special operations." After Operation Barbarossa, when Adolph Hitler invaded Soviet-Russia, the reaction came from Soviet Partisans who arose spontaneously, from cut-off regular troops and ordinary citizens. Freikorps was the Nazi equivalent. Therefore the United Nations approved that any nonmilitary group participating in a spontaneous uprising against an invader is acceptable in international law as self-defense. President Putin has deployed these organized no insignia nonidentifiable Spetsnaz in entirely different ways as insurgents and intelligence operatives. They can remain inactive in a country participating in political parties without exposure as undercover agents to disrupt the political system.

Clandestine use of human intelligence and covert action (HUMINT) is used by Russian Spetsnaz. Inciting civil discord, usually claiming they were not involved, but using the excuse, they saw a spontaneous, partisan reaction to people's routine problems with their government, which they had no role in "just happening to be there." According to Michael Carpenter of The Atlantic, " Russia Is Co-opting Angry Young Men." It can mobilize civil disobedience.[129] This has devastating results when societal leadership acquiesced and became politically anti-Semitic.

The Global Security Organization went a bit further about these operations, summarized in documents that attempt to define Spetsnaz's rules.[130] One example of a human intelligence gathering is Maria Butina. Maria Butina, as reported by *The Washington Post,* may fall under this category. Russian gun-rights activist Maria Butina illustrated a Spetsnaz use in their article, "Russian agent's guilty plea intensifies the spotlight on a relationship with NRA."[131] Her provocation was within Spetsnaz capability, disrupting the normal political process. Since she was not identifiable as a Spetsnaz soldier, she would be tried as a civilian spy. Part of the intelligence operation is the use of comparative discourse examination between herself and known Russian goals.[132] Ms. Butina was an operative conducting the coordination of agreement, a strategic way of making NRA, Russia, and military intelligence goals

---

[129] Carpenter, Michael. "Russia Is Co-opting Angry Young Men." *The Atlantic.* 29 Aug. 2018. in "Mobilizing 'uncivil society': how Russia's 21st Century 'active measures' actually work." Democracy Digest. National Endowment for Democracy. 29 Aug. 2018..

[130] Human Intelligence. Chapter 6. "Definition of HUMINT." *Global Security Organization.* Undated..

[131] Helderman, Rosalind S., Tom Hamburger and Michelle Ye Hee Lee. "Russian agent's guilty plea intensifies spotlight on relationship with NRA." *The Washington Post.* 13 Dec. 2018.

[132] Vivas-Steele, Robert David. "Human Intelligence (HUMINT): *All Humans, All Minds, All the Time."* Author Article [4.0] Article 11 Approved. By DoD CIA. 11 Jul 2009.

one of the same. It is done through speech, writing, friendship, then legislative action.

When a sophisticated nation-state like Russia engages in "co-opting young men," there is attention to what happened. A low command structure far from headquarters can emerge as subcultural entities that act in spontaneous, unplanned ways. For example, Spetsnaz retirees may pose a more significant threat posing as motorcycle gangs. If Spetsnaz, due to their military connection, operated within a country without being identified, as in the United States, they could work customarily inside political parties and partisan organizations. Spetsnaz may also function as a reactivated and retiree force used in Slovenia's forests, recruiting young men for Crimea. If Spetsnaz, due to their military connection, operated within a country without being identified, as in the United States, they could work inside political parties and partisan organizations. Were they to be discovered in deploying a chemical device, they would be subject to ENMOD and could receive intervention by the Hague International Court of Justice. To avoid conflict, the soldier should always identify themselves by an official patch on their uniform, not behave clandestinely.

A Spetsnaz soldier to receive The Geneva Convention protections must be self-identifiable as soldiers with the uniform designation, registering with the United States, when present within its boundaries. In some ways, their weakness is their greatest strength; they are thoroughly indoctrinated to conduct partisan operations such as joining the existing political party in a nation-state. Sometimes the Spetsnaz information influences and policy experts may be referred to as "fellow travelers" by United States police services then expelled from the country. What reaction nations might have comprised none or all retaliatory measures.

To fully understand the Spetsnaz, we have to delve into President Putin's KGB history. He is versed in KGB foreign relations. Therefore, he is quite calculating. Two of his specialties come from asymmetric warfare training or working through others. In *The Atlantic*, Dominic Tierney explains, "We often take it for granted that the greater a country's economic and military resources, the greater its influence. But more capabilities don't always mean getting your way because they inspire resistance from other countries. Sometimes David has more sway than Goliath."[133] This is certainly evident in United States history when foreign governments have interceded in Congress, influencing high-level policies in their efforts to "soften up" political positions.

Russia sidestepped public identification in Slovenia when it did "little green men" recruitment of Nazi-affiliated youth and motorcycle gangs, notably going out of its way to identify Russia's recruiters as *retired soldiers.*[134] Even as retired Spetsnaz, they function as active duty and are identifiable in the country as foreign agents, so they remain on the border in the forests like the Völk. A year before, Russia took Crimea using hooligans and Spetsnaz. This slippery slope not only applies to Russia. The North Vietnamese used the Viet Cong, and Wall Street investors take pride in launching Blackwater's successes (Academi). Headquarters Command sometimes operates on an "as seen" basis, not knowing actual facts. Private "standing armies" inside the United States borders are prohibitive in nearly half of the states. Yet from President Bush to Obama, it was allowed. Eliminating the possibility that on policy decisions, there is no distinction between Republican and Democratic parties.

---

[133] Tierney, Dominic. "Russia's Strength Is Its Weakness." *The Atlantic*. 21 July 2018.
[134] Shevchenko, Vitaly. "Little green men" or "Russian invaders"? *BBC News*. 11 Mar. 2014.

Green men appeared in Syria and attacked United States forces. Ivan Nechepurenko wrote, "Dozens of Russians Are Believed Killed in U.S.-Backed Syria Attack." [135] Russian agents in the United States mask themselves and avoid detection at the highest levels. President Trump should have been asked by Congress to settle whether his emotional support for Russia extended to Ivan Nechepurenko's men in black pajamas. [136]

Spencer Ackerman of *The Guardian Weekly* confirmed that Edward Snowden illustrated how ineffective The Patriot Act was to catch him. One does not appreciate the use of it until, in 2016, Russia hacked the presidential elections. Not just that, they did it, but the methodology happened to involve emails. The Edward Snowden case weakened the ability of the United States to acquire future insurgent emails. Spencer Ackerman reported on this in "Snowden disclosures reduced the use of the Patriot Act provision to acquire email records." [137]

It was apparently no coincidence of the accidental cause and effect relation between the Edward Snowden defection and the 2016 election hacking two events roughly three years apart. Edward Snowden's knowledge of performing government email hacks are well known. Perhaps there are overlooked clues in Edward Snowden and Donald J. Trump's behavior and some other likenesses that went undetected. The most suspicious was their self-interest in The Patriot Act. It had great utility in halting payments of money through intermediary to foreign agents. This was Section 311 setup primarily to stop money laundering and illegal underground economy schemes.

----

[135] Nechepurenko, Ivan. Neil MacFarquhar and Thomas Gibbons-Neff. "Dozens of Russians Are Believed Killed in U.S.-Backed Syria Attack." *The New York Times.* 13 Feb. 2018.
[136] Ibid.
[137] Ackerman, Spencer. "Snowden disclosures helped reduce use of Patriot Act provision to acquire email records." *The Guardian Weekly.* 29 Sept. 2016.

There appears at first profile two men of vastly different genera-tions and interests. Mr. Snowden, the government insider, and Donald J. Trump, a portrayed outsider, is getting ready for Miss America in Moscow. With no desire to represent himself in a public erotic image as part of his publicity like Donald J. Trump displays numerous times. Instead, Snowden has disguised as a college student with stereotypical dark rim glasses, a rehearsed portrayal. This is along the lines of a male version of Maria Butina.

Martin Longman of *The Washington Monthly* reported on the Cha-bad connection in "The Odd Chabad Connection Between Putin and Trump." [138] No physical evidence showed a relationship that suggested he went to Hong Kong (a key Chabad location) to live. He did make a document dump, a strategy well in advance to leak documents there, as he stated to police, he planned to fly-through destined to Moscow air-port. Both were suspected as Russian informants, Donald J. Trump by his intelligence and New York Russia connections, and Edward Snow-den by how he conducted the release of information without explaining why he chose the specific data he did.

The two men are different by upbringing methods, as Mr. Snowden was raised in an intact and cohesive family. Simultaneously, Donald J. Trump was reared as a transactional family member, focusing on in-vestment to financially forward the family organization. In a sense, Donald J. Trump was a category, a face, as the local baseball game catcher. One was born wealthy, and the other almost anonymous. How-ever, most of their differences end and could be the beginning of un-derstanding why Russia decided to work with them.

---

[138] Longman, Martin. "The Odd Chabad Connection Between Putin and Trump." *The Washington Monthly*. 27 Nov. 2017.

Both have profound personal experiences that indicate a strong penchant for self-identifying as victims. They swore persistently in a rehearsed declaration of right and wrong, blaming the government for their dilemmas. In personal and career terms, neither would be specific about that anger, and they naively fantasized about the world, not as a struggle between many competing forces, but a world where they are central to it. In fact, with years of seasoned contacts inside Russia, Brighton Beach, New York, and post-Soviet states, Donald J. Trump was by association well known to crime families overseas. Intelligence portfolio showed Donald J. Trump was much more of a consistent and perpetual overt financial agent than Edward Snowden. Edward Snowden would soon change that perception by going on a timely meeting with Moscow authorities. Vladislav Inozemtsev, a scholar, analyzed Russia's goals today in "Putin's Russia: A Moderate Fascist State." [139]

Reading John R. Shindler of the *Observer* wrote: "The Real Ed Snowden Is a Patsy, a Fraud and a Kremlin-controlled Pawn."[140] From the start, the Edward Snowden case had been clouded by a visible command road map; he did and said things mechanistically, not spontaneously. In synchronicity with Edward Snowden, Donald J. Trump explained why he was in Russia by Edward Snowden. His lines sounded well-rehearsed. They spoke of their actions as repeated and coordinated.

John R. Shindler of the *Observer* noted in Edward Snowden's case taking intelligence from files. At the same time, he did not possess the critical passphrases, raising immediate suspicion. [141] Edward Snowden

---

[139] Inozemtsev, Vladislav. "Putin's Russia: A Moderate Fascist State." *The American Interest*. Volume 12, Number 4. 23 Jan. 2017.
[140] Shindler, John R. "The Real Ed Snowden Is a Patsy, a Fraud and a Kremlin-Controlled Pawn." *Observer*. MEDIA
1 Whitehall Street, Floor 7, New York, New York 10004. 19 Sept. 2016.
[141] Ibid.

was far more effective as an insider operative than Donald J. Trump was at this stage from 2013-2014 since landing in Moscow airport. This was the precise type of data President Vladamir Putin craved. It was original and raw.[142] Only Snowden's handler knew of President Putin's preferences for natural intelligence in KGB.

What Edward Snowden did was to open the door to make intelligence agencies vulnerable. Characteristically President Trump went overboard on President Putin and gave him classified data on Israel from the safe. Edward Snowden acted globally against the United States, undermining The Patriot Act (the USA Freedom Act (known as Section 215 and 311) that allowed for dragnetting the internet, private emails, and phone calls a bit more complicated, creating public hysteria of government incursion. His incursion went directly to attacking the official government policy and practices, not the private system used by corporations.

The searches for "metadata" were curtailed as a result of Edward Snowden's leaks. The process of the FISA (Foreign Intelligence Surveillance Act Section 702) court was established for transnational threats. However, the incidental collection could include referral to law enforcement to surveil data of persons living in the United States.[143] President Trump disclosed (to Congress) he was hesitant to sign the renewal because of a "personally private" concern. His campaign was surveilled; this was the first time a sitting president suggested there was a reason for others to believe his campaign was involved in cooperation with foreign intelligence and criminal organizations. Next, President Trump did not hesitate to attack FISA and the system of checks and

---

[142] Kirillova, Kseniya. "I was told we should work with fascists: former KGB officer Zhirnov." *Euromaiden*. 03 Dec. 2018..
[143] Bischoff, Paul. "A breakdown of the Patriot Act, Freedom Act, and FISA." *Comparitech*. 02 Feb. 2018. Located at Kent, TN15 6AR United Kingdom.

balances. Only after considering FISA would be useful against his personal and corporate enemies did he sign. President Trump also enlisted the rank and file of the Republican National Committee and Senator (Col.) Lindsey Graham to attack FISA.

On June 23, 2013, Edward Snowden arrived at Moscow's International Airport. By a September and November trip, Donald J. Trump met with top Russian officials, generals, and oligarchs, stating this on the Hugh Hewitt Show on 21 September 2015. Still, Donald J. Trump did not disclose why he needed to meet with core Russian intelligence interests for a hotel. The inference from the meeting is that it had to do with intelligence matters. In the Edward Snowden case, he gave original data sets, codes, and knowledge about how United States internal systems worked and those email safeguards.

Donald J. Trump, a man who stated he had no inside political experience, could accomplish the miraculous. He was able to conduct several complicated maneuvers to dissolve the Congress's conservative power and replace it with his own Republican Conservatives. It compared closely to what Leon Trotsky had done between 1934-1936, called the *French Turn*. It was a tactic that allowed Donald J. Trump to negate the existing political party and change it to be responsive to him, denying the former power over the latter. This is a Russian strategic move called entryism.

Edward Snowden and Donald J. Trump accomplished the same goal; both allowed Russia to access the United States' secrets. One by handing data. The other by not funding the United States intelligence apparatus waging an attack on its directors. They are not miraculous actions of coincidence but a strategy with coordination. Russia, in 2016 hacked their own elections.[144] President Trump's efforts match close coordination of agreement to Russia's goals. In two ways, to shift the Republican establishment to friendliness with Russia while weakening the American institutions required to maintain *The Patriot Act* and control its currency transactions, which inflated the value and importance of Trump properties.

---

[144] Polyakova, Alina. "How Russia Meddled in its Own Elections." *The Atlantic.* 18 Mar. 2018.

VLADAMIR LENIN AND YURI V. ANDROPOV

The former Lenin (10 Apr. 1870 – 21 Jan.1924) by himself from 1900 in the Socialist movements in the United States was considered a superior force in revolutionary politics. In New York, Lev Bronstein (Leon Trotsky) published a newspaper with wider circulation than *The New York Times* and highly regarded by Jewish families. Their influence on the Dr. Julius Hammer Jewish family was the source of problems for the United States government.

Eventually, the pressure led to Trotsky and Hammer staying in the Soviet Union as part of the Central Committee of the Communist Party. Among the tactics learned by the Soviet government was how to influence foreign governments through long-term relationships. Undermining was a specialty among conservative socialists with a flair to give voice to the unheard. [145] Anyone can hear and see the Trump family's romanticism and swooning to realize they are directly grafted into these ideas. This seems to translate easily to Mr. Vladamir Putin for good reason because his family has close ties to the Lenin legacy in intimate ways.

Another Dr. Armand Hammer's development, so-to-speak after President Obama, holds particular value if one appreciates and can be satisfied by a cloned species. Knowledge about Lenin's financial plots with the Hammer family and his role in helping President Reagan

---

[145] Mason, Daniel and Smith, Jessica. *Lenin's Impact on the United States.* New World Review. Winter 1970.

served Mr. Putin substantially. Still, in the story, to weaken United States democracy, another slot had to be filled. Mr. Putin coupled his knowledge of expanding communism to returning former member states of the Visegrad's into subservience. That was fulfilled from experience about another talent, the Butcher of Budapest, Hungary.

Unlikely as it first sounds, the Trump family knew Dr. Armand Hammer in Palm Springs and attended many of his functions. Including the New World College Hammer owned that local residents called "a school for the KGB." While Frederick Trump was familiar with the local revolutionary figure Lev Davidovich Bronstein. In 1920-1929 the rumblings of war beneath Adolph Hitler's Germany's regime were felt underground in Moscow well before the West knew. The United States business leaders first heard of Vladamir Ilyich (Ulyanov) Lenin, as Chairman of the Council of People's Commissars of the Soviet Union's New Economic Policy (NEP) 1917-1924. When Head of State, Soviet Union (1922-1924), and currency in Soviet-Russia introduced it as a program that started and energized Moscow's trade.

Bolshevik leader Vladamir Ilyich (Ulyanov) Lenin evolved into the Communist Party. The Communist Party of the Soviet Union did not interfere in this affair. Still, it was informed in Julius Hammer's communique, a physician and friend to the Central Committee to The Communist Party (CCCP) and loyalist to aging Vladamir Lenin. From rumors of war, Julius Hammer, MD, set the framework for regular supplies of medicine, clothing, pharma, wheat, and money to starving Soviet-Russia to repair damages made after World War I.

The distraction for Americans is the same as it is today, a stir among the Nazis. At Vladamir Lenin's end of time, Rudolph Hess was already using Gestapo in the United States through the political system and wedging the Republican National Committee by procedural votes.[146] It established the corporate basis of dual-funding for Adolph Hitler's rise. Republican Conservatives lined up corporate sponsors to help Adolph Hitler's Germany. Later some of them operated factories and research in concentration camps. Dr. Hammer went in an entirely different direction by supporting Soviet-Russia and siphoned off the money that Republican Conservative corporate interest may otherwise have gone directly to the Hitler cause. He became a hated capitalist because it reduced American investment in Hitler's industrialism yes but did not eliminate its function.

Dr. Julius Hammer's son Armand Hammer, MD, instituted a sophisticated system that, over several decades, not only saved Soviet-Russia from the plague but other impoverished Communist countries and specifically addressed the sick and needy. It was adjudicated in the United States Justice Dept. It acts as a "citizen diplomat." In Nazi Germany, at the time, Adolph Hitler was going on a "moderation tour," according to Emil Lengyel in 1932, "The Battlecries of Hitlerism Modified as Election Nears." [147]

Lev Davidovich Bronstein, aka Leon Davidovich Trotsky, played a crucial role in this affair. While in New York in 1917, he received attention from the States Attorney General. He made his way back to Petrograd, where he served as People's Commissar for Foreign Affairs, People's Commissar of War, and the Red Army founder. In the Soviet Union, he was opposed to the Jewish Bund. At one time, his writings were more popular than The New York Times.

---

[146] Yeadon, Glenn. White Rose. *The Nazi Hydra in America: Suppressed History of a Century*. Progressive Press; First Regular Edition. 31 Oct. 2008). ISBN-10: 0930852435.

[147] Lengyel, Emil. "The Battlecries of Hitlerism Modified as Election Nears." *The New York Times*. 10 July 1932.

Armand Hammer looked like the little old man up the street. He was quickly denounced by American business leaders as an anti-war opportunist. Vladimir Ilyich (Ulyanov), Lenin and proponent of Social Democrats, were watchful, particularly over capitalists that tried to exploit the Soviets and reacted to a trade embargo by capitalist nations. Joseph Stalin continued to emphasize this to potential investors. In his conference with Julius Hammer, Vladamir Lenin laid down temporary expedience rules in his first contract with the West. Dr. Julius Hammer would help his 23-year-old son Armand Hammer with a side project. It involved young Armand Hammer when he graduated as a physician to become a Soviet government concessionaire. "If Hammer induced U.S. companies to trade, not only would he be serving Russia, but the commissions would make him rich as well. Abandoning the practice of medicine, Hammer set to work.", Alan Farnham of *Fortune*.[148] Julius and Armand Hammer were strong proponents of people and their dire circumstances, from their early days operating a drug store in the Bronx, New York, to being art collectors and connive the rich.

In between Armand Hammer's busy routine of kissing babies, constructing bridges, and his humanitarian work Vladamir Ilyich (Ulyanov) Lenin trusted him to help build the Soviet economy. Vladamir Ilyich Lenin had a plan that was made on the nature of capitalist greed. Armand Hammer would come to the Soviet Union and exploit it, so Vladamir Lenin and the CCCP could give capitalists a tremendously long rope in their dealings.[149] The laws governing Soviet

---

[148] Farnham, Alan. "Armand Hammer: Tinker, Traitor, Satyr, Spy a Scathing New Biography Paints the Globetrotting Founder of Occidental Petroleum as a Blatant Opportunist, a Womanizer—and Perhaps Even a Soviet Spy." *Fortune*. 11 Nov. 1996.

[149] Komar, M. Boris. "The Journal of Conational Law: America's Journal of International Private Law, Volumes 1-3." Conational Law Publishing Company, 1920. Read Volume 3, January 1922, No.1.

concessionaires had one questionable part: the Soviets to repossess property used in collateral could be foreclosed in the United States. So most of this collaboration took place in the Soviet Union.

It was calculated this would, in turn, cause the greedy capitalists to pressure their governments to export grain, tractors, medicine, and essentials to build the economy. Of course, there was one catch, Armand Hammer would control and yank the rope right around their little capitalist necks. Later, Joseph Stalin, Premier of the Soviet Union, did not continue to work with Armand Hammer. Due to World War II, Armand Hammer turned to other countries that the United States considered communist and continued his charitable mission alongside capitalism.[150] Frederick Trump could not possibly go unexposed to the high publicity and discussions among politicians about the Lenin and Communist Party USA in the New York City Union environment. As his father's influence on him to perpetrate fraud and misrepresentation in Alaska, the secondary recipients of this exposure was Frederick Trump's children.

After Vladamir Lenin's death, one of Armand Hammer's secret ambitions was to sleep in Vladamir (Ulyanov) Lenin's bed. He accomplished this through Mikhail Bruk and Yuri V. Andropov, then KGB Chief, who assigned Armand Hammer to the National Hotel the Vladamir Lenin suite when he moved the government to Moscow. The Moscow Airport Authority also gave Dr. Hammer clearance to fly his Gulfstream jet without escort and customs examination. He was officially named the American "civilian diplomat" of Moscow by the FBI.[151] Armand Hammer's friends speculated on what motivated him.

---

[150] Sudakov, Dimitri. "The Soviet Union that Hammer built." *Pravda*. 23 May 2012.
[151] Epstein, Edward. J. *DOSSIER: The Secret History of Armand Hammer*. Random House. 1996.

The satirical possibilities were endless, and Armand Hammer just could not resist and began with one of the disease outbreaks in the Urals. During this transaction, Armand Hammer bonded to the suffering people. Perhaps it was at this time, pondering Vladamir Ilyich Lenin's deal, he realized the high position he was in. Not only were capitalists greedy, but they had a mental flaw. In their thinking, capitalists would fuel the program themselves as they planned to spread democracy and Bibles.

Instead, they created more Leninism. The more Lenins' capitalists spread, the more commissions Armand Hammer made, and more Bibles came in. In this mix of diplomacy and politics, Armand Hammer received negative notoriety as a spy, passing secrets and using the information he gained to advance his peace purposes, always behind the curtains of politics and capitalist prestige. Joseph Stalin was already communicating with another American. In an overture to a conservative New York Supreme Court Justice Samuel Dickstein, who became Congressman (D-NY) on the House Committee on Un-American Activities, a famous National Socialist (Nazi) hunter aided by Roy Cohn, Esq. an attorney.

Roy Cohn knew where all the fascists were. Anthony Ripley of *The New York Times* in 1974 attempted to explain Armand Hammer's scheme to donate money to the Presidential Candidate Richard M. Nixon.[152] Mr. Ripley left out the seediest parts behind the intrigue of President Nixon's campaign fraud was Roger Stone and 23-year-old Paul Manafort's plan that placed a rope around Armand Hammer's neck. In the amount of what was reported as $54,000.00 in an illegal donation. President Nixon was not in favor of NATO nor a fan of

---

[152] Ripley, Anthony. "Guilt Admitted By A Nixon Donor." *The New York Times.* Archive. 11 Dec. 1974.

Nelson A. Rockefeller, 41st Vice President, and President Dwight D. Eisenhower even less. These dislikes were carried by Roger Stone and Paul Manafort against what they perceived as liberalism in the following scheme.

As a long-standing assistant to President Nixon, Roger Stone went to work on other Republican Conservatives labeled as the "trickster with the Nixon tattoo."[153] This is where operatives could receive training on the psychological mindset needed for corrupt intent and political subversion. Ultimately, their involvement led to events that connected to The Nixon Plumbers. President Nixon began the Strategic Arms Limitation Talks (SALT I) in 1969 with the Soviet Union and went into Détente. President Nixon's efforts set the framework for SALT II, later signed by President Jimmy Carter.

The illegal contributions hid a Lenin-Soviet connected Hammer who received help from the Montana State Republican Committee and the Republican Committee to Elect Nixon. Armand Hammer put in an appeal when he found out his donation was never used. It was a ruse. The report identified pending IRS investigations, and the payment to Nixon was supposed to offset taxes. Still, it showed the FBI another side of Armand Hammer that was much more conspiratorial. FBI Director J. Edgar Hoover alleged treason. Dr. Hammer is suspected of being a Lenin-Soviet communist who was laundering money from Soviet-Russia through Armand Hammer companies dispensing it to Soviet-Russian agents in the United States for roughly 50 years. Armand Hammer was not charged for spying or espionage by FBI Director J. Edgar Hoover, not considering him a political subversive but a capitalist.

---

[153] Ibid.

The funded spies and Armand Hammer era were later popularized in the television shows *The Americans* and *Fargo*. To the FBI, Armand Hammer became a befuddling character, perhaps a conspiratorialist. Although James Jesus Angleton, the CIA's chief of counterintelligence, originated an IRS investigation, nothing came of the spying. Several charges were made by the IRS. Edward Jay Epstein of *The New York Times* was upbraided by Armand Hammer in rebuttal primarily by the apparent fact Armand Hammer asserted he was a capitalist that had no party loyalty, per se, to communism. [154]

It cannot be overlooked how well Vladamir Ilyich (Ulyanov) Lenin knew Western and European capitalists' psychology, especially Republicans, and their propensity for exploitation and greed. Armand Hammer was never prosecuted. For a while, he helped the Soviets, the Western and European capitalists were helping Adolph Hitler. Most of them never fall under any scrutiny for supporting war crimes, which led to another great travesty of incredible privilege. The Soviets wanted to hunt each of them down to prosecute, from the big corporatist to locals. Instead, the United States, not wanting to be called communist supporters, wanted to move on. So under President Harry S. Truman, the Nuremberg Tribunals were ended. [155] A Cold War began with a new perceived military threat, conceived of by theorists, Soviet communism.

At the end of his life, Dr. Armand Hammer was realistic and intentionally died a broken man monetarily. He had given most of his money away to charity and research to cure deadly diseases. When he needed

---

[154] Hammer, Armand. Response. "A Response From Armand Hammer." *The New York Times*. 20 Dec. 1981.

[155] Heller, Kevin and Gerry Simpson. *The Hidden Histories of War Crimes Trials*. Oxford University Press; 1 edition. Oxford University Press. 30 Dec. 2013. Also read Oxford University Online "Capitalism's Victor's Justice? The Hidden Stories Behind the Prosecution of Industrialists Post-WWII." by Grietje Baars.

more money, he leveraged the equity against property and left behind tremendous debt—his most significant monetary accomplishment Occidental Oil. Dr. Hammer had ensured that there was no way his wealth or assets could be captured by the next operative. There must have been the realization that he was one cornerstone of a more comprehensive strategy to make many future Armand Hammers. All of them would have to begin on their own from scratch and leverage their private debt. Later, Albert Gore assisted Occidental Oil to get out of debt ending repayment of Armand Hammer's support.[156]

Under the consignment rules, from the Soviet Union to Russia, they held complete control over capitalists. Vladamir Lenin's view of a corporatist and industrialist was to place them under state control. In Russia, Vladamir Lenin created a succession in line with his initial intent of exchanging gifts with Americans. Based on the idea that American capitalists needed mutual exploits that they could provide.

Yuri V. Andropov, Chief KGB and General Secretary of the Communist Party. Known also as the Butcher of Budapest, Hungary, he was skillful in identifying candidates for psychiatric quarantine and treatments to reverse their social discontent. Mr. Andropov's future in politics was always connected to the Hungary fortunes of eradicating the revolutionary movement. Similarly, President Vladamir Putin's benefits were related to Viktor Mihály Orbán, Hungary Prime Minister and author of Zero Tolerance. President Putin has tutorials with the cloned Prime Minister Orbán, holding similar positions like Trump's family neutrality towards the Eastern European neo-Nazi and Calabria mafia.

---

[156] The Center for Public Integrity. "How the Gores, father and son, helped their patron Occidental Petroleum." 10 Jan. 2000.

According to both countries, Viktor Mihály Orbán, Hungary Prime Minister, is Prime Minister Benjamin Netanyahu; their unity surrounds Zero Tolerance. Another example of people not trusting their government is that Russian Spetsnaz recruited neo-Nazi groups from Slovakian forest motorcycle gangs eventually used in Crimea for years. In no surprise, the Calabria mafia groups' occasional sighting had been noticed coming into the region speaking to neo-Nazis. In Italy, such subtle alliances are outlawed. *Operation Black Shadows* was placed into action after a rumor of the Miss Hitler contest rumored to be an Italian Jew and the appointment to a position of authority by the Sergeant Major of Hitlerism. She had no criminal record and was for all intent and purpose undercover in the Ndrangheta family mafia worth about 70 billion dollars.[157] Sputnik and Google News reported, "The country's anti-mafia and anti-terrorism forces had been investigating the group, linked to similar organizations in the UK, Portugal, Spain, and Greece, for two years. Italian law enforcement's so-called "Operation Black Shadows" saw searches carried out in 16 cities across the country, including Milan, Turin, Padua, and Verona. Reports say that some suspects "had a vast amount of weapons and explosives at their disposal" and tried to recruit new followers on social media, posting anti-Semitic materials. The list of items discovered during the operation includes automatic weapons, rifles, bulletproof vests, grenades, explosives, crossbows, and swords and training materials teaching how to target Jews and gay people." The neo-Nazi fascist groups were extremely well-funded and initiated by a parolee through social media

---

[157] Sputnik International and Google News. " 'Miss Hitler' Winner, Mafia Figure Busted Among Members of Neo-Nazi Ring in Italy" 30 Nov. 2019. Also Tondo, Lorenzo of *The Guardian*, "Italian police uncover Nazi plot as 19 arrested and weapons seized." 28 Nov. 2019.

accounts bearing a resemblance to Mr. Putin and Trump's alignment with the same individuals.

To establish a timeline, early in the 1980's President Ronald Reagan was elected, as was President Mitterand, and Mikhail Gorbachev, Secretary General of the Soviet Communist Party, approximately the same time. In Moscow, the Soviet-Russian government had initiated its first ideological attack against the Mitterand government from 1981 to 1995 using Nazi's in France; Yuri V. Andropov, General Secretary of the Communist Party of the Soviet Union, began election interference into the United States in 1968 while in charge of the KGB.[158] Will Doran has the time-line of election meddling in, "Here's every time Russian or Soviet spies tried to interfere in US elections. How does 2016 compare?" [159]

Yuri V. Andropov, General Secretary, had extensive knowledge of incorporating intelligence operations and psychiatric hospitals by using them against dissidents. He is the first communist to coin the psychiatric term for dissidents as sluggish schizophrenics that required treatment. Yuri V. Andropov was ambassador to Hungary in 1954 during a bloody period to put down an uprising when as Chairman of the KGB on May 10, 1967. Yuri V. Andropov became General Secretary on November 12, 1982, just after Leonid Brezhnev's death. Andropov was elected General Secretary of the Communist Party of the Soviet Union, the first former head of the KGB to become General Secretary; he masterminded the John Walker spy family's approval. General Secretary Andropov died in 1985.

---

[158] Epstein, Jay. "The Andropov Hoax." *The New Republic*. 07 Fed. 1983.
[159] Doran, Will. "Here's every time Russian or Soviet spies tried to interfere in US elections. How does 2016 compare?" *Politifact North Carolina*. 20 June 2017.

In 1986 Soviet society was alarmed by the Chernobyl Nuclear Plant had the first nuclear meltdown, psychologically and biologically stunning the world. The next Secretary-General received word that General Secretary Andropov in 1985 had hoped Mikhail Gorbachev, Secretary General of the Soviet Communist Party, would have great success. President Ronald Reagan previously did not want to meet with Yuri V. Andropov, General Secretary, ostensibly because he could not find any compatibility. Hanging over any meeting was Ronald Reagan's active role as an FBI informant in the Hollywood Actors Guild. There was still the cloud of Hungary, then more recently the incident involving French Nazis and President Mitterrand, an operation the Central Committee of the Communist Party-sanctioned.[160] KGB chairman, Viktor Chebrikov, served from 1982 to October 1988 and told his agents to work with the French Nazis.[161] President Reagan followed suit and recruited Nazis with an Eastern European Emigre program.

Meanwhile, aside from Soviet changes, Armand Hammer's story continued in Palm Beach with President Ronald Reagan and Secretary General Mikhail Gorbachev. The Palm Beach Gala was also a fundraiser front for United World Colleges, where Armand Hammer made pleas for world peace. Afterward, he critiqued the presence of world business leaders as "insensitive." Mixing with those in the group was another face from New York who has said he is not into politics, one donor to the communist cause a Donald J. Trump. [162] By this time, it appeared that Donald J. Trump was deeply involved with Soviet-Russia ten years after marrying Ivana Zelníčková.

---

[160] Kirillova, Kseniya. "I was told we should work with fascists: former KGB officer Zhirnov." *Euromaiden*. 03 Dec. 2018.
[161] Ibid.
[162] Curtis, Charlotte. "Dr. Hammer's Real Concern." *The New York Times*. 19 Nov. 1985.

At this time, Donald J. Trump started making deals with David Bogatin, Soviet-veteran in the Moscow-based New York mob. Rudy Guiliani began The Manhattan Crime Commission that weakened the five Italian New York crime families resulting in ushering the Soviet-Russian mafia into Brighton Beach, New York. [163] In the 1980s, Rudy Guiliani became Republican, followed by Donald J. Trump in July 1987.

The Palm Beach Gala marked the beginning of what later was known as the Intermediate-Range Nuclear Forces agreement. It was Armand Hammer that accompanied President Ronald Reagan to its final signing. Though President Ronald Reagan found Armand Hammer indispensable in his negotiations with Soviet-Russia, it was not without its difficulties for Dr. Hammer found himself in defense of his life against *The New York Times*. 20 Dec. 1981.[164] Dr. Hammer had hoped to be nominated for the Nobel Peace Prize for being against nuclear proliferation and plague. Armand Hammer reiterated he was not interested in political subversion, opinions, and national loyalties. Armand Hammer became an associate of Nancy Reagan in the battle against cancer. In 1987 Armand Hammer went all out for a cancer cure supporting medical research and commented to the Los Angeles Times, "The world is safer today than it was before Chernobyl."[165]

Dimitri Sudakov wrote in, "The Soviet Union that Hammer built." Dimitri Sudakov explained the continuing story, "Mikhail Gorbachev

---

[163] Erickson, Edward Jr. "Discretion Advised: Trump's mob and Russia ties could prove embarrassing for the Donald and the FBI as investigations heats up." *City Paper*. 27 June 2017.

[164] Hammer, Armand. Response. "A Response From Armand Hammer." *The New York Times*. 20 Dec. 1981.

[165] Woutat, Donald. "The Unfinished Business of Armand Hammer : After a Lifetime in the Public Eye, He Still Worries About His Place in History." *Los Angeles Times*. 07 June 1987.

loved to hear about his experiences with Vladimir Lenin."[166] Dimitri Sudakov explained, "It was he who brought to the West the famous series of Faberge eggs that Viktor Vekselberg brought back home for $90 million a few years ago. This time the enterprising crook was not afraid of getting sued because buying stolen goods since the former owners - the imperial family - were destroyed during the Civil War." Mr. Sudakov did not mention the French Legion of Honor pin on Armand Hammer's lapel.

Armand Hammer suggested that Star Wars be given to the Soviets as a bargaining tool. Armand Hammer speaking with President Reagan and Secretary General Mikhail Gorbachev of the Soviet Communist Party was presented with a letter from Margaret Thatcher and encouraged to continue discussions privately about strategic nuclear weapons.[167] This was the productive Palm Beach Gala Dr. Armand Hammer hoped. Armand Hammer was later pardoned by President H.W. Bush for poor health. The fix was to protect the system from the press's further inquiry, making it hard to explain how a Vladamir Lenin protégé helped create peace.

Jonas Salk recalled this about Armand Hammer, "But arteries aside, what accounts for Hammer's drive? Why is he going strong a quarter of a century after most people have retired? As Salk explains, something else propels him from within--some complex impulse reflected in his altruism and ego alike. "Armand Hammer is a man with a purpose," Salk says. "It is that which keeps him alive."[168] Armand Hammer, though received mixed reviews internationally, the EIR from the

---

[166] Sudakov, Dimitri. "The Soviet Union that Hammer built." *Pravda*. 23 May 2012.
[167] Curtis, Charlotte. "Dr. Hammer's Real Concern." *The New York Times*. Archive. 19 Nov. 1985.
[168] Woutat, Donald. "The Unfinished Business of Armand Hammer: After a Lifetime in the Public Eye, He Still Worries About His Place in History." *Los Angeles Times*. 07 June 1987.

Lyndon LaRouche's Movement did an extensive analysis of Armand Hammer's crime influence.[169]

At this point, we need to establish several relevant facts. The Presidential administration of Richard M. Nixon and its operation at Democratic Headquarters in the Watergate Hotel did not capture all the related parties. Behind closed doors, there was the continuity of Roger Stone, Paul Manafort, and in Russia, Viktor Vekselberg, now a Donald J. Trump friend. They became involved in the Iran-Contra Affair during President Reagan and were "out there" doing presidential work. Dr. Zbigniew Brzezinski prevented this team from entering President Jimmy Carter's White House and was therefore labeled "the Russia hater" by Armand Hammer.

KGB Chief General Vladimir Alexandrovich Kryuchkov served from 1988-1991 ordered their agents to sustain the Nazi's operation against Mitterand.[170] It was the first sign of a weakening Central Committee of The Communist Party (CCCP). In some ways, though, CCCP is not quite dead as General Kryuchkov was imprisoned for attempting a coup against Mikhail Gorbachev using the State Committee on the State of Emergency. General Kryuchkov received amnesty in 1994.

In Moscow, a new operation discussed what to do with the annoying American they had under surveillance between 1988-1991, Donald J. Trump. First, they had to do more screening and produce a Dossier on his family background and the status of operations in New York. When the Soviet empire economically collapsed, it reminded many Russians of their history. During the Presidency of Bill Clinton, met

---

[169] Thompson, Scott. "Soviet Fixer from Lenin to the Present." EIR Volume 12, Number 35, 06 Sept. 1985. *EIR News Service*, P.O. Box 17390 Washington, D.C. 20041-0390 Order #85006.

[170] Kirillova, Kseniya. "I was told we should work with fascists: former KGB officer Zhirnov." *Euromaiden*. 03 Dec. 2018.

with Boris Yeltsin, President of the Russian Federation, and held many transcribed phone conferences with him now being made public. According to Dimitri Sudakov, The Kremlin meetings between President Clinton and Yeltsin were secret. Mr. Yeltsin did not mention recommending Vladamir Putin for leadership. The communist hierarchy could also take advantage of undeveloped laws regulating concessionaires.[171]

In theory, an influential politician could help change United States law and bend it in favor of concessionaires in trade and treaty agreements.[172] The Republican National Conservatives were potentially back in the game of exploiting Russia for its minerals. The laws that governed concessionaire agreements that Dr. Armand Hammer used with Vladamir Lenin were newly revised in 2015.

The criminality of primarily business fraud, crime in general, inherent into the family DNA offered a tempting target for any foreign government. Imagine the hatred towards the government that led to the policing of the profitable rackets and drug schemes of New York. The FBI after Director John Edgar Hoover became fearful of bad publicity, which filled theatre screens. On the Soviet-Russian side, there was continuity in the spy businesses. Just as there were cross interests. Seeking to expand global reach had caused the American corporate and energy sector misery after being caught supporting Adolph Hitler. To name a few, I.G. Farben, Shell, and The Bavarian Motor Works, and

---

[171] DLA Piper Law Firm. "Concession law in Russia." *Lexology.* 03 Sept. 2014. See also: World Bank Group. "Public-Private Partnerships Laws / Concession Laws." Public Private Partnership Legal Resources Center. ppp.worldbank.org/public-private-partnership/legislation-regulation/laws/ppp-and-concession-laws.
[172] Rodin, Artem. "Amendments to The Law on Concession Agreements Introduce The Private Finance Initiative (PFI) in Russia." *Roden & Partners* 18 May 2015. 119590, Moscow, Ulofa Palme 1.

Ford was among the notables. This is the Republican Party profile it undoubtedly had on the Trump family.

Friedrich Trump, authoritarian and patriarch of the Trump family and Lutheran Protestants, came to the United States at sixteen from Bavaria, Germany. He made a fortune operating restaurants and whore houses in Alaska during the Klondike Gold Rush. He claimed land already owned by residents to obtain the mineral rights underneath it without purchasing the property. In this scheme, he could force people off their land to mine or sell the mining rights.

Friedrich Trump gained the reputation of "mining the miners." Ultimately, he bought the property and won the election as justice of the peace. Making his way to the Yukon steel supply area, he made his wealth operating a cafeteria and gambling hall. Returning to Bavaria, he was identified as a draft dodger in 1905 by Royal Decree, although he was desirous of staying in Germany with his wife, Elizabeth Christ.[173] Germany deported him for disloyalty. Friedrich Trump wore his money like immunity and stoicism like a small-town judge. He returned to the United States in Queens, New York. He bought a property and rented rooms living among Palatine Germans; the Palatine was initially wealthy families of The Holy Roman Empire, a minority ultimately invaded by France. Friedrich Trump was born in Kallstadt, in the state of Rhineland-Palatinate, in 1869. By May 30, 1918, Friedrich Trump, age 49, contracted the flu during a pandemic and died. His wife Elizabeth Christ Trump at the helm took over the fledgling real estate business and Frederick in tow. In today's currency, his estate would be worth hundreds of thousands. The Trump estate began as a matriarchy, and as such, so long as it was, it reached its highest stature. In its

---

[173] Connolly, Kate. "Historian finds German decree banishing Trump's grandfather." *The Guardian.* 21 Nov. 2016.

feminine identity, it was managed less structurally male and more accountable. Trump Organization was primarily a woman operated business, and Mr. Trump took this strength and worked its political correctness.

Elizabeth Christ Trump, a Bavarian with her son Frederick Jr. in New York, New York, immediately began the matriarchy "Elizabeth Trump & Son." Frederick Christ Trump has just starting to mature in the real estate business and listens to the scurry of a passing Ku Klux Klan Memorial Day 1927 rally. He was caught fighting and arrested. While the radio back at work and *The New York Times* reports on the Nazi movement in New York, the Silver Shirts begin a rampage of violence, and the Jewish community is fighting back viciously. Frederick Christ Trump saw and heard about the Nazi movement as it geared up to February 1939 when it held the Madison Square Garden Hitler Rally.

Frederick Christ Trump Jr. (aka Mr. Green, Fred) was Donald J. Trump's father, born in 1905. Donald J. Trump's father kept the Christ family name, not from his father but the mother. In following the Christ name, Frederick acknowledged his German ancestry. Donald J. Trump's father falsely claimed he was Swedish to avoid criticism from his Jewish tenants. Frederick Christ Trump Jr. married in 1936 to Mary Anne MacLeod. She established a sophisticated business plan and philanthropy with the local community and Jewish organizations.

Woody Guthrie pinned a sign to his guitar, says Will Kaufman of *The Guardian,* "This machine kills fascists."[174] He did this after commenting on the assessment he had on the Trump family. When arrested in 1927 for participating in a KKK rally on behalf of Protestants

---

[174] Kaufman, Will. "Woody Guthrie, 'Old Man Trump' and a real estate empire's racist foundation." *The Guardian.* 22 Jan. 2016. *"I suppose, Old Man Trump knows, just how much, Racial Hate, he stirred up, In the blood pot of human hearts, When he drawed, That color line, Here at his, Eighteen hundred family project."*

(Christian White Evangelicals), he was detained by Catholic police. During Memorial Day celebrations, which in New York meant it was also celebrated by Nazi sympathizers who believed George Washington was the first American fascist. There were little difference and a lot of collaboration between the KKK and the Nazis in those days; they held joint rallies in New York.

Donald J. Trump, as a youth, managed to temporarily leave the family and attend an academy. While there, he did nothing but excel. This tells us that Donald J. Trump had great potential. He could attract friends though he could not draw women before the 1970s in any lasting relationship. Psychologically this represented a significant change in Donald J. Trump's behavior. His apparent lack of family intimacy and conformity, he once stated proudly, punched his teachers, driving his father to separate him from the family. Donald J. Trump feared being separated from his family and required their assurance; it would not happen.

For Frederick Christ Trump Jr., there is no record about his selective service status during the buildup to World War II, meaning he did not serve. War profiteering was seen as dangerous and involved President Dwight Eisenhower. Frederick Christ Trump Jr. 1949-54 transferred money from his housing redevelopment business to his children, to trusts, then back again, swindling the Farm Home Administration (FHA). War veterans who usually paid interest on mortgages of 1% or less Frederick Christ Trump Jr. held at 5%. These transactions allowed his children to receive $60,000 a year from the FHA issuance of leases via a trust.

Frederick Christ Trump Jr. reported itemized expenses paid out to the FHA, suggesting that he charged for building services he already provided in routine maintenance. The evasion of taxes and deductions that he took amounted to a windfall of 4+ million dollars. It received national publicity when it was learned he owned 6 corporations paid by government housing funds, all held by Frederick Christ Trump Jr. His many questionable "profiteering" tax deductions.[175] Later in 1958, a television episode of "Trackdown" featured a cult character giving the Trump name negative national publicity.

Young Donald J. Trumps' account was partially valid. It was a fact that his father tried to structure him and organize his thoughts that were resisted. During puberty, Donald J. Trump had uncontrollable violent incidents, hitting his teachers and pushing a classmate out of a window. Paul Swartzman of *The Washington Post* described Donald J. Trumps' behavior this way, "He had a reputation for saying anything that came into his head," said Donald Kass, 70, a retired agronomist who was a schoolmate. [176] To most classmates, Donald J. Trump's mood was uncontrollable, and his achievement was his phone use.

When Trump misidentified Rocca, the pro wrestler, Kass recalled, "We would laugh at him and tell him he was wrong, and he'd say he was right. The next time, he would make the same mistake, and it would be the same thing all over again."[177] No matter what anyone did to him, Donald J. Trump would return to that time and place of this initial default program. It could also be activated by recalling a series of visualizations and command word sequences, always returning to that default program. Behaviorally his mind operates mechanistically; it goes whirring and buzzing in numerous tasks. Before it rests on considering its

---

[175] FHA Investigation. Hearings Before the Committee on Banking and Currency. United States Senate. 83rd Congress. 2nd Session. Pursuant to S. Resolution 229. Gov't Printing Office 1954. pp. 395-420.
[176] Schwartzman, Paul. and Michael E. Miller. "Confident. Incorrigible. Bully: Little Donny was a lot like candidate Donald Trump." *The Washington Post*. 22 June 2016.
[177]Ibid.

actions, it merely returns to the previous thought. What was happening is that he showed cognitive processing problems. [178]

Notably, one of the most observable behaviors that Donald J. Trump had was with *attribution errors*. A public example of this was when French protesters against President Macron were explained by President Trump as "defending me." It showed itself once more when he received President Nixon's letter to run for office. His statements surrounding his photos with President Reagan and Gorbachev, he was convinced, would meet with him at Trump Tower, not on a whim but a photo vibe. His imagination of the way experience and life come from the visualization—the power he has over actual events transcribing them as totally gothic and conspiratorial. Later was made fun of because no one around him perceived President Gorbachev had shown any sign of interest to Donald J. Trump. Instead, President Gorbachev arranged for Donald J. Trump to meet with KGB Chief General Vladimir Alexandrovich Kryuchkov.

The magical power behind a photo and visualizations over Donald J. Trump remained with him all his life; President Trump used it as a way to base decisions pictorially. He avoided exposing his limitation on understanding, conversing, and managing. President Trump has been remarkably successful in hiding his medical history, but not a descriptive analysis of symptoms; distinct behaviors still point to early cognitive development problems. The world in pictures is not entirely balanced, just a minimally decisive one.

This suggests that the full physical necessary for the position of president has to be approached comprehensively. All party bosses should be excluded, and second opinions sought. Obviously, no one

---

[178] McMillan, Tom M. and Rodger LI. Wood. *Neurobehavioural Disability and Social Handicap Following Traumatic Brain Injury.* Taylor and Francis. 02 Feb. 2017. pp. 10-20. ISBN-13:9781138923935.

can ever have confidence that any military hospital can be trusted to make these evaluations. A case in point, if the president perceives we are at war in pictures, though in facts, no evidence exists. The hazards also exist the other way around when necessary to integrate what is known and seen.

From what is surmised, the Republican and Democratic Party were not estranged from the Trump family. Mr. Trump's persistent involvement in political affairs bears witness to this fact. The same holds true socially among the millionaire class. Using these experiences is a meager way to select a president, but it indicates societal standards. All that was necessary is a man with no particular skill, knowledge, expertise was required, just a cunning personality.

The United States political party also seems to have lapsed memory. In 1973 and 1978, there were significant legal actions against Frederick Trump. Frederick Trump's real estate business had a community association with mob transitions as the Italian families evolved into companies in Queens and Brooklyn, New York. By 1979 organized crime figures exiled from the Soviet Union began arriving in Beach Haven, Brighton Beach, New York, and the neighborhood started somewhat of a decline. He was known as the Henry Ford of New York housing.

During these years, Frederick Trumps' involvement with the arriving Soviet-Russians was limited to just-new arrivals such as Boris Nayfeld, then an insignificant mobster, who came to the community in the 1970s Soviet Jewish refugee under the Jackson-Vanik Amendment. This was the era of Yuri V. Andropov as KGB Chief 1967-1982. There was dissent in the family around their son.

Donald J. Trump's mother asked if she created a monster. Caroline Mortimer reported, "Donald J. Trump's mother asked: 'What kind of son have I created?'"[179] Yelena Akhtiorskaya described some of these characters in the vicinity of Brighton Beach, "Welcome to Брайтон Бич, Brooklyn."[180]

Frederick Trump had established Soviet relationships during this turbulent era, where he owned row houses, apartments near Beach Haven, Brighton Beach, New York. The neighborhood where Soviet-Russian immigrants were located had had well-established neighborhoods. Verka Serduchka detailed life in Little Odessa in "The Soviet and Ukrainian Communities of Brighton Beach."[181] This was the era of Yuri V. Andropov as KGB Chief 1967-1982.

Ivana Marie Zelníčková married Donald J. Trump on April 7, 1977, becoming Ivana Zelníčková-Trump, from Moravia, a town of Zlín (formerly known as Gottwaldov), communist Czechoslovakia. The matriarchy was reinstalled—Donald J. Trump, now 31 years old, with no one interested in marriage. Donald J. Trump was a publicly jovial, pleasant businessman under the tutelage of Ivana. In Berlin's the Guardian, Kate Connolly learned that the Czechoslovakia secret police had the Trump's under surveillance since 1977 at the Soviet secret police's request. They met coincidentally at a social gathering, supposedly having nothing to do with an arranged meeting by the Soviets following Donald J. Trump.

Ms. Ivana Zelníčková-Trump coincidentally brought with her the leadership and administration tools necessary to run the Trump Organization. In 1985 Mr. Trump bought Mar-a-Lago, and Ivana Zelníčková-Trump ran it as though it were second nature. The same year he met

---

[179] Mortimer, Caroline. "Donald Trump's mother asked: 'What kind of son have I created?'." *The Independent.* 04 Nov. 2017.

[180] Akhtiorskaya, Yelena. "Welcome to Брайтон Бич, Brooklyn." The New York Times. 14 Dec. 2018.

[181] Serduchka, Verka. "The Soviet and Ukrainian Communities of Brighton Beach." City University of New York. 04 Nov. 2012.

Armand Hammer. Now ten+ years post marriage. It was just coincidental that the marriage to Ivana Zelníčková-Trump coincided with the most significant influx of Russian mobsters into New York than before. In 1985 they bought Mara-a-Lago Palm Beach, Florida, for 10 million.

Noting that President Ronald Reagan and Armand Hammer met with President Mikhail Gorbachev at the Palm Beach Gayla at the Polo Club in mid-November 1985. It was just two years from when they would sign The Intermediate-Range Nuclear Forces Treaty. Paul Manafort and Roger Stone worked with Ronald Reagan's campaign.[182] In 1989, on a helicopter to return to New York from Atlantic City, the aircraft crashed, killing all on board. His top three high echelon managers Mr. Hyde, Etess, and Benanav, died. Donald J. Trump would never mention them again by name to anyone. Donald J. Trump would never mention them by name. Dr. Hammer shadowed Trump introducing him.

Politically, recovering from President Nixon's impeachment, Ronald Reagan approved Republican Party expansion accepting the Eastern European émigrés. John Dean stated the Republican Party would be a new kind of movement. Donors from this subgroup of Republican Party members supported Paleoconservatism. From the outset, Peter Viereck warned against the change from Republican Conservatism to Reaganomics. In the papers, the government became the problem that created homeless veterans' swaths followed by cuts at

---

[182] Keating, Christopher. "New Britain's Paul Manafort Working To Put Trump in White House." *Hartford Current.* 12 June 2016. "In 1976, Manafort, a New Britain native, helped manage the convention for Gerald Ford, who was fending off a challenge from Ronald Reagan. He performed a similar role for Reagan in 1980, George H.W. Bush in 1988 and Bob Dole in 1996. Here in this Dec. 2, 1976 photograph, Manafort faces unemployment when President-elect Jimmy Carter takes office. For the previous two years Manafort had been President Ford's associate director of the presidential personnel office." -Photo caption.

the Veterans Administration, Medicaid, and Public Health Hospital closures. Just as Peter Viereck foretold, radicalism seeped into the Republican Party, spelling doom for Conservatism.

During the management of Ivana Zelníčková-Trump, the Trump Tower and other businesses "hosted" wealthy mobsters. Donald J. Trump and his spouse had a unique immunity from criminal law in New York City. Not one prosecutor brought charges of criminality and conspiracy, although he had a lengthy history of allegations to both.

Money transfers between countries were being monitored. [183] Rudy Guiliani was in the United States Attorney General's office 1981-1989. In New York, dirty money was on the streets building high-rises and corporate offices that remained vacant. As the title indicates, Michael Hudson followed this history in "How New York Real Estate Became a Dumping Ground for the World's Dirty Money."[184] There was also drug money that made people rich. Steven A. Holmes followed that part writing, "A Drug Dealer Finds Many Eager to Launder His Drug Money."[185] David Cay Johnston reported for *Politico* that David Bogatin, a Soviet army veteran, was arrested in Trump Tower Manhattan. His expertise was gasoline fraud and skirting regulations for money laundering, having bought significant assets over tens of millions in Trump Tower Manhattan luxury apartments.[186]

By 1991 international intelligence agencies confidently reported that when the Soviet economy crashed, the intelligence services and

---

[183] 26 Stat. 209 (1890), 15 U.S.C. §1 (1958): "Every contract, combination in the form of trust or otherwise, or conspiracy, in restraint of trade or commerce among the several states, or with foreign nations, is declared to be illegal."
[184] Hudson, Michael, et.al. "How New York Real Estate Became a Dumping Ground for the World's Dirty Money." *The Nation.* 03 Jul. 2014.
[185] Holmes, Steven A. "A Drug Dealer Finds Many Eager to Launder His Drug Money." *The New York Times.* 24 Jan. 1990.
[186] Johnston, David Cay. "Just What Were Donald Trump's Ties to the Mob?" *POLITICO.* 22 May 2016.

Semion Yudkovich Mogilevich, the Ukrainian named "godfather of the godfathers," extended his reach significantly to New York. Semion Yudkovich Mogilevich was investigated by the US Justice Dept. Donald J. Trump began saying he never met a Russian though he was repeatedly photographed with Mr. Mogilevich. Ukrainian mob boss Marat Balagula ruled the Trump neighborhood rackets before being convicted of gasoline bootlegging in 1991.[187] Now-twenty years of marriage and cultural submersion by Eastern European culture.

Aleksandr Burman, a Ukrainian who scammed the US government out of $26 million in health care, and Leonid Zeldovich, who capitalized on Crimean annexation, bought into Trump properties. Boris Nayfeld rose in the Russian crime syndicate, acquired significant assets over tens of millions in Trump Tower Manhattan luxury apartments, as did other mobsters.[188] Franklin Foer wrote of the relationship between Paul Manafort in The Atlantic, "You have to understand, we've been working in Ukraine for a long time, and Paul has a whole separate shadow government structure … In every ministry, he has a guy."[189] Paul Manafort had the skills of an intelligence officer systems analyst. Donald J. Trump made his upbringing clear, "My legacy has its roots in my father's legacy.", According to Will Kaufman.[190] Ivana Zelníčková-Trump divorced Donald J. Trump in 1992.

Marla Maples, whom he married from 1993-1999, was set adrift from the Trump organizational culture. Donald J. Trump is 17 years older than Marla Maples. In 1999 marked the fourteenth year after he

---

[187] Raab, Selwyn. "Influx of Russian Gangsters Troubles F.B.I. in Brooklyn". *The New York Times*. 23 Aug. 1994.

[188] Johnston, David Cay. "Just What Were Donald Trump's Ties to the Mob?" *POLITICO*. 22 May 2016.

[189] Foer, Franklin. "Paul Manafort, American Hustler." *The Atlantic*. March 2018.

[190] Kaufman, Will. "Woody Guthrie, 'Old Man Trump' and a real estate empire's racist foundation." *The Conversation*. 21 Jan. 2016.

first met President Mikhail Gorbachev with President Ronald Reagan and Armand Hammer. Also scoring since when Donald J. Trump married Ivana Marie Zelníčková-Trump in 1977, just short of twenty years, the couple divorced in 1992; the divorce signaled several significant changes in the Trump organization. Competency, in every respect, took a sharp and abrupt astounding decline.

The way Ivana Marie Zelníčková-Trump ran the organization, it was clear that she was the enabler. Personality-wise, Donald J. Trump was incapable of male competency, which is evident in his failures heretofore. For example, he said, "When I look at myself in the first grade, and I look at myself now, I'm basically the same," the presumptive Republican nominee once told a biographer. He stated, "The temperament is not that different."[191] He has not changed cognitively and is the same now as a boy. Donald J. Trump is actually giving others an invitation to enter his subjectivity, experience him intimately, feel and believe as he, and act as he does. In Donald J. Trumps' imaginative world reality, he is recreated each day in speech and metaphor.

Frederick Christ Trump, Jr. died as Fred, Donald J. Trump's confidant, in June 1999 as headlines referred to him as a philanthropist for his attempt to address his reputation in New York Society. Mary-Anne Macleod Trump and Donald J. Trump started up the real estate business again. Donald J. Trump sitting at the bedside near his father, rewrote portions of the Will so that he would be the primary heir. This was challenged in court by his siblings, and some last words his father spoke

---

[191] Schwartzman, Paul. and Michael E. Miller. "Confident. Incorrigible. Bully: Little Donny was a lot like candidate Donald Trump." *The Washington Post*. 22 June 2016.

about the incident were to his relatives something like, 'Save me from him. Something smells fishy.'[192] These were Fred Trump's children.

Further degradation of *Trump*'s family legitimacy among the New York real estate elite began to push against the Trump brand name. Mr. *Trump,* by 2000, had the bankruptcy schema mastered, efficiently calculating what money he could draw from bankruptcy. Debt overleveraging was not *Trump's* strong suit. It did not help the family credibility of business that Prince Al-Waleed Bin Talal of Saudi Arabia bought into *Trump*'s hotels the entire 45th floor of his Trump World Tower and a yacht. Sale of New York's Plaza Hotel: $325 million. Prince Al-Waleed Bin Talal rarely commented on meetings with Donald J. Trump. He just said he was 'an evil man.' Mary-Anne Macleod Trump died on August 7, 2000, buried as Lutheran and a notable New York philanthropist; in an Irish paper, the obituary was tagged, "Much Missed." No mention of motherhood.[193]

Donald J. Trump's current spouse is Melania Trump (2005), the former Melanija Knavs-Knauss-Trump, a businesswoman model from Slovenia (Yugoslavia). While attending a party Paolo Zampolli, a Clinton friend, met Donald J. Trump. This marriage, like the other, marked social and fiscal crisis points for Donald J. Trump. Donald J. Trump is 70, and she is 47.

From an investment point of view to favor Russians, the acquisition of Melanija Knavs-Knauss-Trump made it possible for President Trump to maintain a great deal of influence. She is famous in Romania, Hungary, Slovakia, Poland lately, the Czech Republic (the Visegrád states) that no one could deny was substantial. The significance of this

---

[192] Touchberry, Ramsey. "Donald Trump Tried to Rewrite His Father's Will to Rescue His Failing Businesses: Report." *Newsweek.* 02 Oct. 2018.
[193] "Mary MacLeod Trump Philanthropist, 88", Obituary. *The New York Times.* 09 Aug. 2000.

is in each one of these countries wherein resides the relatives of former National Socialists (Nazi) are known as the "guardians." They are the Third Reich's surviving families that American Nazis have visited, ostensibly due to their knowledge about undiscovered Nazi artifacts.

The marriage changed Donald J. Trump's personality, and he began to refer to his business as a sovereign state. Trump Tower is the only family he has known. It is somewhat like a person. However, *in some ways, Trump* has risen beyond the street and elevated himself to white-collar crime dealing with Russian Oligarchs operating outside the Visegrád states. [194]   The crime was taking over Russia, and this offered some an opportunity. An American could visit another country to engage in local criminal activity like tax evasion and leave with money stored in shipment. [195] Trump Enterprises were found illegitimate in India. [284]

Enter Trump hotel in Panama amid a standoff by the Army over a legal dispute." [196] This was Ivanka Trump's business dealings.[197] Ms. Trump was labeled a fascist in Panama. An established pattern of working in exchange with the Russians was ultimately a business model.

Father Dearest A Hero's Quest

Before any presidential ambitions, Donald J. Trump is on President Reagan's "acceptable" list invited to the White House dinner with Mikhail Sergeyevich Gorbachev, then Secretary General of the Soviet

---

[194] Galeotti, Mark. "Gangster's paradise: how organized crime took over Russia." *The Guardian*. 23 Mar. 2018.

[195] Gowen, Annie. "Trump Organization's real estate partner in India accused of $147 million fraud." *The Washington Post*. 19 Mar. 2018.

[196] Alesci, Cristina. "Armed authorities enter Trump hotel in Panama amid standoff over legal dispute." *CNN*. 28 Feb. 2018.

[197] Bennhold, Katrin. "Germany's Far Right Rebrands: Friendlier Face, Same Doctrine." *The New York Times*. 27 Dec. 2018.

Communist Party. Mr. Trump receives overtures because he is well-known for his Eastern European émigré connections. John Prados received praise for writing for the US Naval Institute in an article about "The John Walker Spy Ring and The U.S. Navy's Biggest Betrayal." [198] This time frame was when John Anthony Walker and his family had just been caught spying for Soviet KGB forces, an activity lasting 1968 to 1985 during the KGB chairman's administration, Viktor Chebrikov, a conservative. Yuri Andropov was the General Secretary of the Communist Party of the Soviet Union, who approved Armand Hammer's continued involvement in the Soviet Union.

According to the National Security Archive on *The Soviet Side of the 1983 War Scare*, Chairman Andropov said to West German Hans-Jochen Vogel, "After all, at the button that activates the nuclear weapon could be a drunken American sergeant or a drug addict." In Ukraine, Chairman Andropov explained his intent, "The order seems to tacitly acknowledge that the Soviet Union was losing "the culture war," stating, "We ought to patiently and in a targeted fashion influence those among the artistic intelligentsia and young people, who due to their political immaturity and misconceptions and without any hostile intent, spread views foreign to Soviet society."[199]

During 1987 at the Presidential Reagan Dinner, Donald J. Trump mentioned to Mikhail Sergeyevich Gorbachev, Secretary General, he would like to visit the Soviet Union and do business. This came off like it sounds abrasive, arrogant, and no discussion of history or knowledge

---

[198] Prados, John. "The John Walker Spy Ring and The U.S. Navy's Biggest Betrayal." *US Naval Institute News.* 02 Sept. 2014.
[199] Savranskaya, Svetlana, source. "KGB of the USSR to Members of the Politburo, "On Measures to Improve Preventive Work Conducted by the State Security Service." 03 Oct. 1983, Secret.

about the Soviet-Russian history. Donald J. Trump did not know how to speak diplomatically or intelligently about foreign affairs.

In 1987, he arrived in Moscow and was ushered in to meet with Soviet intelligence KGB Chief General Vladimir Alexandrovich Kryuchkov. This seemed arranged in the United States, and Donald J. Trump probably never realized he was shunned by the royalty safeguards surrounding Secretary-General. Someone in the Kremlin simply assigned Donald J. Trump to the department he belonged, the KGB who dealt with criminals. At some level, Donald J. Trump should have realized he was never going to reach the political heights of Armand Hammer. Donald J. Trump did not know how to speak diplomatically or intelligently about foreign affairs keeping his desire to become great silent.

In 1985 John Walker entered a Soviet-Russia embassy for the last time as a free man. Naval Intelligence charged and convicted him for spying ending two decades of leaks. Donald J. Trump visited Moscow in July 1987. He stayed at the National Hotel, in the Lenin Suite like Armand Hammer. This visually signaled the start of the consignment. Roger Stone and Paul Manafort were brought in. By 1988 Donald J. Trump announces his presidential candidacy.[200] It can be realistically construed that Donald J. Trump would help with the Russian economy, which he would have overblown and thought he would run the financial investment sector.

Luke Harding reported on the background and why the meeting with KGB Chief General Kryuchkov was necessary for "The Hidden History of Trump's First Trip to Moscow." [201] This timeline clarified

------

[200] Chaitlin, Daniel. "30 years ago, today Richard Nixon wrote a letter to Trump predicting success in politics." *Washington Examiner.* 21 Dec. 2017.
[201] Harding, Luke. "The Hidden History of Trump's First Trip to Moscow." *Politico.* 19 Nov. 2017.

two points of biographical detail. On this visit, it was July 3, 1987, in Moscow. This was previous to when President Reagan signed the Intermediate-Range Nuclear Forces treaty on December 8, 1987. It was a crucial time in Moscow as it was apparent, they would lose Armand Hammer, and the John Walker case closed doors.

Donald J. Trump seemed to have his New York crime spree tied up as he was the unofficial seller of high-rise condos to the Russian mob. From a practical viewpoint, KGB Chief General Kryuchkov screened Donald J. Trump in the same way as Vladamir Ilyich (Ulyanov) Lenin did Julius Hammer, with an educated eye on his children and finances. There was one exception between the two men as one was a physician and knew how the world operated in its give and take. Donald J. Trump was a taker totally incapable of giving, so he would find a rousing reception for many years, no contact with Russian royalty but the strong arm structure that the Russian intelligence officers were world-renowned for. For the rest of Donald J. Trumps' life, that KGB brand of criminal remained with him. Though he would always try to prove himself better than Armand Hammer. The respected Major Yuri Borysovych Shvets looking to the future, waited until 2021 to disclose his role in developing Mr. Trump along the same lines as Dr. Hammer from a young man.

When Secretary General Gorbachev traveled to New York in 1988, Paula Span covered the event, "From the archives: When Trump hoped to meet Gorbachev in Manhattan."[202] From the 1988 overture to Gorbachev, it appeared Donald J. Trump did not entirely get what he wanted. Things seemed very much in process on the KGB Chief General Kryuchkov side, and Donald J. Trump failed to meet with

---

[202] Span, Paula. "From the archives: When Trump hoped to meet Gorbachev in Manhattan." *The New York Times*. 03 Dec. 1988.

Secretary General Mikhail Gorbachev and once again dismissed. Trump Tower workers arranged instead to have Donald J. Trump attend with an imposter. Armand Hammer was two years away from death.

In 1989 George H.W. Bush became President. As National Security Advisor with Brent Scowcroft, William P. Barr worked with the Republican National Committee under President H.W. Bush. He helped to pardon all individuals involved in Saudi Arabia and the Iran Contra Affair cleaning the record and essentially attempting to erase Iran-Contra from President Reagan's involvement. Later, William P. Barr as U. S. Department of Justice, Assistant Attorney General for the Office of Legal Counsel, an office that functions as the legal advisor for the President and executive agencies when George H . W . Bush pardoned Armand Hammer. David Johnston made headlines, "Bush Pardons 6 in Iran Affair, Aborting a Weinberger Trial; Prosecutor Assails Cover-Up ."[203] William P. Barr fixed everything by contradicting his own office. During talks of a pardon spree, William P. Barr was appointed again in 2019, ostensibly being perceived to rule in favor of the President's Office at the Republican National Committee's request. Suspicions should by now have been cast for all. Still, in 2019 the Democrats in both Houses claimed his records are impeccable.

In summary, thus far, a change in the spy world occurred when, in 1990, Dr. Armand Hammer died as a "philanthropist." John Walker was captured in 1985; Roy Cohn, his lawyer, died in 1986; in 1987, Donald J. Trump visits Moscow with intelligence services. On October 10, 1989, 3 Trump execs, 2 pilots die as helicopter crashes mysteriously reported by The Press of Atlantic City; Ivana Marie Zelníčková -Trump divorces 1992. It was two years after Trump's helicopter pilot was

---

[203] Johnston, David Cay. "Bush Pardons 6 in Iran Affair, Aborting a Weinberger Trial; Prosecutor Assails 'Cover-Up." *The New York Times.* 25 Dec. 1992.

indicted on drug trafficking charges. Federal Judge Maryanne Trump, Donald's sister, recused herself in the drug case, citing helicopter rides and her husband's connections to her brother. Frederick Trump dies in Queens, New York, also as a philanthropist in 1999, and Marla Maples divorced Donald J. Trump in 1999.

A cascade of Donald J. Trump's economic failures began in 1999; his shareholders lost their most considerable amount, and his Trump Marina was $76 million in debt. In the next several years, Donald J. Trump stiffed more shareholders but, in a financial scheme, found out how to turn personal profits from these failures while his shareholders and the communities were laid under a pile of debt in a cascade and maze of emerging corruption and bankruptcy. Donald J. Trump wanted to elevate himself to be President, not just be a spectator. His presidential aspiration has several practical purposes. Donald J. Trump could be as powerful as Armand Hammer, proving himself worthy to Russia. Donald J. Trump had several learning handicaps he may have thought could be compensated for by the dictatorships' dynamic style.

He could not comprehend from his readings and would not understand the character of Russia as Wilhelm Reich explained, "The elimination of individual capitalists and the replacement of private capitalism by state capitalism in Russia has not in the least altered the typical helpless and authoritarian character structure of the masses of people." [204]

Donald J. Trump, through the Palm Beach Gala, set off a series of business events. In turn, he brought Roger Stone, who recruited Paul Manafort that later joined a team of lobbyists called Black, Manafort, Stone, and Kelly circa 1980 that integrated with Martin B. Gold's Gold

---

[204] Reich, Wilhelm. The Mass Psychology of Fascism. Preface Third Edition. Translator Theodore P. Wolfe. Orgone Institute Press. 1946.

& Liebengood in 1996. Paul Manafort began his own conspiracy with Viktor Yanukovych in 2004, who wanted to end NATO; later, Mr. Yanukovych was accused of war crimes.[205] The news was replete with Mark Galeotti's "Gangster's paradise: how the organized crime took over Russia." [206]

When Donald J. Trump ran for the Presidency, his Steve Bannon organizational chart looked like counterintelligence charts. A succession of events occurred early into the campaign. The campaign to Elect Donald J. Trump was clouded by connections to Russia. The messaging was familiar. It sounded like President Putin stated in Romania, Hungary, Slovakia, Poland, and even the Czech Republic. Within two years, Steve Bannon engaged these Visegrad states opening an office called *The Movement* down the street from NATO Headquarters. It began using all the media connections that aired Presidential Candidate and President Donald J. Trump.

Donald J. Trumps' campaign group focused on psychological intervention theory for their candidates in elections. Their plan roughly coincided with Russian intelligence services. The Committee to Elect Trump: Steve Bannon, Wisconsin GOP operative Mark Block, and Alexander Nix, a British citizen CEO of SCL -affiliate Cambridge Analytica, Robert Mercer, and Rebekah Mercer. The Trump family and Jarod Kushner. [207] The Republican Conservatives. White House staff. FOX News. Facebook. Rebranded National Socialists (Nazi) and their affiliates that wanted to become a legitimate political party. It was just as motley as the Bolshevik revolution though it was right-wing radical.

---

[205] Abou-Sabe, Kenzi and Tom Winter and Max Tucker. "What Did Ex-Trump Aide Paul Manafort Really Do in Ukraine?" *NBC News*. 27 June 2017.
[206] Galeotti, Mark. "Gangster's paradise: how organized crime took over Russia." *The Guardian*. 23 Mar. 2018.
[207] Harper, Steven. "A Timeline: Everything We Know About Kushner's Role in the Russia Mess." *Moyers*. 09 April 2018.

From 2008 Vladamir Putin's alleged net worth rose to 70- 200 billion. That also raised questions about young financial investors who wanted their identity hidden, as David DeJong wrote in "The Nazi Shadow Behind the World's Youngest Billionaires." [208] The dream of National Socialists (Nazi) to have a Fourth Reich was hot news, and the method they used was to hide it within Aleksandr Dugin's *The Fourth Political Theory*. Lois Beckett, "My six years were covering neo-Nazis: 'They're all vying for the affections of Russia'." [209] Brandon J. Weichert wrote, "What Yuri Andropov Can Tell Us About Vladimir Putin's Mindset." [210]

David Atkins framed the nature and similarity between the Republican Conservatives in the United States and those in Russia, "Cold War. Racist Plutocrats Won It." *Washington Monthly*. While Republican Conservatives were running away from Americans, they rushed into hard cash relationships with the Russian Oligarchy. In his candidacy, the transparent relationship became evident in a new detente between the Conservatives and Russia. [211],[212] It was so replete with spying conspiracies. Rudy Giuliani appears with Donald J. Trump again almost out of nowhere after decades. In his candidacy, the transparent relationship became evident in a new detente between the Conservatives and Russia. In an oddity in Washington, D.C., there was a disclaimer among elites "We do not know Presidential candidate Trump."

---

[208] DeJong, David. "The Nazi Shadow Behind the World's Youngest Billionaires." *TIME Magazine*. 08 May 2018.

[209] Beckett, Lois. "My six years covering neo-Nazis: 'They're all vying for the affections of Russia'." *The Guardian*. 17 Feb. 2018.

[210] Weichert, Brandon J. "What Yuri Andropov Can Tell Us About Vladimir Putin's Mindset." *Weichert Report*. 16 Oct. 2016.

[211] Atkins, David. "Cold War. Racist Plutocrats Won It." *Washington Monthly*. 22 Dec. 2018.

[212] May, Ruth. "How Putin's Oligarch's Funneled Millions into GOP Campaigns." *The Dallas Morning News*. 08 May 2018.

The Captive Queen

Yugoslavia became known as Slovenia in 1991 as Czechoslovakia and Yugoslavia split into Slovenia and Croatia. Melanija Knavs was born in Novo Mesto, the Socialist Republic of Slovenia, in 1970, so today, it has some notoriety in the United States. Patrick Kingsley of *The New York Times* described it as a country where the business is all about Melania and Slovenia, where she grew up, not what her history and life were.[213] These "now" Melania experiences obscured what impact Yugoslavia had as it turned into Slovenia.

These political reincarnations stood on Pan Slavism's ideology, a populist movement to unite and promote solidarity among Slavic speaking persons. It was also in response to being ruled by non-Slavic rulers from the Balkans, Byzantine Empire, Austria-Hungary, the Ottoman Empire, and Venice. There were several essential parties in these transitions, including family royalties known as *stabilizing rulers.* World War I and the Treaty of Versailles ultimately was the force that created Yugoslavia.

Svetlana Alexievich, Nobel Laureate, in 2015 "On the Battle Lost." Wrote about the atmosphere in the Soviet surrounds where one out of four men died, living in a country of women, hearing stories about how people died and said goodbye. "... I was in a tank crew that made it all the way to Berlin. I remember, we were standing near the Reichstag – he wasn't my husband yet – and he says to me: "Let's get married. I love you." I was so upset – we'd been living in filth, dirt, and blood the whole war, heard nothing but obscenities. I answered: "First make a woman of me: give me flowers, whisper sweet nothings. When I'm

---

[213] Kingsley, Patrick. "In First Lady's Hometown in Slovenia, the Business Is Melania." *The New York Times*. 22 July 2018.

demobilized, I'll make myself a dress." Yaron Ben-Naeh of Jewish History wrote, "Blond, Tall, with Honey-Colored Eyes: Jewish Ownership of Slaves in the Ottoman Empire," going back to the Ottoman Empire during the Slavic slavery trade most Americans do not know.[214]

The intricacy of the Ottoman Slavic slave position went to the Sultan. Once declared as freed, the Sultan could set them in situations, providing specialized training and education to operate their government. Palace schools, proper administrative operations, offices, and executives are specializing in individual tasks. The outcome of this relationship bred formidable loyalties and a fanatic following. Sharia Law permitted slavery and might be used to justify male and female sexual purposes. Overall, slavery was a cruel practice under Ottoman rule. We can see how a person who lived during this history might hold deep resentment and bitterness toward Jewish slave owners and Muslims.

It was not unheard of to return a favor. One could give a slave to dance or model for the ruler and, at the worst unmentionable pleasure. Some Slovenia citizens may be Arab and Turkish descendants, although a recent movement wants to keep Muslims. Given this history, the region was influenced by the Soviets. They were separated, and now under President Putin, they exploited their youth with tethers to National Socialism (Nazi). It is no coincidence that Russia trains within the Slovenia forests, as the völkisch once did. This particular area also has a fear of invasion that they share with Russian paranoiacs who believe invading forces are beyond sight peering in shadows.

In World War II, approximately 225 Jews migrated to Slovenia to escape poverty from the economic depression. Jews, categorized along

---

[214] Ben-Naeh, Yaron. "Blond, Tall, with Honey-Colored Eyes: Jewish Ownership of Slaves in the Ottoman Empire." *Jewish History*, Vol. 20, No. 3/4 (2006), pp. 315-332. JSTOR, Springer, 233 Spring Street, New York, NY 10013.

with undesirable Slovenians when Nuremberg racial laws were imposed, exiled Serbia and Croatia peoples. By May 1942, the exiled Jews were executed, and Serbia and Croatia were designated as the "free from Jews" area. In the fascist Italian sector of Slovenia, 400 Jews and 21,000 other refugees escaping the Germans had arrived, and this number dwindled to around 44 by 1944, then roughly 16 percent of Yugoslavians. The only concentration camp in the Slovenia region was the concentration camp Ljubelj operating with 1800 occupants from around 1941-1945 when it had its crematorium. Reports of 2,300 to 3,000 children reportedly were presumed killed during this period.[215]

In 1955 Yugoslavia became part of the Warsaw Pact with the Soviet Union. Slovenia was part of Yugoslavia and was part of the Warsaw Pact. It was part of the Soviet Sphere of influence as defined by Yalta at the end of WWII. Marshal Broz Tito tried to maintain his independence from the USSR but could never break free of the Soviet Block absolutely and entirely. Slovenia and Croatia both declared formal independence (June 25, 1991). Croatia and Slovenia were diplomatically recognized in January 1992, with Bosnia's independence soon after that; these countries joined the United Nations on May 22, 1992.

Yugoslavia disintegrated because of several factors; ideology was used extensively to gain social control attempting to create passivity and harmony. The Socialist Republic of Serbia (Serbo-Croatian), one of the six constitutional republics of the Socialist Federal Republic of Yugoslavia, was the largest republic regarding population and territory. Its capital, Belgrade, was also the federal capital of Yugoslavia. Slobodan Miloševića, a former banker in Belgrad, Yugoslavia, emerged and drove politics in the region.

---

[215] Rupprecht, Nancy E. and Wendy Koenig. Eds. *The Holocaust and World War II: In History and In Memory*. Cambridge Scholars Publishing; Unabridged edition. 01 Nov. 2012.pp. 109-130.

"In 1987, Serbian communist official Slobodan Milošević was sent to bring calm to an ethnically-driven protest by Serbs against the Albanian administration of SAP Kosovo."[216] In 1991 Slovenia finally broke away from Yugoslavia and wrote its constitution. Russian Federation began in 1991, replacing the Soviet Union as the government with interest in Slovenia. It is one of the countries President Vladamir Putin would like to influence. Mr. Putin has been actively engaged in assigning former Soviet intelligence-military operatives to recruit gangs to serve as insurgents involving his sphere of interest and reverse trends he decides are detrimental to its survival.[217] In a pathological twist to play on Slovenia, the Russians tried to increase the idea that they had many more similarities with Slovenia than they had with the European Union. Both had tethers to National Socialism (Nazi), shared the fear of invasion, and were Slavs. Still, this old appeal to tribalism could not hide the fact that the fear of attack was not from the Ottoman or the Byzantine, nor the Jewish but the Russians.

By 2004 Slovenia had joined the United Nations and the European Union. Yugoslavia and Slovenia were pro-American for their multiethnic origins and coalitions, which allowed them to unify under political attack. Divisive movements created the alley of death through which a maximum of 500,000 people died and up to 3 million displaced. On March 24, 1999, when Melanija Knavs reaches 21 years, the United Nations intervenes and takes Slobodan Milošević for war crimes.

The Hague indicted Slobodan Milošević when President Bill Clinton orders the United States Central Intelligence Agency to intervene with Slobodan Milošević. He was being described as undergoing a

---

[216] Rosenzweig, Roy. "The Memorandum of the Serbian Academy of Sciences and Arts (SANU)." *Center for History & New MediaBreak Up and War.* Undated.
[217] Tamkin, Emily. "The Slovak PM Decried Fascism in His Country. Is He Responsible for It?" FP, *The Slate Group.* 23 Jan. 2017.

significant personality shift compared to his previous position as a banker. Slobodan Milošević turned into an entirely different person from the banker and financial adviser to this person representing the government system to perceived threats made against it. His influence in Yugoslavia placed pressure on sociologists called a "Sense of Community" and safety risk for all residents.[218] This information pointed to the traumatic condition of the Yugoslavian psyche people continued to experience. Slobodan Milošević died March 11, 2006, two months before the conclusion of his trial at the Hague as the communist who perpetrated the genocide.

Steve Bannon has proposed a Western version of ethnic focus through his "The Movement" organization. Only the naïve would say, "it *coincidentally* is the same region where President Trump holds influence." Not that President Trump needed an erroneous criticism of President Bill Clinton, but Clinton did shepherd the Dayton Accords ending the ethnic genocide in the same region Steve Bannon sways politics toward Russia. The intensity of bile for President Clinton from Steve Bannon was looking like a war of National Socialist (Nazi) resentment. Not of cultural and political differences, as its tone gave away a taint of vengeance. Word was that more Nazi gold had been found in the region of Poland. However, if you wanted genocide Clinton's actions would not be something to celebrate.

Steve Bannon has been sent to this region not to interfere and spread democracy but to work with President Putin, Slovakia, to incite fascism. If what Steve Bannon did in the United States is an indication, the intent is to finance an overthrow of the European Union's influence and the United States. Steve Bannon's overarching philosophy is

---

[218] Hueven, Marten van. "Sense of the Community" Report on Yugoslavia. Declassified. NIC-03236-88. CIA File. 31 Oct. 1988.

parallel to Nazi Völksgemeinschaft, attempting to pull together una-ligned and fragmented groups. Into his coalition on the ground as a po-litical party in a similar way. Breitbart Martin Longman wrote: "Steve Bannon Wants to Lead Fascist Movement in Europe."

Donald J. Trump is a brand name for populism in all the Visegrad states. This has not just been a populist surge. Donald J. Trump speaks for President Vladamir Putin's Russian Empire campaign. National Socialist (Nazi) philosophy, including rightist conservatives in Greece, Bulgaria, France, Hungary, Austria, Slovenia, and Marine Le Penn in France, receive campaign loans directly from Russia. However, President Putin's united front on this trip is seen as having a considerable investment of political capital for Donald J. Trump that hasn't yet been elected.[219] What does this mean? In all likelihood, as president, it has been suggested he will betray the region and create what Frida Ghitis of CNN defines as "Yalta 2.0," the Great Betrayal.[220]

For Steve Bannon, Steve Miller, and Sebastian Gorka to be in-volved in Slovenia and the Baltics meant the consolidation of fascist factions. Donald J. Trump did not arrive out of thin air; instead, this was a planned landing in the region. Expectations are Steve Bannon will structure itself as a Brussels based foundation called by DW News as *The Movement* close to NATO Headquarters. Steve Bannon makes no secret he supports the emerging fascist populism in Hungary, Slo-vakia, Poland, and even the Czech Republic.[221] Steve Bannon's

---

[219] Doomstea Diner. Blog. Kollapsnik.com.
[220] Ghitis, Frida. "Putin wants Yalta 2.0 and Trump may give it to him." *CNN*. 17 Jan. 2017. See Yalta on *History*.
[221] Staff Writers. "Steve Bannon plans Brussels-based foundation 'The Movement' for EU far-right." *DW News*. 21 July 2018.

financial supporters in the Republican Conservative sphere also condone a friendly relationship to Vladamir Putin that challenges the West.[222]

The center of the new controversy is Melanija Knavs-Knauss-Trump, whose position on most things Slovenia is silent. *Silence is complicity* has long been the Eastern European political standard among the majority after World War II. Melanija Knavs-Knauss-Trump alludes to her communist past but not its liberation efforts and what she thought about political events during childhood. Viktor Orbán was referenced by Patrick Kingsley of *The New York Times* in their media control coverage and the Breitbart news.[223] Coincidentally Steve Bannon has connections in Hungary.

In Hungary, Victor Orbán has arrived and is campaigning for Slovenian contender Janez Janša. Victor Orbán reiterates that outside non-white "races" were *geschichtslos,* a people without history and origin. He says these outsiders seeking humanitarian assistance will fearsomely change their way of life and construct moral values they do not recognize. His account as a Slav defeat this premise of being "the whites," obviously getting his Slav genetics and geography wrong.

The purpose of this propaganda is to raise fears and anxiety toward immigrants. Still, in reality, it casts looming shadows of conspiracy about President Putin's role in destroying Syria and sending the refugees he created to Europe. Vladamir Putin has so far avoided the wrath of the Slaves for this manipulation. It did reveal a position that chimes well in Donald J. Trumps' behavior of creating a problem, yelling how

---

[222] Weill, Kelly. "Blue Wave or Red Wall, Far-Right Candidates May Be the Real Winners of 2018.*" Daily Beast.* 12 Oct. 2018.
[223] Kingsley, Patrick. "Safe in Hungary, Viktor Orban Pushes His Message Across Europe." *The New York Times.* 04 June 2018.

violated he is, then suggesting a solution to a problem that never was a problem.

The Slovenia First Party of Victor Orbán may be one based on fear. Still, the origin of those fears comes from Russia's machinations to which are alluded by Valerie Hopkins of *Politico* "Slovenian survivor targets victory à la Orbán."[224] Strange enough that Visegrad's politics is beginning to look a lot like those structured in the Southern Strategy. There are other similarities, for Victor Orbán has his own equivalent to FOX News, Trump's propaganda arm.

Leonid Bershidsky from *Bloomberg* reports that Viktor Orbán's economic model is akin to Presidential Nominee Trump's.[225] Viktor Orbán has many personal interests that align well with the Trump administration and FOX News. Patrick Kingsley of *The New York Times* reported, "One, Skandal24, a sensationalist gossip magazine, aimed some of Mr. Jansa's opponents with salacious, thinly sourced articles."[226] It sounded a lot like The Enquirer and Mr. Pecker's views, a friend of Donald J. Trump.

Parallels to Donald J. Trump's media contacts in the United States bear striking similarities. Low-end press sources and fake news are known in the president's circles, as he has many less than reputable resources. Will the unification of these fascist interests, including Steve Bannon's fascist *The Movement, comprise* another scandal? There is a similarity in tactics between Viktor Orbán and the American president, who seem to have struck a media deal they could use to deliver ethnonationalism. This is no small effort to coordinate what people hear

---

[224] Hopkins, Valerie. "Slovenian survivor targets victory à la Orbán." *POLITICO.* 01 June 2018.
[225] Bershidsky, Leonid. "Orban's Economic Model Is Trump's Dream." *Bloomberg.* View. 12 Apr. 2018.
[226] Ibid.

on different continents in different languages. There is a noticeable political resonance to Donald J. Trump's speeches as though they have been synchronized to reach the European Union.

Ruth May of *The Dallas Morning News* found Russian oligarchs gave millions to Republican campaigns to influence foreign policy, explaining why the Republican Conservative Congress in 2017-2018 did not oppose him.[227] Donald J. Trump and his family have publicly stated their preferences for the fringe in those regions of the world where it could sometimes result in real estate transactions such as Panama and money laundering networks in the East.[228] Tom Burgis of the *Financial Times* followed dirty money from President Trump's Kazakh dealings, including the same character representations from foreign governments.[229] They are well funded and even appear in the United States Army.[230] A problem in other countries indicates the Nazis as a movement are on the move globally and are well placed in criminal networks.[231]

Lucie Chládková studying *The Far Right in Slovenia,* explains that there is a great deal of synergy among fascist groups that may give an impression like an individual, and independent uprisings occur

---

[227] May, Ruth. "How Putin's Oligarch's Funneled Millions into GOP Campaigns." *The Dallas Morning News.* 08 May 2018.

[228] Belford, Aubrey. Sander Rietveld and Gabrielle Paluch. "Steppe to Soho: How Millions Linked to Kazakhstan Mega-Fraud Case Ended up in Trump Property." *Organized Crime and Corruption Reporting Task Force.* 25 June 2018.

[229] Burgis, Tom. "Dirty money: Trump and the Kazakh connection." *Financial Times.* 19 Oct. 2016.

[230] Kennard, Matt. "The modern US army: unfit for service?" *The Guardian.* 31 Aug. 2012.

[231] Telegraph Reporters. "Army veteran worked for neo-Nazi group recruiting active soldiers." *The Telegraph.* 02 November 2018.

spontaneously in reality, are orchestrated events.[232] Hungary, Nazi fascist groups, know how to uproot a society by entryism.[233] They vote and participate in elections rather than turn their targets to install a leadership friendly to their position and gradually usurp it and shape its influence on the country. Some of the weak use methods to win wars domestically, and institutionally Ivan Arreguín-Toft details how *the Weak Win Wars: A Theory of Asymmetric Conflict.*[234]

Notably, the Nazi ideology is being reformed to coincide with youth's beliefs, rarely using its name by calling themselves Nazi's opting for "National Socialist" or "Blood and Honour" their real identity and connection to Nazism often obscured. Online "social groups" that promote violence and overthrow do not have reform in mind. Followers may never know who the organizational leaders are or their structure or where the financial support is. As Ann Marie Touma from Balkan Insight has reported, these organizational linkages go overseas to the United States and are supported by those Nazis in Charlottesville, Virginia, from Romania. In this country, Republican Conservatives are present and active.[235],[236]

In her thesis Lucie Chládková, "The Far Right in Slovenia," traced different terror groups, including Nazi movements operating in Austria,

---

[232] Chládková, Lucie. "The Far Right in Slovenia." Supervisor Master's Thesis Miroslav Mareš, Ph.D. *Masaryk Univ.* Faculty of Social Studies Dept. of Political Science. Security and Strategic Studies 2012.

[233] New Statesman. "What does entryism mean?" *The New Statesman.* 10 August 2016.

[234] Arreguín-Toft, Ivan. *How the Weak Win Wars: A Theory of Asymmetric Conflict.* Cambridge Studies in International Relations. Cambridge University Press. 08 Dec. 2005. ISBN-13: 978-0521839761.

[235] Touma, Ann Marie. "Charlottesville Nationalist Leader Inspired by Romanian Fascism." *Balkan Insight.* 15 Aug. 2017.

[236] Weider, Ben and Peter Stone. "GOP leans on rainmaker who courts controversy on two continents." *McClatchy.* 07 Feb. 2017.

Italy, Hungary, and Poland."[237] Lucie Chládková traces them and notes they are far from spontaneous. Each cell uses independently and intricately related to each one another. Coordinating established and maintained headquarters, joint coordination, and friendly inter-group relationships that are sophisticated and purposeful. Groups of this same identity but under different names in the United States frequently visit these countries and are well-financed by wealthy sponsors within established political parties that have a mutual interest in sustaining white power. This interconnected web is global and connected to Republican Conservatives at different levels.

Nazi cells are once again of concern to Michael Carpenter, Senior Director at the Biden Center, wrote in *The Atlantic*.[238] National Socialists (Nazi) identified informal clubs it would work through, such as the alleyway fight club, gangs, and what it termed "soccer hooligans." This implies Russian agents were younger than previously portrayed and more influential at the beginning levels of society. The members can range from any income and all economic backgrounds.

On the role of Republican Conservatism under President Trump, the future is marked by potential disasters for families in the United States. Sunny Hundal of the *Independent* points out, it's not leftists that fund Nazi affiliates and white supremacists but the "center-right" who maintains their organizations, training, and liaison capability.[239] The purpose seems to change the United States from participatory

---

[237] Chládková, Lucie. "The Far Right in Slovenia." Supervisor Master's Thesis Miroslav Mareš, Ph.D. *Masaryk Univ.* Faculty of Social Studies Dept. of Political Science. Security and Strategic Studies 2012.
[238] Carpenter, Michael. "Russia Is Co-opting Angry Young Men." *The Atlantic*. 29 Aug. 2018. in "Mobilizing 'uncivil society': how Russia's 21st Century 'active measures' actually work." Democracy Digest. National Endowment for Democracy. 29 Aug. 2018.
[239] Hundal, Sunny. "White people don't seem to realize that eventually the far right will come for them too." *Independent*. 06 Mar. 2018.

democracy to a police state by creating disturbances. As previously noted, domestic terrorists encouraged by Donald J. Trump's incitement to violence were identified in 2015 speeches. In Donald J. Trump, there are motives masked behind the discourse that only his violent supporters recognize. However, an agreement analysis can identify these motivational phrases when he portrays specific gothic images that are quite vivid.

Julian Lindley-French described strategic *maskirovka* as "a new level of ambition." Established by Moscow to unbalance the West both politically and militarily."[240] When the United Nations and President Bill Clinton began to take action against Slobodan Milošević and Radovan Karadžić, they also set into motion what Michael J. Kelly called *'Defeat of the Sovereign Immunity Defense for Crimes of Genocide.'*[241] After taking away leaders' rights to mass murder their populations, one would think that Donald J. Trump would speak on this. He is talking about himself ignoring Poland's volatile situation where Paul Hockenos is reporting from *The Atlantic.* Poland is now awash in *Trumpism* rhetoric as its centerpiece. Unhealthy and unheard of speeches attacking Jews popular in Nazi Germany are being repeated.[242]

Like the empires ahead of it, there is unmistakably no separation between their mafia-type crimes and Nazi beliefs. The United States was repeating its history when its small faction of +30% chose the Conservatism of Fritz Kuhn, then George Sylvester Viereck, the terror-

---

[240] Lindley-French, Julian. "NATO: Countering Strategic Maskirovka." Senior Fellow, Institute of Statecraft. London Distinguished Visiting Research Fellow, *National Defense University*, Washington D.C. May 2015.
[241] Kelly, Michael J. *Nowhere to Hide: Defeat of the Sovereign Immunity Defense for Crimes of Genocide and the Trials of Slobodan Milošević and Saddam Hussein.* (Teaching Texts in Law and Politics). Peter Lang Inc., International Academic Publishers. 08 Sept. 2005. ISBN-10: 0820478350.
[242] Hockenos, Paul. "Poland and the Uncontrollable Fury of Europe's Far Right." *The Atlantic.* 15 Nov. 2017.

gothic image of National Socialism (Nazi). By this time, Republican Conservatives were identified worldwide as the family and political heirs to their former radical and terroristic base. Wilhelm Reich warned overidentification with the demagogue leads to acclamation. It was beginning to haunt the United States, as evidenced in ways they sounded just like Donald J. Trump from casual supporters to Congress.

Was this the reason Adolph Hitler based his Third Reich on so many American principles? Below the surface, Vladamir Putin realized from just a kernel +30% of supporters a mass movement could be built with Donald J. Trump. Still, caution has to be used in creating our own overwhelming devils while ignoring those who support these ideas with greater hatred in the United States. Melania plays a dual role in the escaping princess in exile. Melanija Knavs-Knauss-Trump escorted her parents out of Slovenia using chain migration.

The strain of politics in the last generation that led to Premier Nikita Khrushchev to lead the Soviet Union's Gulag to *The Great Return* was reconceptualized. The Jackson-Vanik Amendment and Eastern European emigre turned into a criminal opportunity that the system allowed. Mr. Trump running for President first received support from hedge fund managers Bannon and Mercer, the first industry facing reform and possible corruption exposure. First, they would change the meaning of words to what they wanted them to be.

David Smith for *The Guardian* in Washington D.C. underscored what we already knew. Yuri Borysovych Shvets, Master KGB spy for the directorate (Residentiary of the First Chief Directorate), announced they had developed Mr. Trump for over forty years, starting during the President Ronald Wilson Reagan White House.[243]

---

[243] Smith, David. 'The perfect target': Russia cultivated Trump as asset for 40 years – ex-KGB spy." *The Guardian*. 29 Jan. 2021.

EIR International in 1982 as the Lyndon LaRouche movement was responding in one of its editions about the character Chief KGB Yuri V. Andropov. President Reagan refused to meet with him because of his active recruitment of American college students? EIR describes the attempt to liberalize Andropov's image into a cultural figure wrote this.

"The slightly more cautious London Economist editorialized June 5 that Western leaders should contemplate "the possibly beneficent rise" of Andropov, who, as an "enlightened conservative," albeit "no liberal," would be just the man to respond with "flexibility" to W estern pressures to make the Russians lean "towards butter rather than guns."

"Soviet specialists at one London think tank have put into circulation a novel definition of the Soviet "liberaI," in which flexibility hardly figures. According to this version, the KGB for decades (even when under the thumb of the thug Lavrentii Beria in the last years of Stalin's life) has been "exceedingly liberal" because its directors always put top priority on the good life for themselves-and hence cared little for the heavy industry and defense buildup that were the hallmark of Soviet "conservatism!" --- EIR News Service June 22, 1982

THE DAILY STORMERS SONG

In the wildlife, numerous calls only sound at night. The Daily Stormer's Song is a myth to say that only their breed can hear them. In speeches, Dr. Joseph Goebbels described the voices as 'the urgent call from beneath where every creative artist grows out from below. In the earth where he is created by the blood and soil of nationalism. Like the trees in a forest that grow toward the light. The seekers of the hierarchy would bend to the will of one man. For this to be accomplished, a man must lose their identity and purpose for sacrificing ambition for the state.' Family history showed When the Daily Stormers Song was heard, Donald J. Trump first initiated a type of mirroring where the actions of terrorism became indistinguishable from himself and followers. President Trump has seen 20 mass shootings since he became President in January 2017. It was more of a matter of true love.

The cope of heaven seems rent and cloven.
By the inchantment of thy strain,
And o-er my shoulders wings are woven
To follow its sublime career… Percy Bysshe Shelley,
"Letter to Constantia"

Something was changing in the organizational psychology of the Trump organization in 1987. Mr. Trump had already met Dr. Armand Hammer, President Reagan, VP Bush, Secretary General Gorbachev at the White House. The next ambitious step was stated in the public record. Presidential historians have stricken and censored these meetings from the public record.

The Soviet intelligence and diplomatic service arranged for Donald J. Trump to visit Moscow. Indicating approval from the President's State Department. At the legacy offices of General Vladimir Alexandrovich Kryuchkov, KGB Chief, known as *The Center*, sought to establish a package of ideological influences to push back damages done by Presidents Ronald Reagan and George H.W. Bush's end to the Cold War.[244] From 1987 it was difficult to track the Trump activity except that pieces of information leaked out about the business relationship with the Russian mob in New York consisting of the Brooklyn Camorra.

Clara Denina reported in 2014, "Exclusive: Russian central bank buys up domestic gold output as sanctions bite." In 2014 alone, Russia had collected 55 tons of gold when central banks in the world totaled their combined gold assets to 93 tons. It connected this fact that Russia could accumulate based on their oil, uranium, and gas profits.[245] *The Oriental Review* reported, "In 1971, US President Richard Nixon closed the 'gold window,' ending the free exchange of dollars for gold, guaranteed by the US in 1944 at Bretton Woods."[246]Dmitry Kalinichenko posited perhaps this was not about sanctions but a ploy to raise Russia's share of the world's gold reserves by converting.

Sean Illing of *VOX* news in 2018 wrote: "Trump's ties to the Russian mafia go back three decades."[247] This appears to be the organizational reflection of how Moscow functioned as it interfered in its own

---

[244] Harding Luke. "The Hidden History of Trump's First Trip to Moscow." *Politico*. 19 Nov. 2017.

[245] Denina, Clara. "Exclusive: Russian central bank buys up domestic gold output as sanctions bite." *Reuters*. 10 Nov. 2014.

[246] Kalinichenko, Dmitry. "Grandmaster Putin's Golden Trap." *Information Clearinghouse*. 25 Dec. 2014.

[247] Illing, Sean. "Trump's ties to the Russian mafia go back 3 decades." *VOX*. 08 Dec. 2018.

elections reported by Alina Polyakova, "How Russia Meddled in its Own Elections."[248] Shane Harris from *The Washington Post* followed up with investigating why Donald J. Trump never revealed how guests from former Eastern Europe's post-Soviet clientele were increasingly showing up at Trump Tower.[249] Max Abelson wrote in 2016: "Trump Tower a rogue's gallery of criminal tenants."[250] The Trump Tower organization reflected the organizational structure of a bank.[251] No one knows how Russia supported it, given lax laws in the United States.

The biggest obstacle for President Putin's "Good Hitler" is how operative his social psychology is. It is not enough to want to establish a new National Socialist (Nazi) culture. Michael B. Kelley wrote, "12 Prominent People Who Compared Putin To Hitler Circa 1938." [252] Several things need to come into play if someone could be found to create a new Adolph Hitler and lift him into prominence. The message must be scripted and tested on a broad scale to make a racist message for a following but not immediately visible.

That means the parties had to have some correlation and agreement. This takes a messenger who can develop common words under professional advice, an equally powerful influence to establish a bond between the speaker and audience. Notably, due to its volatility and infectious characteristics, there must be a way to create self-immunity

---

248 Polyakova, Alina. "How Russia Meddled in its Own Elections." *The Atlantic.* 18 Mar. 2018.

249 Harris, Shane. "Signs of Trump-Putin collaboration, starting years before the campaign?" *The Washington Post.* 17 Aug. 2018.

250 Abelson, Max, Jesse Drucker and Zachary R Mide. "Trump Tower a rogue's gallery of criminal tenants." *Irish Examiner.* 04 Nov. 2016.

251 Shreck, Carl. "Russian Organized Crime." *Federation of American Scientists.* 11 Nov. 2014. /1112 16th Street NW, Suite 400. Washington, DC 20036..

252 Kelley, Michael B. "12 Prominent People Who Compared Putin To Hitler Circa 1938." *Business Insider.* 22 May 2014.

so the Hitler virus will not kill its host. In no uncertain terms, the speech design had to be generated by an expert.

The Committee to Elect Donald J. Trump began with a unified group. It consisted of his friends and associates Steve Bannon, Wisconsin GOP operative Mark Block and Alexander Nix, a British citizen CEO of SCL-affiliate Cambridge Analytica, Dr. Robert Mercer, and Rebekah Mercer. Roger Stone, Paul Manafort This was the inside circle that lay the United States' initial framework and sought to provide Presidential Nominee Trump with structure. On some subconscious level, his supporters did not understand the fluidity of the situation; they chanted "let Trump be Trump" and unleash his inner hostilities bottled up. The Republican Party fully backed these speaking events while making well-placed statements that they "really didn't know who Trump was."

The alt-right used subliminal messaging to the American people for years; Vladamir Putin's popularity signaled a radical shift primarily among Republicans yearning for a new corporatist era led by strong man authoritarian policies. [253] It was supported by at least 40% of voters in the Republican National Committee franchise, included factions of the Conservative Democrats.[254] The radicalized Republican National Committee franchise endorsed racism, economic ideas, and platform. Any alt-right involvement is dwarfed by the involvement of hedge fund managers.

There must be psychological levels of agreement to build consensus, as Thomas Vetter explained in "Agreement Analysis: What He

---

[253] Altemeyer, Bob. *The Authoritarians*. Cherry Hill Publishing; Unabridged edition ISBN-10: 0972329889. 27 Nov. 2008.
[254] Nussbaum, Matthew. "Poll: Republicans' confidence in Russia's Putin on the rise." *Politico*. 16 Aug. 2017.

Said, She Said Versus You Said."[255] This is how demagogues get peace by building arguments that have a little basis in truth, then they begin to create a more massive structure of false beliefs on top. Often people become confused as they realize what they heard does not match what they do. Eventually, people give in and accept this is how things should be, and everything their government does and says is a matter of "Is what we hear what is being said?"

A mystery seemed to unfold in Moscow 2014 when Donald J. Trump increased his visibility and rudeness on the airwaves. Oleg Shynkarenko filed a story about this change back into totalitarianism, *"Aleksandr Dugin: The Crazy Ideologue of the New Russian Empire: Ideologue Aleksandr Dugin's notion of "Eurasia" is at the heart of Russia's new drive to expand its territory and influence."*[256] Adolph Hitler's National Socialist (Nazi) doctrine has not changed despite the friendly face of fascism and its appeal to Nationalist Youth. The end game is always militarism and subduing populations.

Matthew d'Ancona wrote in *The Guardian*, "Putin and Trump could be on the same side in this troubling new world order." Like Vice Pres-ident Michael Pence, "Dugin is positively millenarian who asserts: "We must create strategic alliances to overthrow the present order of things, of which the core could be described as human rights, anti-hi-erarchy, and political correctness – everything that is the face of the Beast, the anti-Christ."[257] Owen Matthews reported how close Steve

---

[255] Vetter, Thomas R., et.al. "Agreement Analysis: What He Said, She Said Versus You Said." *Anesthesia & Analgesia: June 2018* - Volume 126 - Issue 6 - p 2123–2128. doi: 10.1213/ANE.0000000000002924.

[256] Shynkarenko, Oleg. "Aleksandr Dugin: The Crazy Ideologue of the New Russian Empire: Ideologue Aleksandr Dugin's notion of "Eurasia" is at the heart of Russia's new drive to expand its territory and influence." *Daily Beast*. 02 Apr. 2014.

[257] d'Ancona, Matthew. "Putin and Trump could be on the same side in this trou-bling new world order." *The Guardian*. 19 Dec. 2016.

Bannon's relationship to the Kremlin is writing, "Aleksandr Dugin and Steve Bannon's Ideological Ties to Vladimir Putin's Russia."[258] Linda Kinstler of *Politico* reported, "Why Donald Trump Is Dangerous for Eastern Europe." Ms. Kintsler added, "In Crimea, and in this year's U.S. presidential campaign, all facts are interpretative. When he was the Republican nominee, Donald Trump, compulsively fabricate matters of national security, taking a leaf out of the Kremlin's playbook."[259]

His approach is not an isolated program and has broad ramifications wherever the United States projects its leadership. Following are to-date aspects from the Republican National Committee and other Conservatives of what we know are ideas that have been considered and practices put for implementation in the last two years. These are not a metaphor but actual steps in a program closely associated with "deep" state reforms by the National Socialist (Nazi). The similarity to what occurred in Germany is striking. One of the indications that Donald J. Trump's thinking was drawing its strategy from the National Socialist Party events in Germany when it overtook the Bohemia wing of the National Socialists of Bohemia (Czechoslovakia). See Appendix A.

When the National Socialist (Nazi) party took the next step and disannulled the Social Democrat Party, we know this was an annexation. This can be compared to Trump's dissolution of the traditional Republican Conservative party. Daniel Corluka explained how one influential ideology like Trumpism overtook an acceptably legitimate political party in "The Annexation of National Socialism by Hitlerism."[260] The

---

[258] Matthews, Owen. "Aleksandr Dugin and Steve Bannon's Ideological Ties to Vladimir Putin's Russia." *Newsweek*. 17 Apr. 2017.
[259] Kinstler, Linda. "Why Donald Trump Is Dangerous for Eastern Europe." *Politico*. 12 Aug. 2016.
[260] Sorluca, Daniel. "The Annexation of National Socialism by Hilterism." The University of Sidney. Masters Government and International Relations. 24 Oct. 2014.

Republican National Committee has voluntarily been annexed. Neo-Protestantism is no isolated anti-Semitic program. Most Americans and Israeli media heard the speeches, but few remarked how similar they were to Adolph Hitler. Thomas Idinopulos, "Nazism, Millenarianism, and the Jews."[261]

Most of the processes described above are unnoticeable to most people. They happened then during 1920-1945 and proposed in 2014-2016. The strategy of exercising authority as silently out of view as possible is based on diversion and explained by Chin-Hui Han, writing in *Pointer,* a Singapore journal, primarily military intervention of non-disclosure.[262] This type of polemic propaganda is built on a kernel of truth magnified into a whirlwind known as asymmetric warfare. This type of manipulation hidden in speech and sentences develop a particular train of thought and behavioral pattern in the listener.

Images are crucial to an organic authoritarian regime. From 2015 Donald J. Trumps Republican Conservative policies were based merely on childhood fear appeals. The creation of the liberal monster next door who is a "robber and thief." Hard-earned salaries that support lazy minorities, the "lock her up." Changing the meaning of "a society cannot replenish itself using other people's babies." The "midnight torches of the Klan," "blood and soil chants by Nazi's in the streets." Any alt-right involvement is dwarfed by hedge fund managers.

The aim is to develop a robust and fearful personality and shake-up the feeling of security. It can be correlated to the early ascendency

---

[261] Idinopulos, Thomas. "Nazism, Millenarianism, and the Jews." Academic journal article *Journal of Ecumenical Studies.* 22 Jun. 2003.
[262] Hui Han, Chin. LTA (NS). "Maskirovka In the Information Age." *POINTER,* Journal of the Singapore armed forces. Vol.42 no.1.

period of Adolph Hitler and the coming together of the Völkisch state.[263] Shane Croucher reported in *Newsweek,* "Trump's America feels like just before Adolph Hitler came to power." [264]In almost sequential occurrence, the Presidential Candidacy and Trump's ascendency correlated to National Socialist and Hitler's speeches. The rise and proliferation of Mr. Putin's expansionist thinking he purported byways of Andranik Migranyan, Ph.D., and Aleksander Dugin.

Trump said he was an American and had merely spent time shuttling between Soviet-Russia. Still, his demeanor indicated *Trump* was more like a foreigner on a visit or tourist visa to New York and Washington. There was not one church representative to hold Presidential Candidate Trump in check.[265] Economic self-interest, close coordination of agreement are legal terms that were discussed by *Trump* taking office. As explained by Michael J. Doyle, the presidency could hamper judicial reviews, "Conspiracy: Evidentiary Value of Conscious Parallelism." [266] Doyle explains," The difficulty arises in determining what is sufficient proof of the existence of a conspiracy and then actually obtaining the necessary quantum of proof. It is not essential to prove a conspiracy by direct evidence of an express agreement, written or oral. Circumstantial evidence has always been enough. Evidence of a formal

---

[263] Hitler, Adolph. Mein Kampf. Volume Two: The National Socialist Movement. Chapter 4. Personality and the Conception of the Folkish State. Munich: Verlag. Frz. Eher.

[264] Croucher, Shane. "'I'm A Holocaust Survivor—Trump's America Feels Like Germany Before Nazis Took Over." Newsweek. 09 Apr. 2018.

[265] Connolly, W. (2005) "The evangelical-capitalist resonance machine" Political Theory 33. 6. 869-886

[266] Doyle, Michael J. "Conspiracy: Evidentiary Value of Conscious Parallelism." Vol. 45. Issue 4. Spring 1962. Article 13. *Marquette Law Review.*

agreement is unnecessary and where the law otherwise such conspiracies would flourish...."[267]

Only as He Understood Love

Given William P. Barr, US Attorney General, there was no conspiracy seen. This was the space where Donald J. Trump had lived by standing in the middle and creating polarization between himself and the government, just as Frederick Trump taught him. Unapproved banking system transactions between countries skirted Russian concessionaire law and American banking laws weakening both oversight bodies.[268] We know the system allowed these types of infractions.

Christians support his worst human policies.[269] Hume N. Johnson's work points out this is the behavior intrinsic to illegal groups and the underrepresented, such as the unemployed and ordinary people seeking to infringe on the established civil society identified by scholars as to the "power of disruption."[270] Hume N. Johnson's work is particularly relevant since this underrepresented part is a new Conservative reorganization to use collaborators to keep them in office. The "power of disruption" seen illustrates Trump's signature campaign. [271] This

---

[267] C-O-Two Fire Equipment Co. v. United States, 197 F. 2d 489, 494 (9th Cir. 1952), cert. denied, 344 U.S. 892 (1952).

[268] DLA Piper Law Firm. "Concession law in Russia." *Lexology.* 03 Sept. 2014. See also: World Bank Group. "Public-Private Partnerships Laws / Concession Laws." Public-Private Partnership Legal Resources Center. ppp.worldbank.org/public-private-partnership/legislation-regulation/laws/ppp-and-concession-laws.

[269] Stackelberg, Roderick. *The Routledge Companion to Nazi Germany*. New York: Routledge, 2007.

[270] Johnson, N. Hume. *Challenges to Civil Society: Popular Protest & Governance in Jamaica*. Cambria Press 28 Dec. 2011. ISBN-10: 9781604977820.

[271] Wilson, Erika. "The Great American Dilemma: Law and The Intransigence of Racism." CUNY Law Review. Vol. 20:513. 2017.

"recruitment" of collaborators became his strong support of America's radicalization that could not be accomplished without political party support.

In this belief structure, he interprets caring as abusiveness and aggression. Giving credence, they do not hear what the signals are that define victims from their perpetrators. Joseph Goebbels, the Nazi propagandist, explained this erasure of time. In his relationship with his father and Adolph Hitler as 'the parental love from my father who "only loved me "as he understood love." The father is seen as the solver to all "unsolvable" problems. Manipulating this love metaphor is a matter of artistic ability.[272] In these father-love situations, we turn this around and see the father's love difficulty. Donald J. Trump and Jared Kushner tried to justify their father's conviction. Vladamir Putin receives the same type of love.

When the speaker influences the audience to a close agreement, the listener might eventually believe in the *idiot's delusion*. It is the belief by the idiot that what one is thinking is known by the speaker. Through some mind-reading capability or spiritual awakening in the speaker all along, the idiot is totally unaware of how far they have sunk to the speaker's level and vulgarity just repeating from memorization what they were told or heard once before.

That message plays and repeats itself like a song one cannot forget until another piece replaces it. The singer walks around in their head, explores every crevice, and bangs on the pipes. It is free to rent, and the song stays there, making a disturbance. Then the opportunity arises to act on it, like Gita Sereny's *Journey to Speer* neighbors she knew attacked on cruelty commands.[273]

---

[272] Lakoff, George. *Metaphors We Live By*. University of Chicago Press; 1st edition. 15 Apr. 2003.
[273] Sereny, Gitta. "My Journey to Speer." *The Independent*. 30 Sept. 1995.

It is plausible that how Trump applies his language has a military purpose, particularly. Not so subtly, he mobilizes different forms of military power in his head. Then manipulates them like a game outside their usual scope to prepare for a more massive maneuver, such as using combat soldiers on the border, mobilizing Middle-east locations, changing Naval operations off South Korea and Japan, and issuing military supplies in Ukraine. Trump uses these devices not just as diversions but as warm-up exercises for potential deployment of policy.

Taking a look at how Adolph Hitler and Joseph Goebbels delved into their speeches and whom they consulted. One Ernst Hanfstaengl, nicknamed "Putzi," a Harvard graduate who worked for Franklin Deleanor Roosevelt, made this analysis to the Office of Strategic Services about Adolph Hitler's speeches and those that believed in them. It brings back memory to this and how an enemy uses photo-based memories and metaphor:

"There is only so much room in a brain, so much wall space, as it were, and if you furnish it with your slogans, the opposition has no place to put up any pictures later on because the apartment of the brain is already crowded with your furniture." Hanfstaengl added, "Hitler admired the use the Catholic Church made of slogans and tried to imitate it."[274]

In *Trump's* use of meanings and words, his speeches contain values and instructions that manipulate people to behave in a certain way. For example, the visualizations he communicates are beyond the usual political discourse and are filled with behavioral suggestions that the audience should feel, take action, and agree that a specific type of person is "with me, and this means us."

---

[274] Langer, Walter C. Psychological Analysis of Adolph Hitler. CIA File. *Central Intelligence Agency*. Declassified August 1999.

Analysis of discourse occurs within the societal context of history and culture that influence it. It goes to messaging purpose, and in comparison, with Adolph Hitler to come close, it has to be seen in the light of what he wanted to accomplish. It needs to be placed into a historical examination of the policies that followed. Albert Speer put this in context from an architectural and engineering perspective to declare war on domestic and foreign populations, weaken them, rob them, and imprison them, then ultimately kill them. From the historical record, there is ample evidence of what Adolph Hitler was thinking and doing. Both expressed their inherent uncontrollable, sometimes hysterical violence by using metaphors.

Critical Discourse Analysis is a snapshot of an essential tool for social psychology and psychiatry because it offers insight into power relationships and culture. Therefore, the power relationships in Russia, India, and the United States are different because of regional interpretation. Cultural connections in the same culture offer the behaviorist a tentative understanding of historical reference needed in biographical sketches and psychological analysis.

Comparing Adolph Hitler's speech being made by Donald J. Trump by coordinating similar themes. The production of similarity could be a product of theatrics or a resemblance to someone's personality type. For example, their supporters also may have specific similar receptors. Most profoundly, when supporters chant "let Trump be Trump" to unleash all restraints of his violent nature, it resounds the crowds of Adolph Hitler. There are also possibilities that the Western culture, under its own development, has become governed by a more totalitarian structure of the population. Policies were deliberately developed to express this likeness from the White House, confirming similarity.

For example, does the speech environment and spectacle of Fritz Kuhn and George Sylvester Viereck's speech in Madison Square

Garden elicit the same enthusiasm as it did then as today? What characteristics are different? Observation tells us that the addresses at the Garden continued to draw more massive crowds. Yet, there are many similarities. The abusiveness of Trump's speeches today is more widely accepted. It is not seen as abhorrent to hear immigrants visualized in violent, grotesque ways by audiences today as they would have been then. Although the name Adolph Hitler does not appear, it is evident that the message of metamorphosis is the same. There is a significant number of more initial violence now. Let's discuss the similarity in speech, considering it reflects psychological manipulation toward his supporters. The reverse must also be possible, that supporters now have much more significant influence over the speaker due to the advancement and ever-present technology.

How can we be sure *What We Hear What Was Said?* Daniel de la Cruz Díaz-Valdés had undertaken the research needed to confirm what different speeches communicated linguistically.[275] The study's title is "A study of political manipulation in discourse: Comparing Hitler and Trump's speeches." The location of the research was Universidad Complutense, Madrid. With a computer model, he found a linguist can measure speech in their dimensions of power abuse and what injustice and inequality result from it; this gives a precise but tentative linguistic comparison where their similarities can be measured.[276] He used this approach in his methodology; he took two political discourse samples from Adolph Hitler and Donald J. Trump at different periods. Primarily

---

[275] de la Cruz Díaz-Valdés, Daniel. "A study of political manipulation in discourse: Comparing Hitler and Trump's speeches." Thesis. Degree in English Studies TFG Supervised by Dr. Elena Martínez Caro *Universidad Complutense, Madrid.* June 2017.

[276] Van Dijk, T. A. "Principles of critical discourse analysis." *Discourse and society.* Vol 4(2): 249-283. London. Newbury Park and New Dehli: *Sage.* 1993.

using Van Dijk's theory and measurement of *Critical Discourse Analysis*.[277] With permission from the author, here are some of his results.

Daniel de la Cruz Díaz-Valdés detailed these findings credited to his work in the following breakdown.[278] They are communicated in this writer's own words and are believed to be accurate though not presented verbatim.

- Daniel de la Cruz Díaz-Valdés, closely and linguistically, assessed that Hitler and Trump use the same sophisticated devices to create the polarization.
- They used methods that created allusions when referring to the former and negative ones. For the latter, this included a specific device that victimized the tribe members that followed them and characterized wrong actions toward those outside the tribe.
- Proof of this measured and detailed a pinpointed approach seen in the German's victimization in Hitler's speeches and Americans in Trump's.

Van Dijk calls "Polarization" a notion that can be described, in political terms, as the "movement away from the center toward the extremes."[279] The extreme right is defined as the "New Germany" utopia of Adolph Hitler as the "us." By blood and specific physiological characteristics, Germans made them "look" German-like blond hair and blue eyes, Aryan. The "them" as immigrants, Jews, foreigners, other

---

[277] Ibid.

[278] de la Cruz Díaz-Valdés, Daniel. "A study of political manipulation in discourse: Comparing Hitler and Trump's speeches." Thesis. Degree in English Studies TFG Supervised by Dr. Elena Martínez. *Caro Universidad Complutense, Madrid.* June 2017.

[279] Van Dijk, T. A. "Principles of critical discourse analysis." *Discourse and society.* Vol 4(2): 249-283. London. Newbury Park and New Dehli: *Sage.* 1993.

nations, other political parties, different ethnicities, those that have no part in governance.

Some terms to help understand the purpose of creating this in-group are developing lines of thought that can be framed into policies, politics that serve the ruling political class. These interests went further to mount the in-group as the most loyal in religiosity, nobler in their pursuits, and more worthy than the metaphorical and symbolic terrorist Jew. The "Jew" is a metaphor for the out-group and included Germans, foreigners, and those with "different brains" and anti-Hitler motives. This is similar to *Trump's* views of judicial representatives, Democrats, Europeans, Africans, Immigrants, and others, namely black and brown citizen and noncitizens.

According to Daniel de la Cruz Díaz-Valdés, "Trump and Hitler use metaphorical language to discriminate the members of the out-group and dignify the in-group's (a very usual technique in political discourse). By doing so, the persuading effect of their speech is much more powerful, and as a consequence, new ideologies will be formed."

There are close similarities of comparison that shape the picture in listeners' minds, both adherent and non-adherent. The image is these:

- The verbs defining the in-group are mostly passive (which emphasizes its members) and denote adverse actions, such as deprived, divested, retained, ripped, torn away, or whipped out. These passive verbs portray the out-group members as robbers and destroyers of the in-group's order.

- Hitler and Trump use God's figure as an element to signify the members of the in-group, representing them as if they were some kind of "chosen ones," so to say. In this way, the speaker increases the intended audience's self-esteem and makes them feel secure, confident, and ultimately superior to the out-group members.

A close similarity of identifying Adolph Hitler's thinking to Donald J. Trump is their use of fear and disease. Despite the public opinion that I acknowledge has gripped the country about populism. There are lines of psychological thinking patterns having to do with reflecting the disabling features of rigid authoritarian patterns of domination and racism.

- Jews are related to diseases, thieves, and 15 parasites in Hitler's speech, negative concepts similar to those used for the immigrants in Trump's statement. They are represented as thieves and killers. It is also interesting how both leaders refer to their country as a house/building that should be protected from strangers/menaces that could sneak in, using concepts related to the notion of war. Moreover, both speakers use divine references such as the prophet's figure, in Hitler's case, and God's light of wisdom in Trump's to extol the in-group's members' virtues.

- The invocation of God is a feature directly to a false belief, idolatry, blasphemy. Its use in Trumps' speech comports to a view of the self-inspired trajectory of greatness above the common man. A thought associated with The Holy Roman Empire's destiny---to make a kingdom respectable to the heavens. The implication exists that when a man becomes god, only he determines the rules. I think Donald J. Trump used messages to establish the basis of fear like a political disease. One that might enter a person's mind, their way of life, and home. The intended result was to take civil actions against them as children and younger adults to serve as visible victims permanently mentally disabled and traumatized as a warning to other politically diseased.[280],[281]

The "disease" was used as an anti-Semitic reason for Jewish persecution, wrote Victor Karady, "Political Antisemitism and its Christian Antecedent. Trying to Make Sense of Nonsense."[282] Donald J. Trumps association between his white power and the disabled as infected is a clear relationship to fascist speeches. He implies immigrants are infectious and harmful.[283] This behavior-shaping language also assaults his supporters if they develop the disease.

Daniel de la Cruz Díaz-Valdés, "Both subjects, use the plural form We as if his audience and himself were one entity. This is telling because, by doing this, the leader is showing to his people that he is not different from them, but a common man as well, who has the same feelings and desires of the masses." [284]Trump says he wants to be unrestrained, angry and embittered toward those that interfere. Suggesting punishment, he not only wants to lock them up but pivot to harm them in different ways.

---

[280] Moran, Mark. "Board Approves Statement Against Separation of Migrant Children." *American Psychiatric Association.* 10 Jan. 2019.

[281] Jacobson, Louis. "Are illegal immigrants bringing 'tremendous' disease across the border, as Trump says? Unlikely." *Politifact.* 23 July 2015.

[282] Karady, Victor. *"Political Antisemitism and its Christian Antecedent. Trying to Make Sense of Nonsense",* in The Making of Antisemitism as a Political Movement. Political History as Cultural History (1879-1914) , eds. Werner Bergmann, Ulrich Wyrwa, *Quest. Issues in Contemporary Jewish History. Journal of Fondazione CDEC,* n.3 July 2015.

[283] Ibid.

[284] de la Cruz Díaz-Valdés, Daniel. "A study of political manipulation in discourse: Comparing Hitler and Trump's speeches." Thesis. Degree in English Studies TFG Supervised by Dr. Elena Martínez. *Caro Universidad Complutense, Madrid.* June 2017.

Then the murders and cruelty began as a pattern. To appreciate the planned precision of the "us and them," strategy observe the present self-inflicted conflict's implementation and components and the participants. Congressional collaborators must add the aggressive campaign of policy, such as restrict voting rights—civil disturbance incitement such as murders in Charlottesville, Virginia, the Pittsburgh, Pennsylvania massacre. The provocation was intentional, and the approval from Trump's supporters was overwhelming. This response was indicative of the tie between Mr. Trumps' motivations and the audience's consent to violence. Indicating the listeners are aware they attend a racial rally and not solely a campaign event.

There are other modes of communication, such as mirroring, cues, and body language. Silent agreement between people has been well documented as a form of communication. Jinyuan Liu has done quite a lot of hard work on this very topic that is interesting by her study on connection, "Correlation and agreement: overview and clarification of competing concepts and measures."[285] Presidential Nominee Trump projects what he is thinking in vivid detail but does not explicitly say it.

Jinyuan Liu writes that measurement can be created that correlates between established variables customarily used in medical studies but may be applied in social science research. It could be thought of finding the similarity and differences between President (Nominee) Trump and Putin. We would begin with the hypotheses that they are individually different due to culture and measure them politically. When one of them talks, their speech sounds like they spent their entire lives within

---

[285] Liu, Jinyuan. "Correlation and agreement: overview and clarification of competing concepts and measures." Shanghai Archive Psychiatry. 25 Apr. 2016 28(2): 115–120. doi: 10.11919/j.issn.1002-0829.216045.

the same family. It is both creepy and uncanny. What influence do these leaders rely on to guide their behavior? Why are they so ideally and strictly scripted? This phenomenon has become familiar in the United States; when Trump supporters are asked about opinions, they go into ranting the bullets from a FOX News talking point.

The cruel reality is in the United States, there is an underdeveloped sense of history. Americans often say that they must discount the literature of the world. Particularly that part that is cruel and immoral due to "a polite society." In this formula, everything is patronized. After all, the thinking goes, those that have developed as deviants almost inevitably get a second chance.

Then, 'A Florida Double Murder' was written by Janet Reitman, "All-American Nazis How a senseless double murder in Florida exposed the rise of an organized fascist youth movement in the United States." [286] The Atomwaffen murders were covered by Kyle Swenson, "Suspects in five killings reportedly linked to the macabre neo-Nazi group." [287] President Trump began to have a personality shift and a violent pattern where he has an influence. [288] Sunny Hundal of the *Independent* points out, it's not leftists that fund Nazi affiliates and white supremacists but the "center-right" who maintains their organizations, training, and liaison capability. [289]

---

[286] Reitman, Janet. "All-American Nazis How a senseless double murder in Florida exposed the rise of an organized fascist youth movement in the United States." *Rolling Stone*. 02 May 2018.

[287] Swenson, Kyle. "Suspects in five killings reportedly linked to macabre neo-Nazi group." The Washington Post. 29 Jan. 2018.

[288] Devine, Curt. "Trump's foreign business interests: 144 companies in 25 countries" CNN. 29 Nov. 2016.

[289] Hundal, Sunny. "White people don't seem to realize that eventually the far right will come for them too." *Independent*. 06 Mar. 2018.

Conservatism and this propensity toward populating the Republican Party with extremists, as Senator Lindsay Graham has indicated, "to fight against liberalism" has its current cost. When Conservative candidates make their credentials based on oppressive policies, people's persecutions because of their membership in a specific national, political, social, ethnic, or religious group is considered a crime against humanity.

Intentionally Nazis are recruited as candidates to run under the Republican National Committee. Alan Elsner reported: "Neo-Nazis Look for New Home in Trump's Republican Party."[290] This includes steering them into positions of international police power Bethany Allen-Ebrahimian, "Nazi Sympathizers Pushing to Take Over Europe's Spy Agencies."[291] Republican Nationals have disengaged from interfering in any aspect of the Trump Presidency and have effectively become fascist or enabler to the cause.[292] Nationals recruit youth to radicalize overseas Katrin Bennhold, "Germany's Far-Right Rebrands Friendlier Face, Same Doctrine."[293] There is a funding source Casey Michel, "America's neo-Nazis don't look to Germany for inspiration. They look to Russia."[294] This validates the coordination between political platforms by the Republican National Committee members and the structural framers and authors of neo-Nazi policies.

---

[290] Elsner, Alan. "Neo-Nazis Look for New Home in Trump's Republican Party." *J Street*. 12 Jul. 2018.

[291] Allen-Ebrahimian, Bethany. Et.al. "Nazi Sympathizers Pushing to Take Over Europe's Spy Agencies." *The Daily Beast*. June 26, 2018.

[292] Chait, Jonathan. "How Hitler's Rise to Power Explains Why Republicans Accept Donald Trump." *Intelligencer*. 07 July 2016.

[293] Bennhold, Katrin. "Germany's Far Right Rebrands: Friendlier Face, Same Doctrine." *The New York Times*. 27 Dec. 2018.

[294] Michel, Casey. "America's neo-Nazis don't look to Germany for inspiration. They look to Russia." *The Washington Post*. 22 Aug. 2017.

National Socialism's Policy Integration with Republican Platform

Statement biases and comparisons to Adolph Hitler are depicted in Conservative policies. They include specific themes of social injustices, enthusiasm, anti-Semitism, harmful immigration, and emotion. Mr. Trump's campaign ran parallel to impact; citizen illegitimacy, volatility, vulgarity, violence, and increased incivility. Adding to the weight of mounting evidence, this involves something more substantial than a casual campaign speech. President Trump is changing from the positions of white supremacy and anti-Semitism of Anton Drexler toward Adolph Hitler. He is taking his supporters with him, and this has become a terrorist threat by the increasing number of global victims and the perpetrators who say they were encouraged by Donald J. Trump.

It reveals an aspect of the rage, anger, and resentment that weighs heavily on the racial rally as one motivating the *just call*. One in which is illustrated in words the conservative theatrics of a gothic narrative in mental images. Conservatives attempted to invoke a policy that gives him the executive power to deport sovereign citizens and expects wide-ranging public support. He is quite deliberately rearranging the Republican National Committee's priority of installing judges and connecting that priority to their supporters' dark personal prejudices.

Daniel de la Cruz Díaz-Valdés sensitizes us to Trump's attempt not to describe a situation as it is but drive forceful language to alter how we perceive it. In the following paragraphs, Daniel de la Cruz Díaz-Valdés results are given in quotes.

1. President Trump goes several steps further, unfolding the action people should take when he sets up the scenario of polarization. Using polarization, he establishes the mental foundation used

to create enemies in specific situations like Hitler, *Trump,* and the Jews, Democrats, and immigrants.

2. This discourse signals that President Trump seeks agreement with his followers that they do not have to compromise to accept immigrants in their country, which applies to others such as Jews. Muslims were the first "outsiders" to be placed in this category, followed by the disabled and others "draining the economy." Putting the "other" as an outsider creates a powerful plea for followers to support his plans.

3. Adolph Hitler and *Trump* use "*the* persuading effect of their speech are much more powerful, and as a consequence, new ideologies will be formed. The metaphorical representations of each group will be stored in the individual's episodic memory, affecting his/her cognition and thus influencing the personal conception of reality. This will allow for the creation of new opinions and prejudices that will be socially accepted and shared within the same ideological group." [295],[296]

The civilian population would never imagine being the subject of a military propaganda campaign in 2019. The more this part of President Donald J. Trumps' behavior is examined against human history, we see stark reminders of the uncanny correlation to 1920-1938. There are also some unsettling situations in the Rust Belt. In this region, President Trump is a crucial contributor to incivility and negativism. In particular, this line of thinking about immigrants bears a resemblance to the

---

[295] de la Cruz Díaz-Valdés, Daniel. "A study of political manipulation in discourse: Comparing Hitler and Trump's speeches." pp.5-12, Thesis. Degree in English Studies TFG Supervised by Dr. Elena Martínez. *Caro Universidad Complutense, Madrid.* June 2017.

[296] Lakoff, G. and Johnson, M. *Metaphors We Live By.* 1st ed. Chicago: University of Chicago Press. 2003.

past policies of National Socialism (Nazi), "For hundreds of years (we were) good enough to receive these elements, although they possessed nothing except infectious political and physical diseases.", said Adolph Hitler on January 30, 1939.

In *The Guardian*, Judith Butler wrote of Hannah Arendt at the Nuremberg trials in her article, "Hannah Arendt's challenge to Adolf Eichmann. "Stated that the problem with his supporters and their war crimes against humanity came from automatic response and suggestion of discourse manipulation. Hannah Arendt concluded, "The degradation of thinking worked for hand in hand with the systematic destruction of populations."[297] In this regard, President Trump could be Mr. Putin's best ideological comparison if his emotional volatility turns to military conquest. [298]

President Trump gets weaker as investigations rise, and his policies and threats become stronger. However, this does not reduce his supporters' growing number, and their identification with National Socialism (Nazi) as the approval poll statistics suggest they agree with the same policies.

This year, conservative President Putin, reportedly mild fascist, has spawned gothic images of nuclear catastrophe, his mental picture of devastation in Syria, chemical warfare strategies on children, and other corresponding glossy photographs public eroticism and poisoning. As Casey Michel reported, this has enthralled the Republican Conservatives, "Beyond Trump and Putin: The American Alt-Right's Love of

---

[297] Butler, Judith. "Hannah Arendt's challenge to Adolf Eichmann." *The Guardian.* 29 Aug. 2011.
[298] Savranskaya, Svetlana, source. "KGB of the USSR to Members of the Politburo, "On Measures to Improve Preventive Work Conducted by the State Security Service." 03 Oct. 1983, Secret.

the Kremlin's Policies."[299] These are an illustration of who the Presidential Candidate is and his 30-40% followers. As David Stout reported, these personal attributes coincided with Republican conservatives' history, "How Nazis Tried to Steer U.S. Politics."[300] A theory has developed about the decline among Republican Conservative standards written by Jonathan Chait, "How Hitler's Rise to Power Explains Why Republicans Accept Donald Trump."[301]

There literally is no escape from President Trump's global influences, by design. Therefore, it was necessary to determine whether there were any correlations between President Candidate Trump after becoming President Trump and what he is doing with American policy. France-Presse Agency reported his most active supporters do intend to keep aligned with him, which was explained in, "White supremacists and neo-Nazis: 'We need to have Donald Trump's back.'" [302]

President Trump has mutual feelings. During this book's writing, the Republican Conservatives remained aligned with the radicalization program of theory-based racial politics. In synchronicity, this consent apparently led to immediate reports of suspected crime and corruption. Leading to the suspicion that the inclusion of neo-Nazis' ideas integrated well with criminal activity within the Republican Party structure.

Fourteen policy and political positions were compiled with Mein Kampf and Nazi historical and political records. These were selected

---

299 Michel, Casey. "Beyond Trump and Putin: The American Alt-Right's Love of the Kremlin's Policies." *The Diplomat*. 13 Oct. 2016.
300 Stout, David. "How Nazis Tried to Steer U.S. Politics." *The New York Times*. 23 July 1997.
301 Chait, Jonathan "How Hitler's Rise to Power Explains Why Republicans Accept Donald Trump."[301] *Intelligencer*. 07 July 2016.
302 France-Presse. Agence. "White supremacists and neo-Nazis: 'We need to have Donald Trump's back'." *The Telegraph News*. 16 Aug. 2017.

based on their concordance to the points made in President Trump's speeches and communications. They are cited as commonly known positions of the Third Reich's National Socialist policy platform in its development. Each has their documentation and observation from public records and literature.

Each Nazi Theory below is identified with fascist Germany from 1920-1938 and is publicly voiced by the Republican National Committee members. Tentatively it shows this political body moving toward coordination and agreement of Nazi policy preferences and autocracy. Positions that would have been inconceivable just two years prior but have progressed unilaterally. Footnotes supplement the policy where needed.

1. Policy: Exceeding the legal limits of the presidency and initiating an economy deeply indebted. These decisive and deliberate actions also represent the heart of the Republican Conservative platform.[303], [304],[305]

2. Policy: Fascist mystification of absolute authority *auctoritas* is a declaration of being above the law and embodiment of the law. It is familiar in scope to what Adolph Hitler employed in his ideology, as the god-king with *auctoritas*/Führerprinzip power.[306]

3. Policy: Using the Big Lie theory. "All this was inspired by the principle - which is entirely accurate in itself - that in the big lie there is always an absolute force of credibility; because the broad masses of a nation are always more easily corrupted in the deeper strata of their emotional nature than consciously or voluntarily; and thus in the

---

[303] Tett, Gillean. "Trump and the problem with the new normal." *Financial Times.* 31 Mar. 2017.

[304] Cevallos, Danny. "No, Mr. President, an executive order can't change the Constitution. Here's why." NBC News. 01 Nov. 2018.

[305] Clabough, Raven. "Judge: Trump "Exceeded" Presidential Authority with Executive Orders Targeting Unions the New American." 28 Aug. 2018.

[306] Sheide, R.V. "If Trump Were King Cyrus." *A News-Café Online*. 16 May 2018.

primitive simplicity of their minds they more readily fall victims to the big lie than the small lie, since they often tell small lies in little matters but would be ashamed to resort to large-scale falsehoods. It would never come into their heads to fabricate colossal untruths, and they would not believe that others could have the audacity to distort the truth so infamously."[307]

4. <u>Policy</u>: Establishing and conspiring with authoritarian capitalism's oligarchy to undermine American governance.[308],[309] Plotting, planning, and operationalizing different foreign political contributions to Congressional officials.[310]

5. <u>Policy</u>: Adolph Hitler in speech and propaganda content compares closely. Feedback from the societal guard against fascism. Words were the most obvious. Daniel de la Cruz Díaz-Valdés provided confirmation of what this audience already knew. They compare the National Socialist (Nazi) iconographic identity that voted for Adolph Hitler the 30-40%.

6. <u>Policy</u>: False reporting accusations are levied against the press daily, reminiscent of the Third Reich crackdown. First Amendment Violations.[311]

7. <u>Policy</u>: Donald J. Trump has not followed Congressional Law on limits and separation of powers attempting to undermine the United

---

[307] Hitler, Adolph. *The Big Lie*. in Mein Kampf. p. 134. Munich: Verlag Frz. Eher.
[308] Fuchs, Christian. "Donald Trump: A Critical Theory-Perspective on Authoritarian Capitalism." *Communication, Capitalism & Critique*. 15 (1), 1-72, 2017. University of Forward-Thinking Westminster. Westminster Research.
[309] Baker, Stephanie. "Russian Oligarch's Links to Trump's World Extend Beyond Cohen." *Bloomberg*. 09 May 2018.
[310] May, Ruth. "How Putin's oligarchs funneled millions into GOP campaigns." Dallas News. 08 May 2018.
[311] Blunt, Katherine. "Unrecognized Potential: Media Framing of Hitler's Rise to Power. 1930-1933." *Elon Journal*. Undergraduate Research in Communications, Vol. 6, No. 2 Fall 2015.

States Department of Justice. Addressing the United States in past tense terms replaced *Make America Great Again* as the racialized successor state.[312]

8. Policy: Administrates his duties and anti-immigration policies linking it to preserving white supremacy.[313]

9. Policy: His threats to the United States' external security and encouraging the collapse of NATO.[314]

10. Policy: For his hearts and minds campaign, Donald J. Trump and FOX News allies have fallen for Joseph Goebbels' portrayal as "Adolph Hitler with a soul," modifying Mr. Trump's political stance. Using the immigration applicants and media to shape political levers to create a *geschichtslos,* a people without identity, no history, and no historical record about his opponent President Barack Obama.[315] Violation of United Nations Human Rights agreements.[316]

11. Policy: Instituting trade conflict and "*autarky.*" It could ruin relations with China giving rise to new trade agreements with post-Soviet states and Russia.[317]

12. Policy: Instituting a *Völksgeist*; the uniqueness of nationalists to exclude others speaking other languages or appearing as different

---

[312] Staff Writers. "In His Own Words: The President's Attacks on the Courts." *Brennan Center for Justice.* 05 June 2017.

[313] Serwer, Adam. "The President's Pursuit of White Power." The Atlantic. 13 Jan. 2019.

[314] Kettle, Martin. "Trump is hellbent on destroying the NATO alliance." *The Guardian.* 27 June 2018.

[315] Lengyel, Emil. "The Battlecries of Hitlerism Modified as Election Nears." *The New York Times.* 10 July 1932.

[316] Associated Press. "U.N. Human Rights office to U.S.: Halt Trump policy separating kids from parents at border." *USA Today.* 05 June 2018.

[317] Hunter, Edward. Committee on Un-American Activities, House of Representatives, Eighty-Fifth Congress, Second Session, March 13, 1958, Printed for the use of the Committee on Un-American Activities United States Government Printing Office, Washington 1958.

individuals and through the presidency's institution. There is an element of creating an inflamed speech to encourage vigilantism. Evident in Charlottesville, Virginia, and Pittsburgh, Pennsylvania, Nazi violence and murders.

13. <u>Policy</u>: Vice President Michael Pence misrepresented President Trump's message to the churches and his support for dominionism that underscored their belief in racial theories. Michael Pence has established the basis for national sovereignty based on in-group and out-group theory.

14. <u>Policy:</u> Dissolution and Annexation of the traditional Republican Party using the French Turn.

Mythili Sampathkumar, of the *Independent, wrote,* "Last surviving prosecutor at Nuremberg trials, says Trump's family separation policy is 'crime against humanity.'"[318]

World War II Holocaust survivors confirm:

- Holocaust survivors speak out against President Donald Trump's administration policies on immigration and refugees at a news conference at the Illinois Holocaust Museum and Education Center in Skokie on Feb. 2, 2017. (Chris Walker / Chicago Tribune).[319]

- Holocaust survivor says Trump's America 'feels like 1929 or 1930 Berlin' The president may not be a fascist, the survivor

---

[318] Sampathkumar. Mythili. "Last surviving prosecutor at Nuremberg trials says Trump's family separation policy is 'crime against humanity'." *Independent.* 09 Aug. 2018.
[319] Janssen, Kim. "Trump's immigration order revives horrible memories for Chicago Holocaust survivors." *Chicago Tribune.* 03 Feb. 2017.

told Newsweek, but he is an enabler of hate speech. Monday, 9 April 2018.[320]

- Jews separated from families during the Holocaust condemn US border policy.[321]

- More than 25 Jewish-American organizations published a letter to Attorney General Jeff Sessions on Friday, strongly denouncing the Trump administration's policy of separating migrant children from their families. *Haaretz*. 16 June 2018[322]

National Socialist (Nazi) and their affiliates confirm their understanding of Adolph Hitler and support Trump. There is an expansive narrative of the fascist relationship to Conservatives.

- Neo-Nazis celebrate Trump. *The Baltimore Sun.*16 Nov. 2018.[323]

- Neo-Nazis Look for New Home in Trump's Republican Party. *DW News*. 22 Feb. 2018[324]

- US neo-Nazi groups on the rise under President Donald Trump: report. *J Street*. 12 Jul. 2018[325]

- Rising extremism.[326]

---

[320] Mindock, Clark. "Holocaust survivor says Trump's America 'feels like 1929 or 1930 Berlin'." *The Independent*. 09 Apr. 2019.

[321] Dolsten, Josefin. "Jews separated from families during Holocaust condemn US border policy." *The Times of Israel*. 20 June 2018.

[322] Tibon, Amir. "Separating Migrant Kids From Families" *Haaretz*. 16 June 2018.

[323] France-Presse. Agence. "White supremacists and neo-Nazis: 'We need to have Donald Trump's back'." *The Telegraph News*. 16 Aug. 2017.

[324] Elsner, Alan. "Neo-Nazis Look for New Home in Trump's Republican Party." *J Street*. 12 Jul. 2018.

[325] Neo-Nazi. "US neo-Nazi groups on the rise under President Donald Trump: report." *DW News*. 22 Feb. 2018.

[326] Zurawik, David. "Frontline offers chilling portrait of rising neo-Nazi movement in U.S." *The Baltimore Sun*. 16 Nov. 2018.

No program of economics will stop nearly two years of constant iconography from the White House. They blurt various themes of "do not listen," "to what you hear," "do not believe," "what you see." These are calls for obedience to "whatever we do." Authoritarians use these communication ploys as commands. This phenomenon of "going along with injustice" is explained by Václav Havel. Václav Havel said, "Out of fear for the consequences which came from not supporting the regime, such as loss of employment, being ostracized from the community, or deprivation of secondary education for one's children, people would pretend to support the ideology of the regime."[327]

The thinking behind excusing wealthy industrialists from their part supporting Adolph Hitler has been a long-lived phenomenon. It has played a role in societal conditioning. The rule of law does not apply. It has led the United States to this point of considering immunity for President Donald J. Trump and his Republican National Committee. Liberalism finds it difficult to assert itself and actually make a decision on matters of great importance. Before Mr. Trump took office, there were many escapes offered to him. Among these were the many "psychiatric" excuses for his behavior. By merely overlooking the facts, this movement originated from below and was supported through years of systemic allowances.

In the United States case, Kevin Heller and Gerry Simpson wrote about the "natural and symbiotic immunity between wealth and governance," "The wish—and decision—to try individual industrialists in this changing landscape may seem contradictory at first glance. Below the surface, a deeper US need can be discerned: the need to reassure American industrialists, perhaps counter-intuitively through these

---

[327] Havel, Vaclav. *The Power of the Powerless. October 1978.* Original rough essay. Author deceased 18 Dec. 2011.

trials, that production for the Korean and other, potentially aggressive, wars would not lead to their prosecution. From this perspective, the Tribunals' task was to distinguish culpable involvement with an evil regime from innocent 'business.'"[328] From the time Americans are children, they are taught that it is impolite, and they should be punished by speaking certain words.

The United States never took the European situation seriously by developing legislative barriers to fascism. The United States allowed the racial theories of its beginnings to become part of the law and its educational system. One needs only the mounting evidence of children being kidnapped by United States agents and separated from their parents during infancy, something the United States pledged to Israel. It would "never again" allow what was done in Europe.

Chief US prosecutor Robert Jackson explained only a few defendants did not blame Adolph Hitler for the murders and devastation of the continent. He stood before them in court reading his closing statement to the Nuremberg Tribunal and said:

> "It is common to think of our own time as standing at the apex of civilization from which the deficiencies of preceding ages may patronizingly be viewed in the light of what is assumed to progress. The reality is that in the long perspective of history, the present century will not hold an enviable position unless the second half is to redeem its first. They stand before the record of this tribunal as bloodstained Gloucester stood by the body of his slain king. He begged of the widow, as they beg of you: "Say I slew them not." And the Queen replied: "They say they were not slain. But dead they are." If you were to say of

---

[328] Dubois, above n 10, 20. See also, Jeßberger, 'Die I.G. Farben vor Gericht', above n 1; Jeßberger, 'On the Origins of individual criminal responsibility under international law for business activity: IG Farben on Trial', above n 1.

these men that they are not guilty, it would be as accurate to say that there has been no war, that there are no slain, that there has been no crime." [329]

The Daily Stormer's Song is symbolic as it is memory implanting. The entire Conservative project is evident in the critique of notable psychologists that were mentioned in this book. It is accepted that New York did more to radicalize the different political factions from within the Wall Street hedge fund establishment. The Third Reich publications often are supported by a subculture of Gothicism in the literature used to reinforce a specific thought structure. There is a fascist structure, Stormer's way of thinking that is hierarchical. Norms and practices support the leadership by confirming beliefs to their political platforms—the Republican Party's downfall. The Democratic Party also gained in the recent candidate President Donald J. Trump's ascendency refreshing their ranks with new membership. In this regard, both the Republican and Democratic Party benefitted tremendously from the 45th President's corruption and radicalization.

---

[329] Jackson, Robert. Closing Statement to International Military Tribunal, Nuremberg 1946.

Some general statement about the condition of democracy has to be made. To what end does the West depend on the deviance of outlying groups to forge its progress. For example, we have experienced the collapse of the American economy in 2008. The same JP Morgan Chase culprits were used to revitalizing it. Undoubtedly this trend will exemplify any new presidency in the future. I like to consider this pattern as a car stuck in the sand, and once released, hazardous driving led to being entrapped again. In more psychological ways, Wilhelm Reich wrote of workers caught in fascism 'It amazed me that once getting out of the swamp you reentered again to your detriment." On a positive note, I'd like to believe the problem is forgetfulness about how tragic fascism was that it would be so repulsive to repeat it.

However, this is not always the case, as illustrated below. The events about Republican Conservatives are the second time Americans went onboard with misleading messengers. President Richard Milhouse Nixon, the last practical liberal, was overthrown by the Ronald Wilson Reagan reactionaries. The platform to suppress nuclear war followed the correct path. On social matters, and progress the post-Nixon era was catastrophic. Its legacy still exists in thousands more homeless than the week before. It is still debatable whether President Gerald Ford should have signed the Jackson-Vanik Amendment to the 1974 trade agreement. The Soviets' use hid the Jewish mafia and their thieves-in-law among applicants who established the base of operations among the five mafia families in New York City.

The inclusion of subversives in American democracy continues to this day. It is the most significant impediment to progress on behalf of citizens. One act by President Abraham Lincoln, the characterized the greatest President ever after the Civil War, stopped. President Lincoln allowed the Confederates to remain in the government. This inclusion of traitors included the healing policy proposed by Representative Thaddeus Stevens. He acted in concert with General William T. Sherman to give Confederate lands to slaves while barring them from government service and leadership. Through a veto President, Lincoln blocked the actions and 40 acres and a mule totally undermined. To be in the Republican Party and accept these historical principles meant the continuous investment and fusion with who most Americans considered subversives and traitors. This character trait did not translate to anyone in the population who wasn't white.

The privileges that came from controlling Confederate lands and the preferences it created is not just one of the promises made to America's wealthy families. But to all those in the wealthy class since then. The single attribute of both Republican and Democratic Parties is the first act they do. Pay homage to the wealthy by the symbolism of Republican continuity and preservation. At the same time, the Democratic Party does the same action to invoke the dire necessity of wealthy tax breaks "to strengthen the economy."

It placed law enforcement in New York into a spiral of corruption and ill-gotten profits. Drugs, construction, high-end real estate investment served as cover as my previous book *Deviant-the Web* described. Recruitment of the unsavory continued through President Reagan's attempt to rebuild the Republican Party into a revolutionary force under the auspices of preventing communism (Soviets) from taking control. Reagan's Presidential logic seems to be exercised along the same lines as President Lincoln, who they claim was the first Republican. Therefore, since President Lincoln flourished in history by including traitors in the government. It must be alright to have the extreme right-wing in their government as long as they abided by the Golden Rule of tax breaks to symbolize President Lincoln's loyalty.

Not particularly a success by 1985, President Reagan's administration was known as the "spy years." It was a well-deserved label given the John P. Walker Navy spy case, Iran-Contra, invasion of Grenada, and subversives' involvement in the White House. Most of the following information is "unforgetting" who Ronald Reagan was before the public knew anything about Vladamir Putin's name, the "other" Conservative in the extreme right-wing sphere. There was a persistent one-third of a radical right-wing faction always present among the mainstream Republican Party.

Iran-Contra Affair, exploits of the *Reagan Doctrine* had in some ways duplicated the Democratic Party Congressional mistakes found in the deployment of the Jackson-Vanik Amendment to trade that brought members of the Jewish mafia to New York. Following Germany's pattern of hiring former Nazis, the President Reagan administration recruited a number of them to fight the Cold War against the Soviet Union. With the typical incompetence of government bureaucracy, but not from Germany's same ranks. Instead, the Reagan White House went bold and recruited the most virulent Nazi.

Including members of the Waffen-SS, Nazi Germany's Schutzstaffel's military arm. Even some Iron Cross recipients who, almost immediately after entering the United States, established a small Republican Party club that, in years ahead, tried to steer elections toward the closest racialized conservatism they participated in during the Third Reich. In 1985, President Reagan visited the Bitburg, Germany cemetery he stated commemorated all of Germany's fallen soldiers.

Just how effective the recruitment program was, one has to correlate it to what the Soviet KGB was doing in France. President François Mitterrand became the focus of operatives like KGB Sergey Zhirnov, who was told by the Central Committee of the Communist Party to work with the fascists, which led to an insurgents' development known as today as the neo-Nazis and spin-off groups. This was also true in South and Central America and the post-Cold War drug cartels' expansion into the degradation of United States households.

The Commercial Insurgency

In acknowledgment of what President Reagan's Party wanted to accomplish as part of the Reagan Revolution were goals to tear down the government in favor of corporate dominance. President Reagan accomplished this with the inclusion of his associates in the White House. It included the mentioned Dr. Armand Hammer, Donald J. Trump, Paul Manafort, Roger Stone, Rudy Giuliani, and William P. Barr. All of which played prominent roles in the next forty years of never being prosecuted, investigated for their actions, despite their involvement and peripheral contacts with associates of the Jewish mafia and Eastern European connections. All of which was the Republican Party's future post-Reagan Presidency until this climaxed during President Trump, who issued pardons, except for Rudy Giuliani.

The so-called smart and intelligent in the Republican Party, including former CIA Chief VP George H.W. Bush, either knew or was unmoved about the KGB influence among their new party converts. During President Nixon White House, he used Occidental Oil resources to write checks to distraught Soviet spies. Yuri Borysovych Shvets, the Rezidentura of the First Chief Directorate, in 2021 said the KGB intervened and developed Donald J. Trump into an agent around 1975. Mr. Shvets also reported Mr. Trump would read and repeat whatever they sent him verbatim. Yuri V. Andropov and Sergey Zhirnov, a former Soviet intelligence officer, informed in 2018 through Euromaidan that it was a Soviet operation against President Mitterrand that recreated the neo-Nazi organizations in France.

This seems successful because a subculture of neo-Nazis further developed by the Soviets has been an enduring aspect of American life, to the point that led to the radicalization of the Trump family into the neo-Nazi sphere. It is closely identified as a characteristic of Frederick Trump's fascist thinking and the family's experiences pandering to New York subversive groups. This was covered extensively in *Deviant-the Web*. One could say that Fritz Kuhn and his handler Rudolph Hess, Deputy Fuhrer, have also been brought along the continued legacy of reconstructing the neo-Nazi line.

Credits to Vanity Fair in 1990 that wrote an outline of Mr. Trump's behavior, including how he may have begun an interest in fascist principles of propaganda when Marty Davis from Paramount gave him a copy of Hitler's writings. Following the lies pattern, no one in the Republican Party said they wanted his photo onto My New Order's cov*er* by ISHI Press. Subsequently, following the same logic, no one without a great deal of practice except Donald J. Trump winds up speaking in the nearly identical syntax of Adolph Hitler's speeches or concludes developing 14 closely aligned policies to the Third Reich.

Getting back to the point of Soviet nurturance of the Trump family and their evolving involvement in the Nazi ideological structure, nothing creates a convert of a person that values money than an economic incentive. In this case, it was forty years that Trump Organization accepted mafia tenants disclosed by the FBI, who conducted numerous arrests in Trump Tower. Yet, so far as Donald J. Trump, he remained unharmed by the wheels of justice in both Republican and Democratic cycles of New York governance.

Indicating the value of these relationships, Matthew Heimbach was the first documented case where he contacted the "guardians of Hitler's artifacts and political ideology" in Eastern European circles. His involvement played a part in guessing the link between the alt-right and Eastern European efforts. Through correspondence groups over the internet and during holiday visits, potential fascist activists from American middle-class families visited Eastern Europe to visit fascist landmarks.

The coming together of the subculture around Trump family enterprises included the Jewish mafia, neo-Nazis, and the Klan. It did not fully explain what had transpired that brought about Steve Bannon and Dr. Robert Mercer except that the right-wing became an excellent financial investment it could exploit. Operating as "Hate, Inc.," Bannon and Mercer hoped for consistent funding and investments.

We know that extremist right-wing organizations concealed from the Andropov KGB era became the basis for several organizations that impacted the global economy. Dr. Mercer appears to be a pivotal person. He was an intern at Air Force Weapons Laboratory at Kirtland Air Force Base of the 377th Air Base Wing, whose mission is to execute the nuclear war plan. Owner of Cambridge Analytica, he thrust himself into a new era of espionage and psychological warfare using his access to the military contracting agencies to alter the minds of electorates in the United Kingdom and the United States in Brexit and Trump's campaigns of misinformation. Dr. Mercer also supported the efforts of fellow hedge fund executive that self-acknowledged his quest was to create fascist nation-states. As an artificial intelligence scientist is entirely possible Dr. Mercer could create a sinister AI program to alter populations' behavioral patterns for a fee.

Steve Bannon and Dr. Robert Mercer's name came into the public consciousness in 2015. *Majority Rules* published Mr. Trump was commonly known to read and study *My New Order* and appeared on the cover as the Philadelphia Enquirer published to the world. The event's planning is similar to the purpose of underscoring *When the Daily Stormers Sang* in Charlottesville, Virginia. Both events signified that were he to be elected, he would institute Nazi policy. Significantly no one had made a statement to these events from the Republican Party. Not even the ghosts of past Republican Party officialdom made so much as a peep. It did not seem to dawn on any of the book authors that would later comment, think or remark publicly there were fascist problems ahead.

This American phenomenon of a reactionary group of wealthy individuals in geographic and ideological terms, reconstructing a National Socialist coalition with its roots in the 1920s to the 1930s. Not for any other purpose than to fulfill the Trump family's financial purposes. It's an odd situation, to say the least, where most risk and none of the benefits are generated for those below the hierarchy's highest positions. Akin to a political pyramid scheme. Still, the wealthy individuals connected to Wall Street don't just wither and die away. They rely on the small donations from those on the bottom of this commercial pyramid scheme.

The homogenization of neo-Nazi beliefs and the organized crime family behavior in political candidates also acclimates well to the alleged activities of money laundering representative of Russia's mafia state and the United States wealth immunity laws. On the psychological aspect of the Republican Conservative movement, the dark themes of the gothic and mental illnesses used in campaigns against nonwhite populations bear a close resemblance to history. Not only to what Adolph Hitler liked about America's "racialized identity" but to neo-Nazi compatibility with the 21st Century plans Russia endorses to divide and conquer democracy.

The only caveat to this Conservative mindset in both political atmospheres is the dire lack of psychological insight. The Trump family's demagoguery was not only taken to use by those more politically knowledgeable outside the family boundaries. It was manipulated in such a way that drove people crazy. Never before were so many small upheavals in every state and local government identified as the imaginings from a tiny group's dark and cruel inspiration. It is as though these people's thoughts became formed from the domain of fiction into daily life. They transformed into the bizarre normal dividing and conquering.

Most people would never show their opinions of their hate and resentment, feeling of spite, as markedly superior as the internet editors shaped their language and spoke as though no controls existed. Peter Viereck and Carl G. Jung, MD called this *The Movement of the Godless*; pagan dreams of violence, the rape, and abuse of women, cruelty to children, starvation, and like gangs and cartels forming into the Republican Conservative platform and policy. Congressional House Speaker John Boehner stated in response, "There is no longer a Republican Party as we know it." After he began selling drugs.

The acts, once carefully scrutinized, leads to two possible outcomes. Readers will come to their determination and surmount a theory themselves over what direction of neo-Nazi and organized criminal culture will dominate their homes and workplaces. They will wait and match the record of events and have different interpretations they can discuss. Part of the deliberation will consider the potential that whatever route they take will form their children's future. Have them wear armbands of said organized criminals, artifacts of the Third Reich taught in school, and extra days practice at the Miss Hitler contest's routine. Meanwhile, I want to address a few considerations of my own relative to the overall work.

What compelling reason conservatives have to select a man so incompatible with the Presidency? *The Daily Stormers Sang* say that they represent the re-habitation of former racists and the anti-Semites of the 1920s to the 1930s. This is condoned by President Vladamir Putin's goals of devising a "Good Hitler" out of parts of the 20th Century model and the one created by Yuri V. Andropov's Institute that also benefitted politicians investing in Trump. Logic stands that this is a financial degradation of democratic states in exchange for new prosperity and resource exploitation.

There is an unusual event in time and memorization challenging to explain. An emphasis has been placed on a type of remanufactured fascism being redistributed as democracy. History proves a need to review the United States' position on wealth immunity of corporations that have done business with Americas' enemies. Since World War Two, a billion dollars have been invested in a financial system that expressively places all elite and wealthy individuals out of reach of the law. Under the control of its influences, wars have been waged, millions have been killed, local economies have collapsed, and prisons are filled by minor offenders. While the more giant bugs caught in the web of justice have wiggled free.

Equivalent to 9-11, the intelligence officer remains captive in a logical trap of separating crime from the terrorist's ideology. The Republican Party had already deteriorated by 2008. Just by studying its participants' demographics and age, the Democratic Party has seen its best days as well. It is not surprising that as two organizations about to collapse, there would be efforts to preserve themselves. In this sense, a man like Donald J. Trump epitomized the Wall Street insider who receives just slaps on the wrist as he has a lasting accomplishment by renewing the ranks of both. This is also what the United States has done when it supports dictatorships abroad. Now it reserves it for itself.

For historians, American society being governed by a Republican government, leading to other questions about fascism. Globally, the new fascism is a similarity, not a repetition of older forms closely connected to the extreme conservatism of National Socialism. Though its modernization purports improvement, it has instead ushered in the deterioration of individual freedoms. The condition of new fascism has risen from close geographic proximity to people who formerly inhabited locations that were once strongholds of Nazi fascism. This shows there is little known about the reiteration of fascism as a geographical attribute.

The sophisticated process of electing a president with President Richard M. Nixon's criminal propensity and the Eastern European emigre preferences of Ronald Reagan seems more of a planned event than a random occurrence. Hungarian sociologist Bálint Magyar cautioned; the law can be used to allow a specific purpose in electing a post-moral extremist president. The office can create a type of democratic monarchy based on a perverted interpretation of democracy. A Conservative segment of society with a sharp edge toward organized criminality may adopt a family, giving them government power. Its members include secret service agents, police officers, judges, and insiders trying to profit and facilitate the crime network. It is a political and moral movement that seeks to "understand" the need for enlightenment through visual communities online and a fictional religion. The source is conservatism's "party of true believers."

Theatrics and visual propaganda are carefully re-imagined to resemble the ignoble period under discussion. The idea that Conservatives were inspired by 9/11 to begin the Trump campaign may convince some. I prefer to determine the prominent, contrived multi-media presentation that depicts propaganda of the 20th Century in Republican National Committee ads. This originates from a military source from within the United States' borders. Growing from the other just as George H.W. Bush, former CIA Chief, knew about Mr. Trump Micheal Pompeo, for CIA Chief must have been aware of the Trump Campaign connection to the neo-Nazis white supremacist groups were connected to Moscow. The Conservative declaration of "we don't know anything" has a tight hold on government thinkers. Communication among Conservative groups extends well beyond the United States.

When the Stormers Sang this one segment in the three books series in the next Gothic form *in Politics: Religion, Theory, and Practice,* the following principle is discovered: the collective subconscious and its dark side. The final book addresses the efforts to place the United States in the momentum of steady decline. The regeneration of neo-Nazism began in the Soviet attempt to overthrow President Mitterrand was a new recreated Nazism. This version with a new millennial and American face on new fascism portrays itself as no relationship to its Nazi Germany forbearers. We test this proposition. While meticulously examining the effectiveness of the democratic governing process in the United States. America's disconnection from its past is like a wasp that tried to fly away but couldn't. Realizing what was cut from his was not just wings, but his soul no longer wanted to become elevated toward the sun. To remember, I give this stanza from a history of *What the Daily Stormers Sang* and why.

Josef Magnus Wehner gave a speech of dedication at one memorial in 1932: 'The dying sang! The Stormers sang. The young students sang as they were being annihilated: "Deutschland, Deutschland u¨ber alles," u¨ber alles in der Welt" ... The dead heroes became an omen for the German people.' This gothic message is explored in the next book of this series.

Between Democracy and Gleichschaltung by Ronald von Smelser * ** (1st page only)

We are accustomed to speaking of German National Socialism and Adolf Hitler in the same breath as if to accept the proposition that the two were synonymous. Given the fact that Hitler exercised absolute domination over the movement during most of the period and that he was, for many National Socialists, the embodiment, the myth-person of the movement, there is much truth in this. National Socialism as it came to prominence and power in Germany is unthinkable without Hitler. But this was not always the case. As a set of ideas and attitudes, as a political Organization, National Socialism pre-dates Hitler. Even after he entered politics in 1919, some National Socialists still regarded themselves as the center of the movement by virtue of their seniority, of their political experience and success, and of their ideological development. These pioneers and their conception of National Socialism in the early years were far different from those of Hitler. They were the National Socialists of Bohemia (Czechoslovakia).

Eventually, by 1923, these older Nazis would succumb to Hitler's personal appeal and dazzling regional success and his branch of the movement and accept his leadership. Even then, as they paid homage to Hitler as the Führer, they attached a very different meaning to the word than did the Nazis in Germany. For operating as they were in another country, both beyond the interest and direct influence of Hitler, they were able to hold on to much of their autonomy and independence in practice. They could cherish the not completely unjustified belief that they were still the senior Nazis, the party's conscience, and the not always appreciated heralded outpost of the movement out on the borders of Germandom. Their course was, from the beginning, different from that of the Munich branch of the movement; their relationship with Hitler himself much more ambiguous than that of the Reich Nazis; indeed, it was, at least until 1923, and to an extent even for years after that quite a symbiotic relationship. This symbiosis is significant for two reasons, which have a bearing on understanding the rise of Hitler. First, it underscores the importance of context. Certainly, we recognize the unique importance of Hitler's personality and will. Perhaps so much so that we over-emphasize that factor and forget too easily that Hitler's unique talents were so effective precisely because they meshed with an environment in the early years uniquely suited to enhance them: post-war Bavaria, and in particular, Munich. Had that context been different — or had Hitler been elsewhere — National Socialism would have been a far different movement.

References:

* This is a revised version of a paper presented at the American Historical Association's annual Convention in Dallas/Texas, December 27—30, 1977. --- On Hitler as „myth person," see Orlow, Dietrich: The History of the Nazi Party. Vol. I. Pittsburg 1969, pp. 1—10. --- For a discussion of pre-Hitlerian National Socialism, see Whiteside, Andrew G.: Austrian National Socialism before 1918.

Words of War: Rhetorical manipulation in Goebbels' 'Total War' Speech (2 pages of 3 excerpt)

In his essay 'Education after Auschwitz,' sociologist Theodor Adorno commented that the aggressors behind the genocide at Auschwitz were "hardly able to offer resistance" when the fascist authorities gave the order to murder, in the name "of some ideal in which they half or not at all believe." In short, Adorno postulates that fascism exploited peoples' ignorance to exact such horrors as Auschwitz. This blind subservience to half-truths satisfies columnist Jonah Goldberg's definition of fascism as a "religion" of the state.

The triumph of democracy over fascism after the Second World War has led to the belief that fascism is truly dead, with a greater awareness of racial sensitivity and radical nationalism addressed across governments today. But with increased racist bigotry and a social disparity that demands a negation to class identity, the conjecture of a resurgence of fascism is called into question. Thus, in this case, the study of fascist rhetoric, Nazi propaganda minister Joseph Goebbels' Total War speech, allows us to investigate how deep the nation gets stirred by nationalistic overtures of 'ideal' loyalty and honor. People's individual beliefs become so tied to the jingoistic pride and racist hatred that manipulates them into swearing unconditional fealty. By analyzing different rhetorical techniques used here to incite hostility and ignorant cooperation, we can then understand and detect the presence of such speeches in today's governments and prevent such elements from manifesting again.

The most famous of Goebbels' speeches were delivered at the Berlin Sportpalast in February 1943, shortly after Nazi Germany's military defeat in Stalingrad. German confidence in the country's wartime superiority was shattered; hence the speech made Jewry and Bolshevism convenient scapegoats inflame the crowds and mobilize their total support to continue the war.

In fascist ideology, war fosters national loyalty and unity. It follows, then, that Goebbels impresses upon the significance of aggressive nationalism by manipulating the Germans' security interests towards a common looming threat. He uses Germany's defeat's critical timing by informing them that a disaster is waiting to happen should Germany lose the war. His suspicion of destruction ostensibly turns a potential morale-breaker into encouragement for acts of patriotism amongst the crowd. Goebbels also lays down a stark choice between "living under Axis protection or in a Bolshevist regime." This choice, coupled with the analogy of a medical operation "at the right time than to wait until the disease has taken root." Shows national loyalty as the only way to save Germany from the " "disease" of occupation. Hence, this collective underscore the message that action needs to be taken now; any untimely delay in decision making would lead to a " destruction of the Reich." This aggressive show of patriotism at this crucial time is important in inspiring people to fight back that fear. That the German nation is at stake due to defeat is effectively appealed in uniting the Germans as a single nation, drumming up support for a continuation of war through the forging of national loyalty.

Goebbels follows through nationalistic fervor with a glorification of honor as a reward for loyalty by convincing the audience that they are indispensable to their survival. He appeals to the audience's emotions by using honorific terms as a form of respect for the audience who are being enlightened by the "whole truth" of the war. Such honorific words as "passionate," "holy," and "pure" raise the struggle to one with an epic spiritual quality. Accordingly, these religious overtones of sacredness elevate the Germans' importance to the Reich's salvation, making them feel essential and strengthening their obedience. Conversely, Goebbels uses pejorative language to describe the Bolsheviks, accusing them of governing with "infernal political devilishness" and casting the Bolsheviks as an evil entity that needs to be vanquished by the German people.

Moreover, Goebbels derides Jewry as a "contagious infection" that borders on a ferment of decomposition. Such graphic vilification shocks the audience, intensifying their feelings of hatred towards the enemy and seeing the need to fight against this manifestation of evil; it provokes the Germans to act based on 'honor' against a 'dishonorable' enemy. Goebbels' emotional exaltation conveys sincerity that prides upon civilian participation as a crusade to save their homeland from devastation. ***Jonathan Liautrakul, 20 Oct 201. Civic Discourse in a Fractious World. The National University of Singapore---Alumnus***

Appendix C: Language of the Reich

Presentation of Victor Klemperer, The Language of the Third Reich *Lingua Tertii Imperii*, or LTI.

The LTI only serves the cause of invocation. . .. The sole purpose of the LTI is to strip every one of their individuality, paralyze them as personalities, make them into unthinking and docile cattle in a herd driven and hounded in a particular direction, to turn them into atoms in a gigantic rolling block of stone.

What a vast number of concepts and feelings it has corrupted and poisoned! At the so-called evening grammar school organized by the Dresden adult education center, and in the discussions organized by the Kulturbund and the Freie deutsche Jugend, I have observed again and again how the young people in all innocence, and despite a sincere effort to fill the gaps and eliminate the errors in their neglected education, cling to Nazi thought processes. They don't realize they are doing it; the remnants of linguistic usage from the preceding epoch confuse and seduce them. We spoke about the meaning of culture, or humanitarianism, of democracy and I had the impression that they were beginning to see the light, and that certain things were being straightened out in their willing minds—and then, it was always just round the corner, someone spoke of some heroic behavior or other, or of some heroic resistance, or simply heroism per se. As soon as this concept was even touched upon, everything became blurred, and we were adrift once again in the fog of Nazism. And it wasn't only the young men who had just returned from the field or from captivity. It felt they were not receiving sufficient attention, let alone acclaim. Not even young women who had not seen any military service were thoroughly fascinated with the most dubious notion of heroism. The only thing beyond dispute was that it was impossible to correctly grasp the true nature of humanitarianism, culture, and democracy if one endorsed this kind of conception or a more precise misconception of heroism.

In, *The Problem with Propaganda* by James Thomas Snyder, US State Dept. Diplomat (retired) https://jamesthomassnyder.com/about/ (excerpt)

Abelson, Max, and Jesse Drucker, and Zachary R. Milder. "Trump Tower a rogue's gallery of criminal tenants." *Irish Times*. 04 Nov. 2016.

Abusable, Kenzie, Tom Winter, and Max Tucker. "What Did Ex-Trump Aide Paul Manafort Really Do in Ukraine?" *NBC News*. 27 June 2017.

Ackerman, Spencer. "Snowden disclosures helped reduce use of Patriot Act provision to acquire email records." *The Guardian Weekly*. 29 Sept. 2016.

Akhtiorskaya, Yelena. "Welcome to Брайтон Бич, Brooklyn." The New York Times. 14 Dec. 2018.

Allen-Ebrahimian, Bethany. Et.al. "Nazi Sympathizers Pushing to Take Over Europe's Spy Agencies.*" The Daily Beast*. June 26, 2018.

Allen, Peter. "Russian mafia taking over French Riviera Mafia kingpins from the former Soviet Union have moved into the French Riviera and are taking over with "quasi-military" precision." *The Telegraph*. 31 Aug. 2010.

Altemeyer, Bob. *The Authoritarians*. Cherry Hill Publishing; Unabridged edition ISBN-10: 0972329889. 27 Nov. 2008.

Anderson, Jack. "I.T.T. Said to Seek Chile Coup In '70" *The New York Times*. 22 Mar. 1972.

Andrews, Natalie. "Senate Republicans Block $250 Million Election Security Measure." *The Wall Street Journal*. 01 Aug. 2018.

"Anyplace von Frau Marie B. MacDonald," *Philadelphia Gazette-Democrat*, Luebke, "German-American Leadership Strategies," pp.70-71. 7 Oct. 1933.

Arendt, Hannah. *The Origins of Totalitarianism*, 2nd edition, (New-York: Meridian Books, 1958), p.291.

Arreguín-Toft, Ivan. *How the Weak Win Wars: A Theory of Asymmetric Conflict*. Cambridge Studies in International Relations. Cambridge University Press. 08 Dec. 2005. ISBN-13: 978-0521839761.

Associated Press. "Frank Zeidler, 93; Socialist Was Mayor of Milwaukee." Obituary. *The Washington Post*. 13 Jul. 2016.

Associated Press. "Russia Complains After Polish State TV Links Putin to the Nazis." *Haaretz*. 02 Dec. 2018.

Associated Press. "U.N. Human Rights office to the U.S. Halt Trump policy separating kids from parents at border." *USA Today*. 05 June 2018.

"Asymmetric Warfare: Definition, Tactics & Examples." Study.com.

Atkins, David. "Cold War. Racist Plutocrats Won It." *Washington Monthly*. 22 Dec. 2018.

Axis powers were nations that signed the Tripartite Pact. Referred to as Germany, Italy, and Japan, Bulgaria, Romania, Slovakia, Croatia, Hungary, and Yugoslavia.

Badran, Amneh. *Zionist Israel and Apartheid South Africa*. *Routledge*; 1 edition 17 Sept. 2009. ISBN-10: 9780415489812. p. 64.

Bagli, Charles V. "Trump Paid Over $1 Million in Labor Settlement, Documents Reveal." *The New York Times*. 27 Nov. 2017.

Baker J., Graham. "Christianity and Eugenics: The Place of Religion in the British Eugenics Education Society and the American Eugenics Society c.1907–1940." *Soc Hist Med*. May 2014; 27(2): pp. 281–302.

Baker, Stephanie. "Russian Oligarch's Links to Trump's World Extend Beyond Cohen." *Bloomberg*. 09 May 2018.

Balezdrova, Anastasia. "Golden Dawn and Russian neo-Nazism." *GR Reporter*. 15 Apr. 2014.

Barstow, David. Susanne Craig and Russ Buettner. "Trump Engaged in Suspect Tax Schemes He Reaped Riches From His Father." *The New York Times*. 02 Oct. 2018.

BBC Staff. "Russia nuclear treaty: Gorbachev warns Trump plan will undermine disarmament." BBC News. 21 October 2018.

Beckett, Lois. "Donald Trump warns of 'violence' if Republicans lose midterms." *The Guardian*. 28 August 2018.

Beckett, Lois. "Is there a neo-Nazi storm brewing in Trump's country?" *The Guardian*. 04 Jun. 2017.

Beckett, Lois. "My six years covering neo-Nazis: 'They're all vying for the affections of Russia'." *The Guardian*. 17 Feb. 2018.

Beinart, Peter. "Trump Shut Programs to Counter Violent Extremism." *The Atlantic*. 29 Oct. 2018.

Belford, Aaron. "A Look at The Record: Bernie Sanders in 2011 Denounces Free Trade Pacts." *The Progressive*. 13 Oct. 2011.

Belford, Aubrey. Sander Rietveld and Gabrielle Paluch. "Steppe to Soho: How Millions Linked to Kazakhstan Mega-Fraud Case Ended up in Trump Property." *Organized Crime and Corruption Reporting Task Force*. 25 June 2018.

Bell, Leland. "The Failure of Nazism in America." *Political Science Quarterly*. Vol 85(4). Dec. 1970, p. 585.

Bennhold, Katrin. "Germany's Far-Right Rebrands: Friendlier Face, Same Doctrine." *The New York Times*. 27 Dec. 2018.

Ben-Naeh, Yaron. "Blond, Tall, with Honey-Colored Eyes: Jewish Ownership of Slaves in the Ottoman Empire." *Jewish History*, Vol. 20, No. 3/4 (2006), pp. 315-332. JSTOR, Springer, 233 Spring Street, New York, NY 10013.

Bergman, Jerry. "Darwin's critical influence on the ruthless extremes of capitalism." Creation Ministries International. *Journal of Creation* 16(2):105–109—August 2002.

Bernbaum, John A. "Four Scenarios for Post-Soviet Russia." The February 1995 revised paperback edition of *Russia 2010* is available. Random House Publishers. Maryland. 1995.

Bernstein, Arnie. "6 Things You May Not Have Known About Nazis in America." *The History Reader*. 07 Oct. 2013.

Bershidsky, Leonid. "Orbán's Economic Model Is Trump's Dream." *Bloomberg*. View. 12 Apr. 2018.

Bertrand, Natasha. "A model for civilization: Putin's Russia has emerged as 'a beacon for nationalists' and the American alt-right." *Business Insider*. 10 Dec. 2016.Black, Edwin. "The Horrifying American Roots of Nazi Eugenics." *The Washington Post*. September 2003.

Bischoff, Paul. "A breakdown of the Patriot Act, Freedom Act, and FISA." *Comparitech Online*. 02 Feb. 2018. Located at Kent, TN15 6AR United Kingdom.

Black, Edwin. *War Against the Weak: Eugenics and America's Campaign to Create a Master Race, Expanded Edition*. Dialog Press. Expanded edition. 30 Apr. 2012.

Blakemore, Erin. "The Largest Mass Deportation in History." *History.com* 23 Mar. 2018.

Blunt, Katherine. "Unrecognized Potential: Media Framing of Hitler's Rise to Power, 1930-1933." *Elon Journal of Undergraduate Research in Communications*, Vol. 6, No. 2. Fall of 2015.

Borowitz, Andy. "Trump Angrily Throws Steve Bannon's Signed Copy of "Mein Kampf" in Trash." *The New Yorker*. 03 Jan. 2018.

Boyarsky, Bill. "A Virtual Spy: DOSSIER: The Secret History of Armand Hammer. By Edward J. Epstein." *Los Angeles Times*. 27 Oct.

1996.Braun, Larry. *Who the Hell Is Larry Braun?* Xlibris. 25 de Junio de 2014. ISBN-10: 9781499040210.

Brennan, William. *The Role of the Court — The Challenge of the Future*. In An Affair with Freedom. Atheneum; 1st edition. 1967. ASIN: B0006BRH40.

Bretri, M.L. "Between Politics and Culture: School of Fascist Mystic." *Contemporary History*. 1-2, 1989. pp. 377-89.

Browne, Gareth. "Orban is the original Trump, says Bannon in Budapest." *The National World*. 24 May 2018.

Burgis, Tom. "Dirty money: Trump and the Kazakh connection." *Financial Times*. 19 Oct. 2016.

Burns, Ken. "The Dust Bowl." Biographies Woody Guthrie. PBS Documentary. See also Library of Congress. Smithsonian Folkways.

Burton, Tara Isabella. "The biblical story the Christian right uses to defend Trump." VOX. 05 Mar. 2018.

Butler, Judith. "Hannah Arendt's challenge to Adolf Eichmann." *The Guardian*. 29 Aug. 2011.

Canedy, Susan. *America's Nazis: A Democratic Dilemma: A History of the German-American Bund*. Menlo Park: Markgraf Publications Group, 1990.

Cain, Áine. "Before he became the president of Russia, Vladimir Putin was a KGB spy — take a look at his early career." *Business Insider*. 16 Jul. 2018.

California Newspaper Collection. "Exiled Bund Leader Fled Internment Fritz Kuhn Disappears from Camp Where Held for Trial by Germans." *Madera Tribune*, Number 273, 4 February 1948.

Camera, Lauren. "Lawmaker Calls on DeVos to Resign." *US News*. 01 Apr. 2019

Caplan, Jane. "Unsettling Echoes: Joseph Goebbels (1933), Sean Spicer (2017), Steve Bannon (2017)." *Historians Watch*. 30 Jan.

2017.Carlson, John Roy, Avedis Boghos Derounian, in *Under Cover: My Four Years in the Nazi Underworld of America--the Amazing Revelation of How Axis Agents and Our Enemies Within Are Now Plotting to Destroy the United States*. E. P. Dutton. 1943. p.118.

Carpenter, Michael. "Russia Is Co-opting Angry Young Men." *The Atlantic*. 29 Aug. 2018. in "Mobilizing 'uncivil society': how Russia's 21st Century 'active measures' actually work." Democracy Digest. National Endowment for Democracy. 29 Aug. 2018.

Casey, Nicholas. "Nazi Past of Long Island Hamlet Persists in a Rule for Home Buyers." *The New York Times*. 19 Oct. 2015.

Cay Johnston, David. "The Drug Trafficker Donald Trump Risked His Casino Empire to Protect." *The Daily Beast*. 16 Oct. 2016.

Center for American Progress Action Fund. "A Timeline of Trump's Deals and Investments in Eastern Europe and Central Asia." *The Moscow Project Org*. 18 May 2018.

Central Intelligence Agency. "Order of Battle Handbook Czechoslovak Army." 50 year declassified. Headquarters U.S. Army Europe. Office of A/C of S, G2. 01 Aug. 1958. *Central Intelligence Agency*. Wash. D.C. 03 Apr. 2004.

Cevallos, Danny. "No, Mr. President, an executive order can't change the Constitution. Here's why." NBC News. 01 Nov. 2018.

Chait, Jonathan. "How Hitler's Rise to Power Explains Why Republicans Accept Donald Trump." *Intelligencer*. 07 July 2016.

Chiu, Allyson. "Trump revives 'Willie Horton' tactic with ad linking illegal immigrant killer to Democrats." *The Washington Post*. 01 Nov. 2018.

Chládková, Lucie. "The Far Right in Slovenia." Supervisor Master's Thesis Miroslav Mareš, Ph.D. *Masaryk Univ*. Faculty of Social Studies Dept. of Political Science. Security and Strategic Studies, 2012.

Clabough, Raven. "Judge: Trump "Exceeded" Presidential Authority with Executive Orders Targeting Unions." *The New American*. 28 Aug. 2018.

Clarkson, Frederick. "Dominionism Rising: A Theocratic Movement Hiding in Plain Sight." *Political Research Associates*. 18 Aug. 2016.

C-O-Two Fire Equipment Co. v. United States, 197 F. 2d 489, 494 (9th Cir. 1952), cert. denied, 344 U.S. 892 (1952).

Cohn, Norman. "Apocalypticism Explained, Nazism and Marxism." *WGBH Boston. PBS Channel 13*. Undated.

Connolly, Kate. "Historian finds German decree banishing Trump's grandfather." *The Guardian*. 21 Nov. 2016.

Connolly, W. "The evangelical-capitalist resonance machine" *Political Theory*. 33. 6. 869-886. 2016.

Correia, Rion B., K. N. Chan, & L.M. Rocha [2015]. "Polarization in the US Congress." The 8th Annual Conference of the Comparative Agendas Project (CAP). Lisbon, Portugal, June 23-24, 2015.

Corn David and Andy Kroll. "Fuck You, Tyrants!": Ron Paul Supporters Rebel on Convention Floor." *Mother Jones*. 28 Aug. 2012.

Cowell, Allen. "Swiss Say Nazis Stole More Victim Gold Than Believed." *The New York Times*. 02 Dec. 1997.

Croucher, Shane. "I'm A Holocaust Survivor—Trump's America Feels Like Germany Before Nazis Took Over." *Newsweek*. 09 Apr. 2018.

Curtis, Charlotte. "Dr. Hammer's Real Concern." The New York Times. 19 Nov. 1995.

d'Ancona, Matthew. "Putin and Trump could be on the same side in this troubling new world order." *The Guardian*. 19 Dec. 2016.

Daley, Jason. "Footage Recalls the Night Madison Square Garden Fills with Nazi's." *Smithsonian.Com*. 13 Oct. 2017.

Davis, Mark. "Commentary: The uneasy relationship between the early church and the empire." *Los Angeles Times*. 08 Sept. 2016.

Davis, Tasha. Trump, Pence, & Jr. "Exploit Dead Girl Killed by Immigrant; Now Her Family Is Fighting Back." *Bipartisan Report*. 22 Aug. 2018.

DeJong, David. "The Nazi Shadow Behind the World's Youngest Billionaires." *TIME Magazine*. 08 May 2018.

de la Cruz Díaz-Valdés, Daniel. "A study of political manipulation in discourse: Comparing Hitler and Trump's speeches." Thesis. Degree in English Studies TFG Supervised by Dr. Elena Martínez Caro *Universidad Complutense, Madrid*. June 2017.

Demirjian, Karoun. "Republicans on Russia Trip Face Scorn and Ridicule from Critics at Home." *Washington Post*. 05 Jul. 2018.

Denina, Clara. "Exclusive: Russian central bank buys up domestic gold output as sanctions bite." *Reuters*. 10 Nov. 2014.

Devine, Curt. "Trump's foreign business interests: 144 companies in 25 countries." *CNN*. 29 Nov. 2016.

Diamond, Anna. "The Nazis' Plan to Infiltrate Los Angeles And the Man Who Kept Them at Bay." *Smithsonian Magazine*. 26 Oct. 2017.

DLA Piper Law Firm. "Concession law in Russia." *Lexology*. 03 Sept. 2014. See also: World Bank Group. "Public-Private Partnerships Laws / Concession Laws." Public-Private Partnership Legal Resources Center. ppp.worldbank.org/public-private-partnership/legislation-regulation/laws/ppp-and-concession-laws.

Docherty, Neil. And Gillian Findlay. "Putin's Way." *PBS Frontline*. 13 Jan. 2015.

Dolsten, Josefin. "Jews separated from families during Holocaust condemn US border policy." *The Times of Israel*. 20 June 2018.

Doran, Will. "Here's every time Russian or Soviet spies tried to interfere in US elections. How does 2016 compare?" *Politifact North Carolina*. 20 June 2017.

Doyle, Michael J. "Conspiracy: Evidentiary Value of Conscious Parallelism." Vol. 45. Issue 4. Spring 1962. Article 13. *Marquette Law Review*.

Duffy, Peter. "The Congressman Who Spied for Russia." *Politico Magazine History Dept.* 06 Oct. 2014.

Dugin, Alexander. And Alain Sorel. *The Fourth Political Theory*. Arktos Media Ltd. 16 July 2012.

Eatwell, Roger. The University of Bath. "Explaining Fascism and Ethnic Cleansing: The Three Dimensions of Charisma and the Four Dark Sides of Nationalism." *Political Studies Review*: 2006. Vol. 4. pp. 263-278.

Elsner, Alan. "Neo-Nazis Look for New Home in Trump's Republican Party." *J Street*. 12 Jul. 2018.

Engels, Fredrick. *The End of Classical German Philosophy*. 1886.

ENMOD. The Center for Media and Democracy. "Environmental warfare." Source Watch. Note: The 1977 Treaty is the "United Nations General Assembly Resolution 31/72, TIAS 9614 Convention on the Prohibition of Military or Any Other Hostile Use of Environmental Modification Techniques."

Epstein, Edward. J. *DOSSIER: The Secret History of Armand Hammer*. Random House. 1996.

Epstein, Jay. "The Andropov Hoax." *The New Republic*. 07 Fed. 1983.

Epstein, Edward Jay. "The Riddle of Armand Hammer." *The New York Times*. 29 Nov. 1981. See FOIA Reques.t

Erickson, Edward Jr. "Discretion Advised: Trump's mob and Russia ties could prove embarrassing for the Donald, and the FBI as investigations heats up." *City Paper*. 27 June 2017.

Evans, Richard. *The Third Reich in Power*. New York: Penguin Press, 2005.p. 216.

"Evangelicals and Apartheid." *Evangelical Alliance*. 176 Copenhagen Street, London N1 0ST Tel: 020 7520 3830 (Mon - Fri, 9am - 5pm) Fax: 020 7520 3850. 11 Dec. 2013.

Everett, Burgess. "Like a Soviet-type economy: GOP free traders unload on Trump." *POLITICO*. 24 July 2018.

European Christian Political Movement (ECPM) founded in November 2002 in Lakitelek, Hungary.

Fairweather, Nicolas. "Hitler and Hitlerism: Germany Under the Nazis." *The Atlantic*. April 1932.

Fairweather, Nicolas. "Hitler and Hitlerism: A Man of Destiny." *The Atlantic*. March 1932.

Farley, Harry. "Donald Trump's former advisor Steve Bannon: I'm a proud 'Christian Zionist.'" *Christian Today*. 13 Nov. 2017.

Farnham, Alan. "Armand Hammer: Tinker, Traitor, Satyr, Spy a Scathing New Biography Paints the Globetrotting Founder of Occidental Petroleum as a Blatant Opportunist, a Womanizer—and Perhaps Even a Soviet Spy." *Fortune*. 11 Nov. 1996.

"FBI Milwaukee History. Field Office Histories." *FBI Headquarters Washington D.C.* is 935, Pennsylvania Avenue, Northwest Washington, DC 20535-0001, United States.

Ferris-Rotman, Amie. "Can Russia, with its history of racist attacks and hooligans, put on a World Cup welcome?" *The Washington Post*. 12 Jun. 2018.

Ferris-Rotman, Amie. "Slovenians for Trump. In Melania's home country, the political far-right loves The Donald—and hopes he'll reciprocate." *POLITICO*. 04 Jun. 2016.

Festinger, L. & Carlsmith, J. M. (1959). "Cognitive consequences of forced compliance." *Journal of Abnormal and Social Psychology,* 58, pp. 203 – 210.

FHA Investigation. Hearings Before the Committee on Banking and Currency. United States Senate. 83rd Congress. 2nd Session. Pursuant to S. Resolution 229. Gov't Printing Office 1954. pp. 395-420.

Final Statement. Arthur Seyss-Inquart, International Military Tribunal, Nuremberg 1947.

Flood, Alison. "Hitler speeches published with Donald Trump as cover illustration." *The Guardian*. 03 Oct. 2016.

Foer, Franklin. "Paul Manafort, American Hustler." *The Atlantic*. March 2018.

France-Presse. Agency. "White supremacists and neo-Nazis: We need to have Donald Trump's back.'" *The Telegraph News*. 16 Aug. 2017.

French, Anne English. "Trials in Times of War: Do the Bush Military Commissions Sacrifice Our Freedoms?" *OHIO STATE LAW JOURNAL* [Vol. 63: 1225 (2002)}.

Friedländer, Saul. *Nazi Germany and the Jews Volume I*. Harper Collins. 1997, pp. 1-2.

Fuchs, Christian. "Donald Trump: A Critical Theory-Perspective on Authoritarian Capitalism." Communication, Capitalism & Critique, 15 (1), 1-72, 2017. *The University of Forward-Thinking*.

Westminster. Westminster Research.

Galeotti, Mark. "Gangster's paradise: how organized crime took over Russia." *The Guardian*. 23 Mar. 2018.

Gellately, Robert, and Ben Kiernan. Eds. *The Specter of Genocide: Mass Murder in Historical Perspective*. New York: Cambridge University Press, 2003.

Gera, Vanessa. "Hoosier survivor won't miss Putin at Auschwitz liberation ceremony." *IndyStar*. 27 Jan. 2015.

Giles, Geoffrey J. STUNDE NULL, "The End and the Beginning, Fifty Years Ago." *GERMAN HISTORICAL INSTITUTE* 1607 New Hampshire Ave., NW Washington, DC 20009. 1997.

Ghitis, Frida. "Putin wants Yalta 2.0 and Trump may give it to him." *CNN*. 17 Jan. 2017.

Goble, Paul. "Russian Defender of Hitler No Longer to 'Defend' Human Rights in US." The Interpreter. 29 June 2015.

Goldensohn, Leon and Gellately, Robert., from *The Nuremberg Interviews*. 14 Apr. 1946. Reprint edition Vintage. 25 Oct. 2005. ISBN-10: 1400030439.

Goldman, Shalom. "Mike Pence on the "American Heartland" and the Holy Land." *Patheos*. 20 Jul. 2016.

Goldstein, Judith S. *The Presence of the Past: Confronting the Nazi State and Jim Crow*. In Humanity in Action: Collected Essays and Talks, pp. 32-42. New York: Humanity in Action Press, 2014. ASIN: B00MOIO318.

Goodman, Alana. "Rand Paul's Russian Connection." *Washington Free Beacon*. 20 Aug. 2014.

Gray, R. "Freud and the Literary Imagination." Lecture Notes: Freud, "The Uncanny" (1919).

Gray, Rosie. "Pro-Putin Think Tank Based In New York Shuts Down" *Stop Fake Org.* 30 Jun. 2015.

Greer, Broderick. "Billy Graham's legacy is the evangelical pursuit of politics instead of Jesus: The limitations of relegating the gospel of

Christ to little more than eternal fire insurance was on full display in Graham's lifetime." *NBC Think*. 25 Feb. 2018.

Guzman, Timothy Alexander. "Creating a "New Israel" Jewish State in Southeast Texas." *Global Research*. 29 Apr. 2014.

Haija, Rammy M. "The Armageddon Lobby: Dispensationalist Christian Zionism and the Shaping of US Policy Towards Israel-Palestine." *Holy Land Studies*. A Multidisciplinary Journal, Vol. 5, Number 1, May 2006.

Hall, Allen. "Court papers shed light on the killing of Goebbels children." Berlin Bureau. *The Telegraph*. 08 Oct. 2009.

Hammer, Armand. Response. "A Response From Armand Hammer." *The New York Times*. 20 Dec. 1981.

Haney-Lopez, Ian. "The racism at the heart of the Reagan presidency." *Salon*. 11 Jan. 2014.

Hankins, Barry. *Francis Schaeffer And the Shaping of Evangelical America*. Library of Religious Biography. Pp. 193-196. Eerdmans. 03 Nov. 2008. ISBN-10: 0802863892.

Harden, Blaine, and Gall, Carlotta. "Crisis in The Balkans: The Serbian Orthodox. Church of Milosevic's Rise Now Sends Mixed Message." *The New York Times*. 04 Jul. 1999.

Harding, Luke. "Czechoslovakia ramped up spying on Trump in late 1980s, seeking US intel." *The Guardian*. 29 Oct. 2018.

Harding Luke. "The Hidden History of Trump's First Trip to Moscow." *POLITICO*. 19 Nov. 2017.

Harper, Steven. "A Timeline: Everything We Know About Kushner's Role in the Russia Mess." *Moyers*. 09 April 2018.

Harris, Catherine, and Mason Clark. "Russian Military Doctrine and Lessons Learned in Syria. Institute for the Study of War." 09 Nov. 2018.

Harris, Shane. "Signs of Trump-Putin collaboration, starting years before the campaign?" *The Washington Post.* 17 Aug. 2018.

Havel, Vaclav. *Living in Truth: 22 Essays Published on the Occasion of the Award of the Erasmus Prize to Vaclav Havel.* Faber & Faber; Reprint edition. 01 Mar. 1990. ISBN-10: 0571144403.

Havel, Vaclav, *The Power of the Powerless. October 1978.* Original rough essay. Author deceased 18 Dec. 2011.

Hawley, George. "Some Conservatives Have Been Against Capitalism for Centuries: *They just haven't been that effective." The American Conservative.* 01 Oct. 2017.

Hedding, Malcolm Rev. "The History of Christian Zionism the roots of the movement." *International Christian Embassy*, 20 Rachel Imeinu Jerusalem · Ph. 02-539-9700.

Hedges, Chris. *American Fascists: The Christian Right and the War on America.* Free Press. 2006. p.13.

Heinze, Kristin, and Carsten Heinze. "The Educational Conceptualization of the Ethnic Community Volksgemeinschaft in National Socialist Primers by the Example of Presentations of Adolf Hitler – Methodical Prospects." In History of Education & Children's Literature», IX, 2 (2014), pp. 185-200. ISSN 1971-1093 (print) / ISSN 1971-1131.

Helderman, Rosalind S., Tom Hamburger, and Michelle Ye Hee Lee. "Russian agent's guilty plea intensifies spotlight on relationship with NRA." The Washington Post. 13 Dec. 2018.

Heller, Kevin, and Gerry Simpson. The Hidden Histories of War Crimes Trials. Oxford University Press; 1 edition. Oxford University Press. 30 Dec. 2013. Also, read Oxford University Online "Capitalism's Victor's Justice? The Hidden Stories Behind the Prosecution of Industrialists Post-WWII." by Grietje Baars.

Heneghan, Tom. 'Neo-Protestant' challenge seen in France's political upheaval.' CRUX Taking the Catholic Pulse. 13 Sept. 2017. Religious News Service.

Heschel, Susannah. *The Aryan Jesus: Christian Theologians and the Bible in Nazi Germany*. Princeton University Press (03 Oct. 2010). ISBN-10: 0691148058.

Hess, Rudolf. "Walter Richard Rudolf Hess, (born April 26, 1894, Alexandria, Egypt—died August 17, 1987, West Berlin, West Germany, German National Socialist who was Adolf Hitler's deputy as party leader." *Encyclopedia Britannica*.

Hitler, Adolph. *Mein Kampf*. Volume Two: The National Socialist Movement. Chapter 3. Subjects and Citizens. Munich: Verlag. Frz. Eher.

Hitler, Adolph. Mein Kampf. Volume Two: The National Socialist Movement. Chapter 4. Personality and the Conception of the Folkish State. Munich: Verlag. Frz. Eher.

Hitler, Adolph. "Public Speech, Munich." Cited in The Bulletin of International News, *Royal Institute of International Affairs*, XVIII, No 5, 1941, p 269. Nov. 1941.

Hitler, Adolph. *The Big Lie*. in Mein Kampf. p. 134. Munich: Verlag Frz. Eher.

Hitler, Adolph. "The Settlement [of Accounts]," or "Revenge" in *Mein Kampf*. Munich: Verlag Frz. Eher.

Hockenos, Paul. "Poland and the Uncontrollable Fury of Europe's Far Right." *The Atlantic*. 15 Nov. 2017.

Holmes, Steven A. ," A Drug Dealer, Finds Many Eager to Launder His Drug Money." *The New York Times*. 24 Jan. 1990.

Hopkins, Valerie. "Slovenian survivor targets victory à la Orbán." *POLITICO*. 01 Jun. 2018.

Horsfield, John. "Social Civil Disobedience-Social Change." *Alliance Research Group* 3212 Cutshaw Ave. Ste. 210, Richmond, VA 23230.

Hui Han, Chin. LTA (NS). "Maskirovka In the Information Age." *POINTER, Journal of the Singapore armed forces.* Vol.42 no.1.

Hudson, Michael, et al. "How New York Real Estate Became a Dumping Ground for the World's Dirty Money." *The Nation.* 03 Jul. 2014.

Hueven, Marten van. "Sense of the Community" Report on Yugoslavia. Declassified. NIC-03236-88. CIA File. 31 Oct. 1988.

Human Intelligence. Chapter 6. "Definition of HUMINT." *Global Security Organization.*

Hundal. Sunny. "White people don't seem to realize that eventually, the far-right will come for them too." *The Independent.* 06 Mar. 2018.

Hunter, Edward. *Testimony.* Committee on Un-American Activities, House of Representatives, Eighty-Fifth Congress, Second Session, 13 Mar. 1958, Printed for the use of the Committee on Un-American Activities. United States Government Printing Office, Washington, 1958.

Huntington, Samuel P. *Religious Persecution and Religious Relevance.* in "The Influence of Faith: Religious Groups in US Foreign Policy." Elliott Abrams, Rowman, and Littlefield. 2001.

Ibrahim, Muhktar. "A look at Wisconsin's 'hate' groups." *Wisconsin Center for Investigative Journalism.* 12 Nov. 2017.

Idinopulos, Thomas. "Nazism, Millenarianism, and the Jews." *Journal of Ecumenical Studies.*

Illing, Sean. "Trump's ties to the Russian mafia go back 3 decades." *VOX.* 08 Dec. 2018.

Inozemtsev, Vladislav. "Putin's Russia: A Moderate Fascist State." *The American Interest.* Volume 12, Number 4. 23 Jan. 2017.

Israel, Josh. "20,000 Republicans just voted for an actual Nazi." *ThinkProgress.* 21 Mar. 2018.

Isidore, Chris. "Krispy Kreme owners admit to family history of Nazi ties." *CNN.* 25 Mar. 2019.

Ivanyi, Gabor. "There's nothing Christian about Orban's democratic values." Euronews. 09 May 2018.

Jackson, Robert. Closing Statement to International Military Tribunal, Nuremberg 1946.

Jacobson, Louis. "Are illegal immigrants bringing 'tremendous' disease across the border, as Trump says? Unlikely." *Politifact.* 23 July 2015.

James, Lamond. "The Origins of Russia's Broad Political Assault on the United States." *Center for American Progress.* 03 Oct. 2018.

Janssen, Kim. "Trump's immigration order revives horrible memories for Chicago Holocaust survivors." *Chicago Tribune.* 03 Feb. 2017.

Jewish Telegraphic Agency. "Nazis Drill N. J. School Children in Hitler Tactics, Police Told." 13 Jun. 1934.

Jewish Telegraph Agency. "War Veterans Reply to Steuben Society Threat." *Jewish Daily Bulletin.* 05 May 1933. p.8.

Jewish Telegraphic Organization. "Steuben, Societies Council Bids Jews Here Halt Mass Protests Against Hitler's Reign." 07 May 1933. p.8.

Johnson, Daryl. "Hate In God's Name." Southern Poverty Law Center. 25 Sept. 2017.

Johnson, N. Hume. *Challenges to Civil Society: Popular Protest & Governance in Jamaica.* Cambria Press 28 Dec. 2011. ISBN-10: 9781604977820.

Johnston, David Cay. "Just What Were Donald Trump's Ties to the Mob?" *POLITICO.* 22 May 2016.

Johnston, David. "Bush Pardons 6 in Iran Affair, Aborting a Weinberger Trial; Prosecutor Assails 'Cover-Up'". *The New York Times*. 25 Dec. 1992.

Jonas, Susanne. "Cuban Exiles & Watergate: Opening a Can of Worms." *North American Congress on Latin America*. 25 Sept. 2007.

JPost Staff. "Nazi Goebbels' descendants are hidden billionaires." *The Jerusalem Post*. 27 Aug. 2017.

Jung, G. Carl. Wotan, Neue Schweizer Rundschau (Zurich). n.s., III March 1936, 657-69. Republished in AUFSATZE ZURZEITGESCHICHTE (Zurich, 1946), 1-23. Trans. by Barbara Hannah in ESSAYS ON CONTEMPORARY EVENTS (London, 1947), 1-16; this version has been consulted. Motto, trans. by H.C. Roberts.

Kaczynski, Andrew. "Mike Pence's moral case for removing a president from office." *CNN*. 06 Aug. 2018.

Kalinichenko, Dmitry. "Grandmaster Putin's Golden Trap." *Information Clearinghouse*. 25 Dec. 2014.

Kaldor, Mary. "Imagining Global Governance: Alternatives to Trump, Brexit, and New Wars." *Univ. California Santa Barbara*. Public Imagination. 23 Jan. 2018, |Volume11 |Issue5. 21st Century Global Dynamics Initiative at the Orfalea Center of the University of California, Santa Barbara.

Kara-Murza, Vladamir. "Putin and the 'Good Hitler." *World Affairs*. 04 Apr. 2014.

Karady, Victor. *"Political Antisemitism and it's Christian Antecedent. Trying to Make Sense of Nonsense"*, in The Making of Antisemitism as a Political Movement. Political History as Cultural History (1879-1914), eds. Werner Bergmann, Ulrich Wyrwa, *Quest. Issues in Contemporary Jewish History. Journal of Fondazione CDEC*, n.3 July 2015.

Kaufman, Will. "Woody Guthrie, 'Old Man Trump' and a real estate empire's racist foundation." *The Conversation.* 21 Jan. 2016.

Keating, Christopher. "New Britain's Paul Manafort Working To Put Trump in White House." Hartford Current. 12 June 2016. "In 1976, Manafort, a New Britain native, helped manage the convention for Gerald Ford, who was fending off a challenge from Ronald Reagan. He performed a similar role for Reagan in 1980, George H.W. Bush in 1988, and Bob Dole in 1996. Here in this Dec. 2, 1976 photograph, Manafort faces unemployment when President-elect Jimmy Carter takes office. For the previous two years, Manafort had been President Ford's associate director of the presidential personnel office." -Photo caption.

Kelley, Michael B. "12 Prominent People Who Compared Putin To Hitler Circa 1938." *Business Insider.* 22 May 2014.

Kelley, Michael B. "Europe's Russian Nightmare Is Starting to Come True.*" Business Insider.* 12 May 2014.

Kelly, Michael J. *Nowhere to Hide: Defeat of the Sovereign Immunity Defense for Crimes of Genocide and the Trials of Slobodan Milošević and Saddam Hussein.* (Teaching Texts in Law and Politics). Peter Lang Inc., International Academic Publishers. 08 Sept. 2005. ISBN-10: 0820478350.

Keneally, Meghan. "A timeline of Trump and Bannon's turbulent relationship." *ABC News.* 05 Jan. 2018.

Keneally, Meghan. "A look back at Trump comments perceived by some as encouraging violence." ABC News. 19 Oct. 2018.

Kershaw, Ian. *Hitler.* Routledge. 2013. p. 33.

Kershaw, Ian. "How Hitler Won Over the German People." *Spiegel.* And Spiegel Online. 30 Jan. 2008.

Kershaw, Ian. *Hitler 1889-1936 Hubris.* W.W. Norton and Company. New York. 1999.

Kessler, Glenn, et al. "President Trump has made more than 5,000 false or misleading claims." *The Washington Post*. 13 Sept. 2018.

Kettle, Martin. "Trump is hellbent on destroying the NATO alliance." *The Guardian*. 27 Jun. 2018.

Khalili-Tara, Daniel. "Hungarian prime minister Viktor Orban vows to create 'Christian homeland' on the eve of the election." The Independent. 07 April 2017.

Khoshkish, A. *The Socio-Political Complex: An Interdisciplinary Approach to Political Life* (Pergamon international library of science, technology, engineering, and social studies). Pergamon; 1st edition 22 Oct. 2013.

Kingsley, Patrick. "In First Lady's Hometown in Slovenia, the Business Is Melania." *The New York Times*. 22 Jul. 2018.

Kingsley, Patrick. "Safe in Hungary, Viktor Orban Pushes His Message Across Europe." *The New York Times*. 04 Jun. 2018.

Kingsley, Patrick, and Novak, Benjamin. "The Website That Shows How a Free Press Can Die." *The New York Times*. 24 Nov. 2018.

Kinstler, Linda. "Why Donald Trump Is Dangerous for Eastern Europe." *POLITICO*. 12 Aug. 2016.

Kirillova, Kseniya. "I was told we should work with fascists: former KGB officer Zhirnov." *Euromaidan*. 03 Dec. 2018.

Kohl. Diane. "The Presentation of "Self" and "Other" in Nazi Propaganda." *Psychology & Society*, Vol. 4 (1), 7 – 26. The University of Stirling. 2011.

Komar, M. Boris. "The Journal of Conational Law: America's Journal of International Private Law, Volumes 1-3." Conational Law Publishing Company, 1920. Read Volume 3, January 1922, No.1.

Kopp. Eliot A. "Fritz Kuhn The American Führer and The Rise and Fall of the German-American Bund." Thesis. *Florida Atlantic University*. Boca Raton, Florida May 2010.

Krastev, Nikola. "In the Heart Of New York, Russia's 'Soft Power' Arm Gaining Momentum." *Radio Free Europe-Radio Liberty*. 15 Feb. 2009.

Kramer, Andrew E. "Gorbachev Calls Trump's Nuclear Treaty Withdrawal 'Not the Work of a Great Mind.'" *The New York Times*. 21 Oct. 2018.

Kubizek, August. *The Young Hitler I Knew: The Definitive Inside Look at the Artist Who Became a Monster*. Arcade; Reprint edition 13 July 2011.

Kupsky, Gregory J., MA. "The True Spirit of The German People": German-Americans and National Socialism, 1919-1955." Dissertation Graduate School. *The Ohio State University*. 2010.

Ladd, Christopher. "Pastors, Not Politicians, Turned Dixie Republican." *Forbes*. 27 Mar. 2017.

LaFraniere, Sharon, and Kenneth P. Vogel and Maggie Haberman. "The Rise and Fall of Paul Manafort: Greed, Deception, and Ego." *The New York Times*. 12 Aug. 2018.

Lakoff, G. and Johnson, M. *Metaphors We Live By*. 1st ed. Chicago: University of Chicago Press. 2003.

Langer, Walter C. "Psychological Analysis of Adolph Hitler. CIA File." *Central Intelligence Agency*. Declassified August 1999.

Lebor, Adam. "Revealed: The secret report that shows how the Nazis planned a Fourth Reich in the EU." *Daily Mail*. 09 May 2009.

Lengyel, Emil. "The Battlecries of Hitlerism Modified as Election Nears." *The New York Times*. 10 July 1932.

Levin, Hank. "Anti-Semitism in German 'Volk' Culture by Propaganda through the Pen and Screen." *The Earlham Historical Journal Volume VII: Issue I*. Fall 2014.

Library of Congress. "Revelations from the Russian Archives: Perestroika." 31 Aug. 2016.

LIFE. "U.S. Communist rally. November 09, 1939." Old Life Magazines Company, Chris Palmer, 1-800-023-6433.

Lindley-French, Julian. "NATO: Countering Strategic Maskirovka." Senior Fellow, Institute of Statecraft. London Distinguished Visiting Research Fellow, *National Defense University*, Washington D.C. May 2015.

Littell, Franklin H. "Kirchenkampf" and Holocaust: The German Church Struggle and Nazi Anti-Semitism in Retrospect." *Journal of Church and State*. Vol. 13, No. 2. Spring 1971. pp. 209-226.

Liu, Jinyuan. "Correlation and agreement: overview and clarification of competing concepts and measures." Shanghai Archive of Psychiatry. 2016 Apr 25; 28(2): 115–120. DOI: 10.11919/j.issn.1002-0829.216045.

Lockett, Jon. "Lord of The World. Psychic Baba Vanga, who predicted 9/11 terror attacks, also foretold 'unstoppable' Vladimir Putin will one day rule Earth." *The Sun*. 19 Mar. 2018.

Longhurst, John. "Trump's presidency, 'Christian supremacism' criticized at Parliament of World Religion." Religious News Service. 06 Nov. 2018.

Longman, Martin. "Steve Bannon Wants to Lead Fascist Movement in Europe." *Washington Monthly*. 23 Jul. 2018.

Longman, Martin. "The Odd Chabad Connection Between Putin and Trump." *The Washington Monthly*. 27 Nov. 2017.

Lowery Contreras, Raoul. "Russian meddling in the 2016 election – with Armenian lobby's support?" *Foreign Policy News*. 30 May 2018.

Lyubansky, Mikail. "Studies of Unconscious Bias: Racism Not Always by Racists." *Psychology Today*. 26 Apr. 2017.

MacDonnell, Francis. *Insidious Foes: The Axis Fifth Column and the American Home Front*. Oxford University Press, New York: 1995.

Mac Farquhar, Neil. "Russia Revisits Its History to Nail Down Its Future." *The New York Times*. 11 May 2014.

Mackel, K. A. "Fascism: A Political Ideology of the Past." *Inquiries Journal/Student Pulse*, *2*(11). 2010.

Macklin, Audrey. "Citizenship Revocation, the Privilege to Have Rights and the Production of the Alien," *Queen's Law Journal* 40, no.1, October 2014: 1-54.

Marcuse, Harold. "*First, they came for the communists ... *", In Berenbaum, Michael (ed.) et.al. Remembering for The Future: Armenia, Auschwitz, and Beyond. Paragon House. 01 Apr. 2016. ISBN-10: 1557789231.

"Martin Niemöller: Biography," United States Holocaust Memorial Museum website, last modified 09 Jan. 2016.

"Mary MacLeod Trump Philanthropist, 88", Obituary. *The New York Times*. 09 Aug. 2000.

Masters of the Universe. Name given to identify The World Economic Forum at Davos, Switzerland by themselves.

Mathias, Christopher. "Murders by U.S. White Supremacists More Than Doubled In 2017, New Report Shows." *HUFFPOST*. 18 Jan. 2018.

Mathis-Lilley, Ben. "How Trump Has Cultivated the White Supremacist Alt-Right for Years." *Slate*. 14 Aug. 2017.

Matthews, Owen. "Alexander Dugin and Steve Bannon's Ideological Ties to Vladimir Putin's Russia." *Newsweek*. 17 Apr. 2017.

May, Ruth. "How Putin's Oligarch's Funneled Millions into GOP Campaigns." *The Dallas Morning News*. 08 May 2018.

Maylon, John. Art Cuclopedia Com Oct.

McFaul, Michael. *From Cold War to Hot Peace: An American Ambassador in Putin's Russia*. New York: Houghton Mifflin Harcourt, 2018.

McLaughlin, David. "Romania's de facto leader Liviu Dragnea survives party rebellion." *Irish Times*. 21 Sept. 2018.

McMillan, Tom M., and Rodger LI. Wood. *Neurobehavioural Disability and Social Handicap Following Traumatic Brain Injury*. Taylor and Francis. 02 Feb. 2017. pp. 10-20. ISBN-13:9781138923935.

Means, Russell. *Welcome to The Reservation*. Video. YouTube.

Memo Reading: "Seminar with Russia's Andranik Migranyan. On June 22, 2015. Andranik Migranyan, director of Russia's government-connected Institute for Democracy and Cooperation, spoke about U.S.-Russian relations at a Center seminar moderated by President Dimitri K. Simes. Russian Ambassador Sergey Kislyak also participated in the discussion." A summary of the meeting is available—Center for The National Interest, 1025 Connecticut Avenue NW Suite 1200, Washington, DC 20036.

Michel, Casey. "Beyond Trump and Putin: The American Alt-Right's Love of the Kremlin's Policies." *The Diplomat*. 13 Oct. 2016.

Michel, Casey. "America's neo-Nazis don't look to Germany for inspiration. They look to Russia." *The Washington Post*. 22 Aug. 2017.

Mikyung Lee, Margaret. "An Overview of Judicial Review of Immigration Matters." *Congressional Research Service*. 11 Sept. 2013.

Miller, Anna. "Socialism and Milwaukee's Amnesia." *Milwaukee Independent*. 05 Dec. 2016.

Miller, Joan Irene. "Spies in America German Espionage in the United States 1935-1945." Master's Thesis. Portland State University. 1984.

Miller, Manjari Chatterjee; "The Role of Beliefs in Identifying Rising Powers." *The Chinese Journal of International Politics*. Volume 9. Issue 2. 1 June 2016. pp. 211–238.

Mindock, Clark. "Holocaust survivor says Trump's America 'feels like 1929 or 1930 Berlin'." *The Independent*. 09 Apr. 2019.

Moran, Mark. "Board Approves Statement Against Separation of Migrant Children." *American Psychiatric Association.* 10 Jan. 2019.

Mortimer, Caroline. "Donald Trump's mother asked: 'What kind of son have I created?'." *The Independent.* 04 Nov. 2017.

Mosse, George L. *The Crisis of German Ideology: Intellectual Origins of the Third Reich.* Knopf Doubleday Publishing Group. Sept. 1987. ISBN:0805206698.

Murphy, William. "AG: Yaphank German-American group settles a housing discrimination case." Newsday. 17 May 2017.

Murray, Henry. "Subject: Adolph Hitler" CIA File. *Central Intelligence Agency.* Declassified. 18 May 2000.

Myre, Greg. "America First': From Charles Lindbergh To President Trump." *NPR.* 06 Feb. 2017.

Nakamura, David, Min Kim, Seung, McAuley, McAuley, James. "In World War I, remembrance, France's Macron denounces nationalism as a betrayal of patriotism." *The Washington Post.* 11 Nov. 2018.

National Constitution Center Staff. National Constitution Center. 23 Jan. 2017.

Nazi Germany – "Anschluss." *History on the Net.*

Nazi Rise to Power. Holocaust Encyclopedia 100 Raoul Wallenberg Place, SW. Washington, DC 20024-2126.

Nechepurenko, Ivan. Neil Mac Farquhar and Thomas Gibbons-Neff. "Dozens of Russians Are Believed Killed in U.S.-Backed Syria Attack." *The New York Times.* 13 Feb. 2018.

Neo-Nazi. "US neo-Nazi groups on the rise under President Donald Trump: report." *DW News.* 22 Feb. 2018.

Neumann, Franz L. *Behemoth: The Structure and Practice of National Socialism 1933-1944.* Ivan R. Dee; Book Club Edition. 16 May 2009). ISBN-10: 1566638194.

New King James Bible. St. Mark 11.23.003

New Statesman. "What does entryism mean?" *The New Statesman.* 10 August 2016.

Nippert, Regina, "Mixing Christianity and Politics Is Killing the Church." *The Hill.* 29 May 2015.

Nisbet, Eric C., and Olga Kamenchuk. "3 charts explain how Russians see Trump and US." *The Conversation.* 13 July 2018.

Noack, Rick. "Former Trump aide Sebastian Gorka listed as 'wanted' on the Hungarian police website." *The Washington Post.* 18 Jan. 2018.

Nom de plume. Watson narrates the tale. He begins with Sherlock Holmes, lost in thought, looking at a letter from 'Porlock.' Watson asks who Porlock is. Holmes explains it is a nom-de-plume; Porlock is important in that he is connected to an influential man: Professor Moriarty.

Norton-Taylor, Richard, and Nicolas Kent. "Nuremberg: The War Crimes Trial." Drama. (1997).

Nussbaum, Matthew. "Poll: Republicans' confidence in Russia's Putin on the rise." *Politico.* 16 Aug. 2017.

Office of The Historian. "The Breakup of Yugoslavia, 1990–1992." *United States Department of State.*

Oppenheim, Maya. "22 Million Americans Support Neo-Nazi's, New Poll Indicates." *Independent.* 22 Aug. 2017. Independent Digital News & Media, 2 Derry Street, London W8 5HF, United Kingdom.

Pace, Eric. "Armand Hammer Dies at 92; Industrialist and Philanthropist Forged Soviet Links." *The New York Times.* 12 Dec. 1990.

Percy, Martyn. "To know Donald Trump's faith is to understand his politics." *The Guardian.* 06 Feb. 2018.

Perovšek. Jurij (ed.) and Bojan Godeša. "Between the House of Habsburg and Tito a Look at the Slovenian Past 1861–1980." *Institute of Contemporary History.* 21 November 2016.

Peterson, Anne Helen. "Donald Trump Showed His Hand In 1999, But No One Was Looking." *Buzzfeed*. 06 Jan. 2017.

Petkova, Mariya. "The death of the Russian far right." *Aljazeera*. 16 Dec. 2017.

Pfaff, William. "Is Romania's New President A Fascist?" *Chicago Tribune*. 22 June 1990.

Photo. C27275-33, President Reagan talking with Donald Trump and Ivana Trump at a state dinner for King Fahd of Saudi Arabia in the blue room. 2/11/85. Reagan Library Archive.

Pick, Daniel. ""In pursuit of the Nazi mind?" The deployment of psychoanalysis in the Allied struggle against Germany" Psychoanalysis and history vol. 11,2 (2009): 137-57.

Piekkola, Brad. "Conceptual and Historical Issues in Psychology." *SAGE Publications Ltd;* 1 edition 07 Dec. 2016 ASIN: B01JZ7ISWA. p.252.

Pietikäinen, Petteri. "The Völk and It's Unconscious: Jung, Hauer and the 'German Revolution'." *Journal of Contemporary History* 35.4 October 2000: 523–539, p. 524.

Poenaru, Florin. "Friends and Foes. Traditional and Alt-Right in Romania." *Lefteast*. 24 Oct. 2017.

Polyakova, Alina. "How Russia Meddled in its Own Elections." *The Atlantic*. 18 Mar. 2018.

Prados, John. "The John Walker Spy Ring and The U.S. Navy's Biggest Betrayal." *US Naval Institute News*. 02 Sept. 2014.

Raab, Selwyn. "Influx of Russian Gangsters Troubles F.B.I. in Brooklyn." *The New York Times*. 23 Aug. 1994.

Rampe, David. "Armand Hammer Pardoned by Bush." The New York Times. 15 Aug. 1989.

Rao, Shrenik. "Hitler's Hindus: The Rise and Rise of India's Nazi Loving Nationalists." *Haartz*. 14 Dec. 2017.

"Reich Conference of German Christians at the Sportpalast in Berlin." 13 Nov. 1933). *German History in Documents and Images.* ghdi.ghi-dc.org/sub_image.cfm?image_id=2059

Reich, Walter. "The World View of Soviet Psychiatry." *The New York Times.* 30 Jan. 1983.

Reich, Wilhelm. And Vincent R. Carfagno. *The Mass Psychology of Fascism. Farrar, Straus, and Giroux.* 3 edition 01 Nov. 1980.

Reich, Wilhelm. *The Mass Psychology of Fascism. Preface Third Edition.* Translator Theodore P. Wolfe. Orgone Institute Press. 1946.

Reich, Wilhelm. William Steig, Ralph Manheim. *Listen, Little Man.* First Published 1946. Noonday/Farrar, Straus & Giroux (NYC). 01 Jan. 1974.

Reiss, Tom. "The First Conservative: How Peter Viereck inspired-and lost-a movement." *The New Yorker.* 24 Oct. 2005.

Reitman, Janet. "All-American Nazis How a senseless double murder in Florida exposed the rise of an organized fascist youth movement in the United States." *Rolling Stone.* 02 May 2018.

Religious News Service. "Trump to top evangelicals: 'I'm on your side.'" 21 Jun. 2016.

Remak, Joachim. "Friends of New Germany: The Bund and German-American Relations," *The Journal of Modern History.* 29, no. 1. 40. March 1957.

Remnick, David. "KGB Head Warns Republics." *The Washington Post.* 23 Dec. 1990.

Reuters. "Ex-Trump strategist Bannon says to work with Hungary PM Orban." 16 Nov. 2018.

Reuters. "U.S. judge allows Mueller case against Russian company to proceed." *Reuters News Agency.* 13 Aug. 2018.

Reuters. "Russian professor sacked over criticism of actions in Ukraine." *Reuters News Agency.* 24 Mar. 2014.

Rice, Andrew. "Stash Pad: The New York real estate market is now the premier destination for wealthy foreigners with rubles, yuan, and dollars to hide." *New York Magazine.* 29 Jun. 2014.

Riebling, Mark. "Conservatism Turned Upside Down: Sam Tanenhaus's critique of conservative reason." *City Journal.* 16 Oct. 2009.

Ripley, Anthony. "Guilt Admitted by A Nixon Donor." *The New York Times.* Archive. 11 Dec. 1974.

Rockwell, John. "Friedelind Wagner, 73, Opponent of Nazism Despite Family's Ties. The New York Times. 09 May 1991.

Rodin, Artem. "Amendments to The Law on Concession Agreements Introduce The Private Finance Initiative (PFI) in Russia." Roden & Partners 18 May 2015. 119590, Moscow, Ulofa Palme 1.

Rosenberg, Alfred and Wilhelm Weib, *Reichsparteitag der NSDAP Nürnberg 19. /21.* Munich: Verlag Frz. Eher. August 1927. pp. 30-32.

Rosenzweig, Roy. "The Memorandum of the Serbian Academy of Sciences and Arts (SANU)." *Center for History & New Media Break Up and War.*

Ross, Alex. "How American Racism Influenced Hitler: Scholars are mapping the international precursors of Nazism." *The New Yorker.* 30 April 2018.

Ross Reid, Alexander. "Opinion: Hitler in Brasilia: The U.S. Evangelicals and Nazi Political Theory Behind Brazil's President-in-waiting." *Haaretz.* 28 Oct. 2018.

Rubin, Daniel. "Lou Diskin, Marxist educator, working-class activist" *People's World.* 08 Aug. 2003.

Rupprecht, Nancy E., and Wendy Koenig. *The Holocaust and World War II: In History and In-Memory.* Cambridge Scholars Publishing; Unabridged edition. 01 Nov. 2012.pp. 109-130.

Rushdoony, R.J. Rev. *Sovereignty.* Vallecito, CA: Ross House Essays, 2007. p. 149-153.

Ryback, Timothy W. "Hitler's Forgotten Library: You can tell a lot about a person from what he reads. The surviving—and largely ignored—remnants of Adolf Hitler's personal library reveal a deep but erratic interest in religion and theology." The Atlantic. May 2003.

Sampathkumar. Mythili. "Last surviving prosecutor at Nuremberg trials says Trump's family separation policy is 'crime against humanity.'" *Independent.* 09 Aug. 2018.

Samuel Dickstein. "The Congressman Who Spied for Russia." *POLITICO.* 06 Oct. 2014.

Savranskaya, Svetlana, source. "KGB of the USSR to Members of the Politburo, "On Measures to Improve Preventive Work Conducted by the State Security Service." 03 Oct. 1983, Secret.

Scales-Trent, Judy. "Racial Purity Laws in the United States and Nazi Germany: The Targeting Process.", 23 Hum. Rts. Q.259 (2001). University at Buffalo School of Law Digital Commons @ University at Buffalo School of Law. Human Rights Quarterly. 23 (2001) 259-307 © 2001 by The Johns Hopkins University Press.

Schaeffer, Edith. *The Tapestry: The Life and Times of Francis and Edith Schaeffer.* Pp. 258-59. W Pub Group; Special memorial ed edition. 01 May 1985. ISBN-10: 0849930162.

Schaeffer, A. Francis. "Soundword Labri Conference Video on Names and Issues." Video.

Schaeffer, Frank. "With God on Our Side-Christian Zionism Exposed." *HuffPost.* 25 May 2011.

Schreckinger, Ben. "The Happy-Go-Lucky Jewish Group That Connects Trump and Putin." POLITICO. 09 Apr. 2017.

Schulze, Rainer. "Hitler and Zionism: Why the Haavara Agreement does not mean the Nazis were Zionists." Independent. May 02, 2016.

Schwartzman, Paul, and Michael E. Miller. "Confident. Incorrigible. Bully: Little Donny was a lot like candidate Donald Trump." *The Washington Post*. 22 June 2016.

Selk, Avi et al. 'I just want to kill Jews:' Documents detail the Pittsburgh synagogue massacre and name the dead.' *The Washington Post*. 28 Oct. 2018.

Serduchka, Verka. "The Soviet and Ukrainian Communities of Brighton Beach." *The City University of New York*. 04 Nov. 2012.

Sereny, Gitta. "My journey to Speer." *The Independent*. 30 Sept. 1995.

Serwer, Adam. "The Nationalist's Delusion." *The Atlantic*. 20 Nov. 2017.

Several Nazi youth camps were organized in Camp Siegfried in Yaphank, New York, Camp Hindenburg in Grafton, Wisconsin, Camp Nordland in Andover, New Jersey, the Deutschhorst Country Club in Sellersville, Pennsylvania, Camp Bergwald in Bloomingdale, New Jersey, and Camp Sutter near Los Angeles.

Serwer, Adam. "The President's Pursuit of White Power." *The Atlantic*. 13 Jan. 2019.

Seyss-Inquart, Arthur. Final Statement. International Military Tribunal, Nuremberg 1947. Trials of The Major War Criminals. Before the International Military Tribunal. 14 November 1944- 1 October 1946. Published Nuremberg Germany 1947.

Sharkey, Joe. "Word for Word/The Case Against the Nazis; How Hitler's Forces Planned To Destroy German Christianity." *The New York Times*. 13 Jan. 2002.

Sheide, R.V. "If Trump Were King Cyrus." *News-Café Online*. 16 May 2018.

Sheffield, Hazel. "The tiny German town fighting back against neo-Nazis." *BBC*. 29 Nov. 2018.

Sherwood, Harriet. 'Toxic Christianity': the evangelicals creating champions for Trump." *The Guardian.* 21 Oct. 2018.

Shevchenko, Vitaly. "Little green men" or "Russian invaders"? *BBC News.* 11 Mar. 2014.

Shindler, John R. "The Real Ed Snowden Is a Patsy, a Fraud and a Kremlin-controlled Pawn." *Observer MEDIA*, 1 Whitehall Street, Floor 7, New York, New York 10004. 19 Sept. 2016.

Shreck, Carl. "Russian Organized Crime." *Federation of American Scientists.* 11 Nov. 2014. /1112 16th Street NW, Suite 400. Washington, DC20036.

Shynkarenko, Oleg. "Alexander Dugin: The Crazy Ideologue of the New Russian Empire: Ideologue Alexander Dugin's notion of "Eurasia" is at the heart of Russia's new drive to expand its territory and influence." *Daily Beast.* 02 Apr. 2014.

Sizer, Stephen. *Christian Zionism: Road-map to Armageddon?* IVP Academic. ISBN-10: 0830853685. 01 Jan. 2006.

Sizer, Stephen R. 'Lindsey's Literalistic Dispensationalist Hermeneutic', *Hal Lindsey: The Father of Apocalyptic Zionism* (updated 11 April 1999).

Sizer, Stephen. "The Theology of the Land by Stephen Sizer." *The Balfour Project.*

"Slobodan Milosevic: More or Less. heroes & killers of the 20th century." 2018.

Smith, Chris. "His Truth is Marching On." *California Magazine.* Fall 2012 Politics Issue.

Smith, David. "Donald Trump: the making of a narcissist." *The Guardian.* 16 July 2016.

Smith, Marie-Danielle. "Russia Tweets About 'Nazi' Monuments in Canada Amid Ongoing Concerns Over Political Interference." *National Post.* 30 Oct. 2017.

Sorluca, Daniel. "The Annexation of National Socialism by Hitlerism." *The University of Sidney*. Masters Government and International Relations. 24 Oct. 2014.Sorn, Mojca. "Life in Occupied Slovenia During World War II." *Sistory SGODOVINA SLOVENIJE and Institute of Contemporary History*. Kongresni trg 1, Ljubljana.

Span, Paula. From the archives: "When Trump hoped to meet Gorbachev in Manhattan." *The Washington Post*. 03 Dec. 1988.

Spark, L. Clara. "Klara Hitler's Son: Reading the Langer Report on Hitler's Mind." *Social Thought and Research*, Volume 22, Number 1&2 (1999), pp. 113-137

Speech. Judge Learned Hand-delivered on May 31, 1944, at *"I Am an American Day" at ceremonies in Central Park, New York City.*

Speer, Albert. Trials of The Major War Criminals. Before the International Military Tribunal. 14 November 1944- 1 October 1946. Published Nuremberg Germany 1947.

Stackelberg, Roderick. *The Routledge Companion to Nazi Germany*. New York: Routledge, 2007.

Stahl, Leslie. "What the last Nuremberg prosecutor alive wants the world to know." *CBS*. 07 May 2017.

Staff Writer. "German Nazi Heir and Billionaire Friedrich Karl Flick Dies at 79." *Reuters*. 06 Oct. 2006. HAARETZ.

Staff Writer. (J.C.) "How Germany responds to "blood and soil" politics." *The Economist*. 13 Aug. 2017.

Staff Writer. "In His Own Words: The President's Attacks on the Courts." Brennan Center for Justice. 05 June 2017.

Staff Writers. "Steve Bannon plans Brussels-based foundation 'The Movement' for EU far-right." *DW* News. 21 July 2018.

Steinmetz-Jenkins, Daniel, Pheiffer-Noble, Brittany. "Steve Bannon's Would-Be Coalition of Christian Traditionalists." *The Atlantic*. 23 Mar. 2017.

Stern, Rachel. "Hitler's Bid to Create Lebensraum by the Sea." Spiegel. 08 Nov. 2012.

Steuben Society membership platform 2018.

Stewart, Katherine. "Eighty-One Percent of White Evangelicals Voted for Donald Trump. Why?" *The Nation*. November 17, 2016.

Steinberg, Ben. "Antitrust Law Could Help Mueller Prove That Trump Officials Conspired With Russia." *Slate*. 21 Feb. 2019.

Strenger, Carlo. "Netanyahu and the Mystics of." *Haaretz*. 17 Jun. 2011.

Steil. Ben. "Who Lost Czechoslovakia?" *History Today*. 09 May 2018.

Stout, David. "How Nazis Tried to Steer U.S. Politics." *The New York Times*. 23 July 1997.

Sudakov, Dimitri. "The Soviet Union that Hammer built." *Pravda*. 23 May 2012.

Sudakov, Dimitri. "Why did Yeltsin lie to Clinton about Putin?" *Pravda*.31Aug.2018.

Suvorov. Viktor. *Spetsnaz: The Inside Story of the Soviet Special Forces*. W. W. Norton & Company 01 Sept. 1988. ISBN-10: 9780393335576.

Swenson, Kyle. "Suspects in five killings reportedly linked to macabre neo-Nazi group." *The Washington Post*. 29 Jan. 2018.

Tamkin, Emily. "The Slovak PM Decried Fascism in His Country. Is He Responsible for It?" FP, *The Slate Group*. 23 Jan. 2017.

Taylor, Jarod. "Sowing the Seeds of Destruction: Gunnar Myrdal's Assault on America." *The Renaissance Magazine*. Vol 7, No. 4. April 1996.

Taylor, Melissa Jane. "Bureaucratic Response to Human Tragedy: American Consuls and the Jewish Plight in Vienna, 1938–1941."

Holocaust and Genocide Studies. *Oxford University Press*. Volume 21, Number 2, Fall 2007, pp. 243-267. United States Holocaust Museum.

Tenold, Vegas. *Everything You Love Will Burn: Inside the Rebirth of White Nationalism in America*. Nation Books. 20Feb. 2018). ISBN-10: 1568589948.

Tett, Gillean. "Trump and the problem with the new normal." *Financial Times*. 31 Mar. 2017.

The Center for Public Integrity. "How the Gores, father and son, helped their patron Occidental Petroleum." 10 Jan. 2000.

The Editors of Encyclopedia Britannica. "Steve Bannon." Encyclopedia Britannica, Inc. 23 Nov. 2018.

"The Mark of German-Americans," *Steuben News*, July-August 1970.

The New York Times time machine. "Hoover Blunt to Hitler on Nazism; Says Progress Demands Liberty; Tells Fuehrer in a 40-Minute, Talk That the Principles of His Doctrine Would Be Impossible to Tolerate in U. S. Hoover Speaks Out to Hitler On Nazis." 09 Mar. 1938.

"The Sinister Face of Neutrality. The Role of Swiss Financial Institutions in the Plunder of European Jewry." *Institute of the World Jewish Congress*. Jerusalem.

Thompson, Scott. "Soviet Fixer from Lenin to the Present." EIR Volume 12, Number 35, 06 Sept. 1985. EIR News Service, P.O. Box 17390 Washington, D.C. 20041-0390 Order #85006.

Tibon, Amir. "Separating Migrant Kids From Families" *Haartz*. 16 June 2018.

Tierney, Dominic. "Russia's Strength Is Its Weakness." *The Atlantic*. 21 July 2018.

Times Archive. "The Riddle of Armand Hammer." *The New York Times Magazine*. 29 Nov. 1981.

Times Archive. "The Stain of Nazi Gold." *The New York Times*. 08 May 1997.

Touchberry, Ramsey. "Donald Trump Tried to Rewrite His Father's Will to Rescue His Failing Businesses: Report." *Newsweek*. 02 Oct. 2018.

Touma, Ann Marie. "Charlottesville Nationalist Leader Inspired by Romanian Fascism." *Balkan Insight*. 15 Aug. 2017.

Trew, Bell. "Israel's Netanyahu criticized for wooing Hungary's far-right prime minister Orbán." *The Independent*. 19 Jul. 2017.

"Trump predicts 'riots' if Republicans deny him the nomination." *BBC*. 16 March 2016.

TV Guide News. "Here's a Timeline of Every Time Donald Trump Ran for President." *CBS Interactive Inc*. 28 July 2015.

Umansky, Eric. "The Many Red Flags of Trump's Partners in India." Trump Inc. Podcasts. *ProPublica*. 28 Mar. 2018.

Ungar, Rick. "Dramatic, Little Known GOP Rule Change Takes Choice of Presidential Candidate Away from Rank-and-File Republicans and Hands It to Party Elite." *Forbes*. 07 Apr. 2014.

Unger, Craig. "Understanding Trump vs. Bruce Ohr: Think Russia's top crime boss, Semion Mogilevich." *Just Security Org*. 30 Aug. 2018.

"U.S. and Coalition Forces." *Counterinsurgency in Afghanistan: RAND Counterinsurgency Study--Volume 4*, by Seth G. Jones, RAND Corporation, Santa Monica, CA; Arlington, VA; Pittsburgh, PA, 2008, pp. 87–110. *JSTOR*, Open Access.

Van Dijk, T. A. "Discourse and manipulation." *Discourse and society*. Vol 17(2): 359–383. London. Newbury Park and New Dehli: Sage. 2006.

Van Dijk, T. A. "Principles of critical discourse analysis." *Discourse and society*. Vol 4(2): 249-283. London. Newbury Park and New Dehli: Sage. 1993.

Van Ells, Mark D. "Americans for Hitler: The Bund." *America in World War II Magazine*. August 2007.

Van Ells, Mark D. "How Milwaukee's German-Americans Faced Down Fascism Eighty Years Ago." *Milwaukee Independent*. 17 Mar. 2017.

Varagur, Krithika. "Why Bannon Is Meddling with Bosnia." *The New York Review of Books*. Crisis Reporting. 05 Sept. 2018.

Vetter, Thomas R., et al. "Agreement Analysis: What He Said, She Said Versus You Said." Anesthesia & Analgesia: June 2018 - Volume 126 - Issue 6 - p 2123–2128. DOI: 10.1213/ANE.000000000 0002924.

Viereck, Sylvester George. *THE KAISER ON TRIAL*. The Greystone Press. 1937. Reprinted and translated in "It Can Happen Again!" By the William Byrd Press, Inc. Richmond, Virginia.

Viereck, George Sylvester. "Speech at Madison Square Garden." 17 May 1934. RG 59, Box 4729, Folder 3, *National Archives and Records Administration*.

Vivas-Steele, Robert David. "Human Intelligence (HUMINT): *All Humans, All Minds, All the Time.*" Author Article 4.0, Article 11 Approved. By DoD CIA. 11 Jul 2009.

Voigt, Fritz. *Unto Caesar*. New York, G.P. Putnam's Sons, 1938. p.303.

Wagner, Ludwig: *Hitler, Man of Strife*. New York. Norton, 1942, 331.

Wadsworth, D. Nancy. "The racial demons that help explain evangelical support for Trump." *VOX*. April 30, 2018.

Walton, Gregory, and Matthew Day, "Nazi gold train: Russia may lay claim to any treasure." *The Telegraph*. 29 Aug 2015.

Waxman, Matthew. "Cyber Strategy & Policy: International Law Dimensions. Testimony Senate Armed Services Committee." *Lawfare*. March 01, 2017.

Webb, James. *The Harmonious Circle: The Lives and Work of G. I. Gurdjieff, P.D. Ouspensky, and Their Followers*. Shambhala; 1St Edition (September 12, 1987). ISBN-10: 0877734275.

Weichert, Brandon J. "What Yuri Andropov Can Tell Us About Vladimir Putin's Mindset." *Weichert Report*. 16 Oct. 2016.

Weider, Ben, and Peter Stone. "GOP leans on rainmaker who courts controversy on two continents." *McClatchy*. 07 Feb. 2017.

Weill, Kelly. "Blue Wave or Red Wall, Far-Right Candidates May Be the Real Winners of 2018.*" Daily Beast*. 12 Oct. 2018.

Weil, Patrick. "Can a Citizen be Sovereign?" Humanity. *Humanity Journal*. 02 Jan. 2016.

Weiss, Michael. "What Russia Understands about Trump." *The New York Review of Books*. 02 Aug. 2018.

Weiser, Benjamin, and Daisy Hernandez. "Drug Money Laundered into Gold, U.S. Says." *The New York Times*. 06 June 2003.

Whitman, Q, James. *Hitler's American Model: The United States and the Making of Nazi Race Law*. Princeton University Press. 21 Feb. 2017.

Widle, Robert. "Who Were Hitler's Supporters? Who Backed the Führer and Why?" *ThoughtCo*. 10 Apr. 10, 2018. About, Inc., 1500 Broadway, 6th Floor, New York, NY, 10036.

William J Brennan Jr, Associate Justice, US Supreme Court, *NY Times* (October 6, 1963).

Williams, Daniel. *God's Own Party: The Making of the Christian Right*. Oxford Scholarship Online. September 2010. ISBN-13: 9780195340846.

Williams, Anne. *Art of Darkness: A Poetics of the Gothic*. Chicago: University of Chicago Press. 1995. p. 67.

Wilde, Robert. "The Early Development of the Nazi Party." *ThoughtCo.* 14 Jun. 2018,

Wolfe, Audra. "Psychological Warfare: By working for the CIA, a crack team of researchers honed the United States' first formal peace-time campaign of propaganda and manipulation." *The Atlantic.* December 01, 2018.

Woutat, Donald. "The Unfinished Business of Armand Hammer: After a Lifetime in the Public Eye, He Still Worries About His Place in History." *Los Angeles Times.* 07 June 1987.

Yeadon, Glenn. White Rose. *The Nazi Hydra in America: Suppressed History of a Century*. Progressive Press; First Regular Edition. 31 Oct. 2008). ISBN-10: 0930852435.

Zentner, Christian, Bedürftig, Friedemann (1991). *The Encyclopedia of the Third Reich*. Macmillan, New York. ISBN 0-02-897502-2.

Zimmermann, Augusto. "Adolf Hitler's Debt to Karl Marx." *Quadrant.* May 09, 2018.

Zurawik, David. "Frontline offers chilling portrait of rising neo-Nazi movement in U.S." *The Baltimore Sun.* 16 Nov. 2018.

8 U.S. Code § 1226a - Mandatory detention of suspected terrorists; habeas corpus; judicial review.

INDEX

A

agents, former Russian, 70
American National Socialism, 15
American National Socialists, 21, 60
American Russophobia, 53
Andropov, Yuri, 110, 116, 130
Andropov's Institute, 171
Annexation of National Socialism by Hitlerism, 136
Apocalypticism Explained, 189
Arendt, Hannah, 153, 187
Austrian National Socialism, 204

B

Balagula, Marat, Ukrainian mob boss, 106
Brzezinski, Zbigniew, Carter's National Security Advisor, 95
Butina, Maria Russian gun-rights activist, 72

C

Camorra, Brooklyn Mafia, 132
Christian White Evangelical and Republican Conservatives, 50
Christ Trump Jr, Frederick, 98-100
church aesthetics movement, 44
Civil Rights church movement, 41
Cohn, Roy Attorney, 86, 113
Committee on Un-American Activities, 86, 198
Confederate lands, 164

Conscious Parallelism, 138, 191
Corruption Reporting Project, 58, 185
Critical discourse, analysis, 142-44, 219
cruelty commands, 140

D

Daily Stormers Song, 131
Davidovich Bronstein, Lev (aka Leon Trotsky) local revolutionary figure, 82
Democratic cycles of New York governance, 167
Democratic Party Congressional mistakes, 165
detente, new, 116
Díaz-Valdés Cruz, Daniel, 143-44, 151,156
Dijk, Van, T.A. Ph.D. 144
Dominionism, 36
Dragnea, Liviu, 61, 206
drug cartels, post-Cold War, 166
Dugin, Aleksandr, 11-12, 38, 47, 64, 116, 135–36

E

Eichmann, Adolf, 153 See Arendt, H. 153
Eisenhower, President Dwight, 38, 99
ENMOD, Environmental Modification Convention, 38, 73, 191

Ethnic Community Volksgemein-
    schaft, 196
eugenics movement, 15
European Christian Political Move-
    ment (ECPM), 43
Evangelical Alliance, 43

F
family separation policy, 158, 212
fearsome threesome, evangelicals,
42
Folkish State, 138
folkish state concept, 14
folkloric nationalism Trump-style, 61
Foreign Intelligence Surveillance Act
    Section (FISA), 78Fourth Polit-
    ical Theory, Russia, 8, 12, 116,
    191 See Dugin, Aleksandr
Freikorps, 21

G
Geli Raubal, half-niece, 29
Germany's Far Right Rebrands, 109,
    150
Geschichtslos, 24, 123, 157
Global Security Organization, 72,
    198
Goebbels, Joseph, Ph.D., 19, 22, 28-
    31, 131
Golden Dawn, 8, 185
Gorbachev, Mikhail Sergeyevich,
    General Secretary, President,
    109-110
Gorka, Sebastian, 122, 208
Gothic, 52-53,
Graham, Billy, Reverend, 35, 52, 194
Graham, Lindsay, Senator, 150
groups, macabre neo-Nazi, 63, 149
    216
Guardians, Hitler's Legacy, 109, 167
Giuliani, Rudy, Attorney General,
    116, 166
Guthrie, Woody, 98, 187, 201

H
Haavara Agreement, 212
Hanfstaengl, Ernst, 20, 21,141
Hammer, Armand, 17, 81–89, 92–96,
    104, 107, 110–14, 131
Hammer, Julius, 70, 81, 82-84, 112
Havel, President Václav, 160
Hitler's Forgotten Library, 22
Hitlerism Modified, 83
Hitlerputsch, 20, 26
Holocaust, 54, 158
Holocaust Survivor, 158, 190, 206
Hoover, John Edgar, FBI Director,
87, 96
Human Intelligence (HUMINT), 71-
    72, 219

I
idiot's delusion, 140
Ilyich Ulyanov Lenin, Vladamir, 17
Immigrants, 144, 147, 152
India's Nazi Loving Nationalists, 12,
    209
Industrialists, 160, 196
intelligence, operations, 70-73. 91

J
Jackson-Vanik Amendment, 102,
    129, 163, 165
Jews, 24, 27, 32,38, 146-8
John Walker Spy Ring, 110, 209
Jews area, free, from, 119

K
Knavs-Knauss-Trump, Melanija,
    108, 123, 129
Khrushchev, Nikita, Premier, 129
Kislyak, Ambassador Sergey, 206
Kubizek, August, 19
Kuhn, agent Fritz, 15
Kryuchkov, Vladimir Alexandrovich
    Soviet intelligence KGB Chief,
    132

L

law, skirted Russian concessionaire, 139

Lenin, Vladamir, 11, 81–82, 84, 88, 95, 111–12

Lindbergh, Charles To President Trump, 207

Lindsay, Hal, 37 Dispensationalist Hermeneutic, 37, 214

Liu, Jinyuan, Ph.D.,148

M

Macleod Trump, Mary-Anne, 107–8

Magyar, Bálint Hungarian sociologist, 172

Manafort, Paul, 201 See Bibliography

maskirovka, strategic, 128, 198, 204

Mass Murder in Historical Perspective, 194

Master Race, 186

McConnell, Mitch Senate, 56–57

Memory and Memorization, 141, 162

Mercer, Rebekah (Robert Ph.D.), 115, 129, 134, 168

Migranyan, Andranik, Ph.D., 11, 57–59, 62, 64, 138

Mikhail Gorbachev, Secretary General, 92, 94, 113

Miller, Stephen, 39, 50, 122

Milošević, Slobodan, 120–21, 128

Miss Hitler, in Italy, 90, 170

Mitterrand, François Maurice Adrien Marie, President, 63, 92, 165, 167, 173

Mogilevich, Semion, Boss of Bosses, 106, 218

Moral Majority, 41-42

myth-person, 33, 131, 176

N

Netanyahu, Benjamin Prime Minister, 90

Navalny, Alexei Anatolievich, 64

National Socialism, Practice, 48, 207

National Socialists, 115-116

NATO Headquarters, 115, 122

Navalny, Alexei Anatolievich, 66

Navy's Biggest Betrayal, 110, 209

Nazi movement, 98, 126, 221

Nazi America beginnings, 167, 202

Nazi violence and murders, 158,

Nayfeld, Boris, 102, 106

New York Supreme Court Justice Samuel Dickstein, 86, 212

Nix, Alexander, 134

O

Obama, President Barack, 157

Office of Strategic Services (OSS), 20, 23, 27, 141

Operation Black Shadows, 90

P

Paleoconservatism, 104

Palm Beach Gala, 92-94, 114

Paul, Rand, Senator, 56–57, 62

Paul Manafort, Ex-Trump Aide, 115, 183

Pence, Michael, Vice President, 36-37, 158, 183

Penn, Marine Le, President of the National Rally, 122

Poenaru, Florin, 61

Psychiatric Association, American, 89, 147, 207

Psychological Analysis, 26, 29, 36, 38, 39, 50

Disinformation, psychological, 35, 65, 87, 134, warfare, 221

Pushkov, Alexey, Sanctioned, 62

R

Reagan, President Ronald, 42, 92–93, 104, 107, 132

Republicans Accept Donald Trump, 154, 188

Republicans on Russia Trip, 190

Romanian Fascism, 61, 218

Rushdoony, Rousas John, 37, 45

S

Sessions, Jeff Attorney General, 159
Snowden, Edward, 75–79
Schaeffer, Francis, Rev. 44-46, 49-
    50, 51
School Children in Hitler Tactics,
    199
Sereny, Gita, 22-24,
Sense of the Community Report, 20
Seyss-Inquart, Arthur Gestapo, 193,
    213

Sizer, Stephen, 37, 214
Slovenia During World War II, 118-
    119

Snowden, Edward, 75-77
Soviet Psychiatry, World View of,
    210
Span, Paula, 112, 215
Speer, Albert, 32, 215
Spetsnaz, Russia Special Forces, 55,
    70-74
 states, völkisch, 20, 118, 138
Stevens, Thaddeus, Representative,
    164
subversive groups, Russia's use of,
    58, 167

T

thieves-in-law, 6, 163
Theocratic Movement, 50, 189
theory, the Good Hitler, 8, 59, 133,
    171, 200
Trump, Elizabeth Christ, 17, 98
Trump, Frederick Christ, 17, 98, 107
Trump, Maryanne, Judge Federal,
    114
Trump Tower Manhattan, 105-106,

V

Vanga, Baba, 35-36, 204
Viereck, George Sylvester, 15, 59–
    60, 128, 142
Vladamir Ilyich, Bolshevik leader, 82
Vladamir Putin, President, 6, 58, 64
Völk, 74, 209

W

Al-Waleed Bin Talal, Prince, 108
Wagner, Friedelind, 211, 219
Walker, John Anthony, 110
Wall Street, 74, 162, 169, 171
war crimes, 26, 88
White, Pastor Paula, 47
white power, sustaining, 127, 147
World Bank Group, 190

Y

Yudkovich Mogilevich, Semion, 106
Yuri Borysovych Shvets, Major, 112

Z

Zelníčková-Trump, Ivana, Marie 107
Zionism Exposed, Christian, 48, 50
Zionism, Apocalyptic, 37, 48, 50
Zionism, nationalist, 212, 214